ROBIN '89

The Kitchen of the Governor's Palace at Williamsburg.

PLATE I.

E. JONES.

THE
WILLIAMSBURG ART OF COOKERY

OR,

Accomplish'd Gentlewoman's
COMPANION:

Being a Collection of upwards of Five Hundred of the moſt Ancient & Approv'd Recipes in *Virginia* COOKERY.

Soups & Sauces,	Preserving,
Flesh & Fish,	Confectionery,
Breads,	Cakes,
Garden Stuff,	Puddings,
Pastry,	Wines, Punches, &c.

AND ALSO

A Table of favorite *Williamſburg* Garden HERBS.

To which is Added,

An Account of *Virginia* Hoſpitality; Treatiſes on the various Branches of Cookery; an Account of Health Drinking; ſome Conſiderations on the Obſervation of *Chriſtmas* in *Virginia*, with traditional Recipes for this Seaſon; with the Author's Explanation of the Method of Collecting & Adapting theſe choice Recipes; and an alphabetical INDEX to the Whole.

By Mrs. *HELEN BULLOCK*

WILLIAMSBURG:

Publiſhed by *Colonial Williamſburg*, and printed by *The Dietz Press, Inc.*, at *Richmond, Virginia.*

MCMXC

LC: 43-6700; ISBN: 0-910412-30-8

PREFACE.

THE *first* American *Book on the Art of Cookery,* The Compleat House-wife, or Accomplifh'd Gentle-woman's Companion, *was printed in the Year 1742, by* William Parks *in* Williamfburg *in* Virginia. *Mr.* Parks *in his Preface, begged leave to inform his Readers that he had collected the Volume from one much larger, by Mrs.* E. Smith, *printed in* England. *He omitted Recipes containing Ingredients or Materials not to be had in* Virginia, *printing only thofe ufeful or practicable here and leaving out fuch as would merely ferve to* "*fwell out the Book and* "*increafe its Price.*"

In a City which is attempting to recapture a Paft that was enriched by fuch able Craftfmen as Mr. Parks, *it feems fitting that any Attempt to produce a* Williamfburg Art of Cookery *fhould be guided by Purpofes fimilar to his own. This cookery Book, then, is intended as a Compilation of favorite* Virginia *Recipes, collected from Books known to have been ufed in* Virginia *Houfeholds. Some of thefe Books were printed in* England *and fold in the local Shops, while others were printed in* Virginia. *The beft*

Source

PREFACE.

Source of Virginia *Recipes proved to be the little handwritten Books kept by early Housewives and cherished by their Descendants. Recipes on Scraps of Paper pinned into printed Books or tucked between Pages often gave Directions beyond mere Cookery.* Mrs. B's *Recipe for* Cocoanut Pudding *in* Mrs. Coalter's *cook Book concluded, "Now the most im-"portant Recipe is to take care of yourself, not only "for your own Family's Sake but for that of my "whole Household."* Mrs. Taylor *warned* Mrs. Bruce *of the Potency of General* Taylor's Fish House Punch — *"Walter says look out for swell "Head next Morning."*

An Effort has been made to select, as Mr. Parks *would have selected, "only such Recipes as are useful "and practicable here" — but the Author being intere- sted also in a History of Cookery has been tempted to include a few such Monuments of Cookery as* An Egg as big as Twenty, Solomon's Temple in Flummery, Snail Broth, Lisbon Cake *and* Plumb Porridge for Christmas. *It is hoped that these Curiosities will divert and amuse the Reader without confusing the Cook.*

Some present-day Recipes are included with their Prototypes, showing, for Example, how Veal Glue, *or* Cake Soup for the Pocket, *may find its Way to the modern Table as tasty, clear Broth or jellied Consommé.*

The Recipes have been tested carefully and all those which have been proved in the Kitchens of the Market Square *Tavern, the* Travis House *and* Blair House *have been marked thus* (✳). *The professed Cook may attempt some of the unproved Recipes or may choose*

PREFACE.

choose to adapt them in her own Way, while the less Experienced may proceed with the proved Recipes.

Any Worth in the present Volume may be attributed to the Generosity of the many Virginians who contributed to it their most treasured Recipes, cookery Books and old Letters. Much Gratitude is due to those who skillfully aided in testing and adapting the Recipes—and still Others who worked with great Pains and Patience in the Preparation and Printing of this Volume.

The Author would add only one Word more before offering this Volume as the Accomplish'd Gentlewoman's Companion—*lest a Failure in Cookery be attributed to any Lack of Management in the Preparation of this Book:*

"HEAVEN SENDS GOOD MEAT,
but the DEVIL SENDS COOKS."

H. B.

Contents.

CONTENTS.

Favorite

CONTENTS.

ILLUSTRATIONS.

"The Inhabitants

THE
WILLIAMSBURG
Art of Cookery:
OR,
Accomplifh'd Gentlewoman's
COMPANION.

OF *VIRGINIA* HOSPITALITY

"THE Inhabitants are very courte-
"ous to Travellers, who need no
"other Recommendation but the
"being human Creatures. A
"Stranger has no more to do, but
"to inquire upon the Road, where
"any Gentleman, or good Houfekeeper lives, and
"there he may depend upon being received with
"Hofpitality."

When *Robert Beverley*, Gent., a Native and Inhabitant of that Place, wrote thefe Words in 1705
in his *Hiftory of Virginia*, he was writing of a Tradition of Hofpitality already firmly eftablifhed on
Virginia's Soil. It is little Caufe for Wonder, then,
that

that there was a Law of the *Virginia* Colony called
"An Act concerning Entertainment of Strangers",
which was deſigned to protect Strangers from ava-
ricious Perſons by providing that "every one ſhall
"be reputed to entertayne thoſe of Curteſie with
"whome they make not a certaine Agreement."

And ſuch was the Courteſy of theſe early *Virginians* that ſcarce a Traveller's Account or a Hiſtory written in that Day may be found which fails
to mention in ſome Way their open-handed Liber-
ality. In the *London Magazine* printed in July,
1746, an obſerving Traveller in *Virginia* wrote:

> All over the Colony, an univerſal Hoſpitality
> reigns; full Tables and open Doors, the kind
> Salute, the generous Detention, ſpeak ſomewhat
> like the old Roaſt-beef Ages of our Fore-fathers,
> and would almoſt perſuade one to think theſe
> Shades were wafted into theſe Regions, to enjoy
> with greater Extent, the Reward of their Virtues.
> (What is ſaid here is moſt ſtrictly true, for their
> Manner of living is quite generous and open:
> Strangers are ſought after with Greedineſs, as
> they paſs the Country, to be invited. Their Break-
> faſt Tables have generally the cold Remains of
> the former Day, haſh'd or fricaſſeed; Coffee, Tea,
> Chocolate, Veniſon-paſty, Punch, and Beer, or
> Cyder, upon one Board; their Dinner, good Beef,
> Veal, Mutton, Veniſon, Turkies and Geeſe, wild
> and tame, Fowls, boil'd and roaſted; and perhaps
> ſomewhat more, as Pies, Puddings, &c., for
> Deſſert: Suppers the ſame, with ſome ſmall Addi-
> tion, and a good hearty Cup to precede a Bed of
> Down: And this is the conſtant Life they lead,
> and to this Fare every Comer is welcome.)

When *Williamſburg*, in 1699, became the Capital of the Colony and Dominion of *Virginia*, it
became

became alſo the Center of its official Hoſpitality. The Capital City was actually planned for the Accommodation of the great Concourſe of People who would naturally be called to the Place where the General Aſſembly and Courts were held. Pub- lick Houſes, or Taverns, flouriſhed in *Williamſburg* and the private Dwellings in Publick Times were open for the Entertainment of the Thouſands who poured into the City. Within the magnificent Palace, which had been built at publick Expence as a Houſe for the royal Governors, there was a fine Appearance of Ladies and Gentlemen, good Diverſion and ſplendid Entertainment.

It is not ſurpriſing that this Reſponſibility for official Hoſpitality occaſionally reſted heavily upon the royal Governor in his Palace. His Politeneſs was ſuch that no Intimation of its Burdenſomeneſs eſcaped him except in his moſt intimate Letters. The popular Governor *Gooch* wrote Home in 1727 to his Brother (later Biſhop of *Norwich*):

> My firſt Introduction is attended with a great Charge, for the very Moment I was ſworn and ſwore all the Council, we proclaimed His Majeſty after which I did according to Cuſtom entertain the Town and all the Neighbours around us, and tho' I can't as yet ſend over any Money, you may depend upon it the very firſt Opportunity I have.

Two Months later the Governor was ſtill apolo- gizing for his Delay in the Matter of Remittances, explaining it as owing to his conſtant great Expence of Houſekeeping, proclaiming His Majeſty at firſt and keeping very magnificently his Birthday ſince. His Maintenance of his Station, he affirmed, was

as

as expenfive and ftately as any in this Part of the World—fo much fo, in Fact, that he wrote frequently to his Brother of his Apprehenfions that the Charge of his prefent Grandeur would prevent, in his old Age, his fecuring a fair Retreat to keep him from conftantly walking on Foot after riding fo long in his Coach and Six.

That the Governor enjoyed this Burden muft not be doubted. He told his Brother that the Gentlemen and Ladies of *Virginia* were perfectly well bred, and there was not an ill Dancer in his Government.

When News reached *Williamsburg* of the Battle of *Culloden*, Governor *Gooch*, though confined to the Palace fuffering from an old Wound received in the *Carthagena* Campaign, faw fuch an Occafion for Rejoicing amongft loyal Subjects of the King that he contributed handfomely to the Feftivities. The *Virginia Gazette* of July 18, 1746, defcribes the Celebration:

> On receiving the News, in this City, of the glorious Victory gain'd over the Rebels, by his Royal Highnefs, the Duke of *Cumberland*, an univerfal Joy diffuf'd among all Ranks of Perfons; the General Affembly being met, and much Company in Town, a grand Entertainment was made at the Capitol, on *Tuefday* Night, fuitable to the extraordinary Occafion, by the Honourable the Prefident and Council, Mr. Speaker, and the reft of the Houfe of Burgeffes; to which his Honour the Governor, who continues indifpof'd, was pleaf'd to contribute very largely. In the Evening a very numerous Company of Gentlemen and Ladies appear'd at the Capitol, where a Ball was open'd, and after dancing fome Time, withdrew to Supper,

Supper, there being a very handſome Collation
ſpread on three Tables, in three different Rooms,
conſiſting of near 100 Diſhes, after the moſt delicate Taſte. There was alſo provided a great Variety
of the choiceſt and beſt Liquors, in which the
Healths of the King, the Prince and Princeſs of
Wales, the Duke, and the reſt of the Royal Family, the Governor, Succeſs to his Majeſty's Arms,
Proſperity to this Colony, and many other loyal
Healths were cheerfully drank, and a Round of
Cannon, which were remov'd to the Capitol for
this Purpoſe, was diſcharg'd at each Health, to
the Number of 18 or 20 Rounds, which laſted 'til
near 2 o'Clock. The whole Affair was conducted
with great Decency and good Order, and an un-
affected Chearfullneſs appeared in the Counte-
nances of the Company. All the Houſes in the
City were illuminated, and a very large Bon-fire
was made in the Market-Place, 3 Hogſheads of
Punch given to the Populace; and the whole concluded with the greateſt Demonſtrations of Joy
and Loyalty.

Hoſpitality was not the excluſive Virtue of the
Gentry who attended the elegant Birthnight Balls
or other Entertainments at the Palace, or who
made ſuch a handſome Appearance at Dancing
Aſſemblies in the Capitol and the *Raleigh* Tavern—
it characteriſed all Ranks of People.

Lord *Adam Gordon* wrote in his *Journal* in 1765
of the extreme Civility of the People of *Williamsburg* toward Strangers; and many Years after the
Turmoil and Excitement of Publick Times had
ſubſided in the former Capital, *William Wirt*, in
1806, wrote affectionately of the old City, "*Wil-
"liamſburg is juſt as beautiful and hoſpitable as
"ever."

Williamſburg,

Williamsburg, as a reſtored City, is ſo remindful of the City which ſerved as a Capital and Metropolis for *Virginia* from 1699 to 1780, that a modern Author can find no better Words with which to deſcribe it than thoſe firſt written more than a Century ago:

"*Williamsburg* is juſt as beautiful and hoſpitable "as ever."

✿✿✿✿✿✿✿✿✿✿✿✿✿✿✿✿✿✿✿✿

Obſervations upon SOUPS.

WHEN one reflects that two Centuries ago Soup was of ſuch Importance in the Diet that the Soup Tureen was upon practically every Table and the wiſe Traveller carried Soup in his Pocket on long Journeys, it ſeems ſtrange to find it of ſo little Conſequence Today.

The thoughtful Reader who is alſo an accompliſh'd Cook would find much Profit in ſtudying the Herbs, Seaſonings and Vegetables that gave theſe old Soups their Diſtinction. He may not find Pocket Soup as neceſſary as did that compleat Gentleman, *William Byrd* of *Weſtover* in *Virginia*, Eſquire, who, in 1729, recommended his favorite Recipe to Foreſters in his *Hiſtory of the Dividing Line*, ſaying:

"... This Glue is ſo ſtrong, that two or three Drams, diſſolv'd in boiling Water, with a little Salt, will make half a Pint of good Broth, & if
you

you ſhou'd be faint with Faſting or Fatigue, let a ſmall Piece of this Glue melt in your Mouth, and you will find yourſelf ſurpriſingly refreſhed.

One Pound of this Cookery wou'd keep a Man in good Heart above a Month, and is not only nouriſhing, but likewiſe very wholeſome. Particularly it is good againſt Fluxes, which Woodſmen are very liable to, by lying too near the moiſt Ground, and guzzling too much cold Water. But as it will be only uſ'd now and then, in Times of Scarcity, when Game is wanting, two Pounds of it will be enough for a Journey of ſix Months.

But this Broth will be ſtill more heartening if you thicken every Meſs with half a Spoonful of Rockahominy, which is nothing but *Indian* Corn parched without burning, and reduced to Powder. . . . "

Soup had alſo its Place in the Literature of the Day and in 1760 when the Life and Opinions of *Triſtram Shandy*, Gent., were on every Tongue, The *Gentleman's Magazine* appropriately publiſhed

A Recipe for a Soup for Tristram Shandy

TAKE a Knuckle of Veal,
  You may buy it, or ſteal;
In a few Pieces cut it,
In a Stewing-pan put it;

Salt, Pepper, and Mace,
  Muſt ſeaſon your Knuckle;
Then, what's join'd to a * Place,
  With other Herbs muckle.

That which † killed King *Will*,
And what ‡ never ſtands ſtill:
Some § Sprigs of that Bed,
Whence Children are bred.
This much you will mend, it
Both Spinnage and Endive,

---

*Salary. †Sorrel ‡Thyme. §Parsley.

And

And Lettice and Beet,
With Marygolds, meet.
Put no Water at all,
For it maketh things ſmall;
Which, leſt it ſhould happen,
A cloſe Cover clap on;
Put your Pot, of *Wood*'s Metal,
In a boiling-hot Kettle.

And there let it be,
   (Mark the Doctrine I teach)
About (let me ſee)
   Thrice as long as you preach.

Then ſkimming the Fat off,
Say Grace with your Hat off;
Oh then with what Rapture,
Will it fill Dean and Chapter!

Soups & Sauces

Aſparagus Soup

TAKE four large Bunches of Aſparagus, ſcrape
it nicely, cut off one Inch of the Tops, and lay
them in Water, chop the Stalks and put them on
the Fire with a Piece of Bacon, a large Onion cut
up, Pepper and Salt, and two Quarts of Water; boil
them till the Stalks are quite ſoft, then pulp them
through a Sieve, and ſtrain the Water to it, which
muſt be put back in the Pot; put into it a Chicken
cut up, with the Tops of Aſparagus which had
been laid by, boil it until theſe laſt Articles are ſufficiently done, thicken with Flour, Butter, and
Milk, and ſerve it up.

(Mrs. *Mary Randolph*'s Virginia Houſewife, 1831)

Another

Another Way *

WASH and remove the Tips from a Bunch of fresh green Asparagus, and simmer them until tender in a little Milk. Cut up the Stalks of the Asparagus, add one fourth Cupful of chopped Onion and one fourth Cupful of chopped Celery, and boil about half an Hour in six Cups of Meat Broth. Rub through a coarse Sieve, and place your Pan over boiling Water. Add a rich Cream-sauce made of three Tablespoonfuls of melted Butter, three of Flour and half a Cup of Cream. Add the Tips last.

(Mrs. *Randolph's* Recipe, 1831.
Adapted *Blair* Kitchen, 1938.)

To make Scotch Barley-broth

TAKE a Leg of Beef, chop it all to Pieces, boil it in three Gallons of Water with a Piece of Carrot and a Crust of Bread, till it is half boiled away; then strain it off, and put it into the Pot again with half a Pound of Barley, four or five Heads of Celery, washed clean and cut small, a large Onion, a Bundle of Sweet-herbs, a little Parsley, chopped small, and a few Marigolds. Let this boil an Hour. Take a Cock or large Fowl, clean picked and washed, and put into the Pot; boil it till the Broth is quite good, then season with Salt, and send it to Table, with the Fowl in the Middle. This Broth is very good without the Fowl. Take out the Onion and Sweet-herbs before you send it to Table.

Some make this Broth with a Sheep's-head instead of a Leg of Beef, and it is very good; but you must chop the Head all to Pieces. The thick Flank

(about

(about six Pounds to six Quarts of Water) makes good Broth; then put the Barley in with the Meat, first skim it well, boil it an Hour very softly, then put in the above Ingredients, with Turnips and Carrots clean scraped and pared, and cut in little Pieces. Boil all together softly, till the Broth is very good; then season it with Salt, and send it to Table, with the Beef in the Middle, Turnips and Carrots round, and pour the Broth over all.

(Mrs. *Glasse's* Art of Cookery, *London*, 1774.)

Or do it thus *

TAKE three Pounds of Beef and one Pound of Veal. Chop it all to Pieces and put it on to boil softly in one Gallon of cold Water with a Carrot and a Crust of Bread till it is half boiled away; then strain it off and add two Cups of Celery washed clean and chopped small, a large Onion, a Bundle of Sweet-herbs and a little Parsley chopped small. Let this cook an Hour then strain again. Then add one Tablespoonful of Barley to each Quart of the Broth and cook thirty or forty Minutes until the Barley is enough.

(Mrs. *Glasse's* Recipe, 1774, adapted *Market Square Tavern* Kitchen, 1937.)

Barley Soup *

PUT on three Gills of Barley, three Quarts of Water, few Onions cut up, six Carrots scraped and cut into Dice, an equal Quantity of Turnips cut small; boil it gently two Hours, then put in four or five Pounds of the Rack or Neck of Mutton

ton, a few Slices of lean Ham, with Pepper and
Salt; boil it ſlowly two Hours longer and ſerve it
up. Tomatoes are an excellent Addition to this
Soup.

(Mrs. *Mary Randolph's* Virginia Houſewife, 1831.)

Beef Broth*

TAKE off the Fat and Skin of a Pound of lean
Beef, and cut it into Pieces. Then put it into a
Gallon of Water, with the Under-cruſt of a Penny-
loaf, and a very little Salt. Let it boil till it be reduced to two Quarts, then ſtrain it off, and it will
be very nouriſhing. In ſome Caſes, when the ſick
Perſon be very weak, the Phyſician will order Beef-
tea, which muſt be made thus: Take a Piece of
lean Beef, cut it croſs and croſs, and then pour on
it ſcalding Water. Cover it up cloſe, and let it ſtand
till it be cold. Then pour it off as you want it,
ſeaſon it moderately, and give it to the ſick Perſon, having firſt warmed it.

(Mr. *Farley's* Recipe, 1787, adapted
Market Square Tavern Kitchen, 1937.)

Beef Soup*

PUT four pounds good Rump Steak in a Pot. Add
five Quarts of cold Water and bring to boil.
When boiling, add one Spoonful Salt, and boil for
two Hours. Prepare and cut in large Pieces and
add ſlowly three Onions, two Carrots, one Turnip,
one Parſnip, one ſmall Cabbage, one ſmall Head of
Celery, four Cloves, Bundle of Parſley, Bay-leaf,
Thyme, Marjoram, and twenty Peppercorns. Cook
another two Hours. Strain and cut up Vegetables
into

into small Cubes excepting the Cabbage. Cut two
Rolls in Slices and toast in Oven. Put all in a large
Tureen and heat thoroughly. Sprinkle over with
one Spoonful chopped Parsley and serve. Place
Meat and Cabbage on separate Dish and serve it up.

(A *Richmond* Family Recipe. Prov'd.)

Beef Soup *

TAKE the hind Shin of Beef, cut all the Flesh
off the Leg-bone, which must be taken away
entirely, or the Soup will be greasy. Wash the
Meat clean and lay it in a Pot, sprinkle over it one
small Tablespoonful of pounded black Pepper
and two of Salt; three Onions the Size of a Hen's
Egg, cut small, six small Carrots scraped and cut
up, two small Turnips pared and cut into Dice;
pour on three Quarts of Water, cover the Pot close,
and keep it gently and steadily boiling five Hours,
which will leave about three Pints of clear Soup;
do not let the Pot boil over, but take off the Scum
carefully, as it rises. When it has boiled four Hours,
put in a small Bundle of Thyme and Parsley, and a
Pint of Celery cut small, or a Teaspoonful of
Celery-seed pounded. These latter Ingredients
would lose their delicate Flavour if boiled too
much. Just before you take it up, brown it in the
following Manner: put a small Tablespoonful of
nice brown Sugar into an iron Skillet, set it on the
Fire and stir it till it melts and looks very dark,
pour into it a Ladlefull of the Soup, a little at a
Time, stirring it all the While. Strain this Browning
and mix it well with the Soup, take out the Bundle
of

of Thyme and Parſley, put the niceſt Pieces of
Meat in your Tureen, and pour on the Soup and
Vegetables; put in ſome toaſted Bread cut in Dice,
and ſerve it up.

(Recipe, 1831, Prov'd Market
Square Tavern</i> Kitchen, 1937.)

Savoury Tomato Soup*

TO four Pounds of Beef Knuckles and Briſket,
add ſeveral Sprigs of Parſley, ſome Celery Tops,
four Stalks of Celery, one Onion, one Tableſpoon of
pickling Spices, Salt and Pepper. Cover with cold
Water and ſimmer gently for about five Hours.
Add one Tableſpoon each of Marjoram and Thyme
and one Blade of Mace. Cook about thirty Minutes. Settle with Egg Shells and ſtrain through a
Cloth. To this Stock add one Part of ſtrong Tomato
Juice to two Parts of Stock.

(Mrs. Randolph's Recipe, 1831,
Adapted <i>Travis</i> Houſe, 1938.)

Calf's Head Soup*

WASH well and ſcald one Calf's Head. Put it to
boil in three Quarts of cold Water. Boil gently for five Hours, taking off Scum as it riſes; then
add one Onion, a Bunch of Parſley and Marjoram,
one Bay-leaf and Salt and boil one more Hour.
Strain and cool. Make ſmall Forc'd-meat Balls the
Size of a Walnut of Meat chopped from the Head,
grated Lemon Rind, chopped Parſley, one Egg, one
Tableſpoonful of Flour and Salt and Pepper. Fry
theſe well in Butter. Boil Soup and thicken with
three Tableſpoonfuls of Butter mixed with Flour.
Put

Put Forc'd-meat Balls into Tureen, pour boiling Soup over them, add one Glaſsful of Sherry or *Madeira* and ſerve it up.

(Old Recipe from *Kenbridge, Virginia*.)

Cheſtnut Soup

TAKE a Half Hundred of Cheſtnuts and notch them; put them in an earthen Pan, in a warm Oven for Half an Hour. Stew them one Hour in a Quart of Veal or Beef Broth; in the Meantime, take three or four Pieces of lean Ham or Bacon and put them at the Bottom of the Stew-pan, one Pound of Veal, one Pound of Beef, a Pigeon cut into Pieces, two Onions ſtuck with Cloves, two Blades of Mace, a Bundle of Sweet-herbs over the Ham, with half a Pint of Water; ſtew it gently till it ſticks, but muſt not burn; pour off boiling Water, and ſkim it well; ſtuff two Pigeons with Forc'd-meat, and ſtew them in the Soup till tender; then take the Pigeons out and ſtrain the Soup to the Cheſtnuts; ſeaſon it with Pepper and Salt to your Palate, and boil it up for five Minutes; put the Pigeons into the Tureen, the Cheſtnuts round them and pour the Soup, boiling hot, over them. Add two or three Pieces of criſp Bread at the Top; garniſh the Edge of the Diſh with some of the Cheſtnuts, ſplit in two.

N. B.—If you have a Partridge, you may uſe it inſtead of the Pigeons cut to Pieces.

(Recipe, 1797, from *Cheſter, Virginia*.)

Chowder,

Chowder, a Sea Dish *

TAKE any Kind of firm Fiſh, cut it in Pieces ſix
Inches long, ſprinkle Salt and Pepper over each
Piece, cover the Bottom of a ſmall *Dutch* Oven
with Slices of Salt-pork about half boiled, lay in
the Fiſh, ſtrewing a little chopped Onion between;
cover with Crackers that have been ſoaked ſoft in
Milk, pour over it two Gills of white Wine, and
two of Water; put on the Top of the Oven, and
ſtew it gently about an Hour; take it out carefully,
and lay it in a deep Diſh; thicken the Gravy with
a little Flour and a Spoonful of Butter, add ſome
chopped Parſley, boil it a few Minutes, and pour
it over the Fiſh—ſerve it up hot.

(Mrs. *Mary Randolph*'s Virginia Houſewife, 1831.)

Cat Fiſh Chowder *

WASH the Fiſh in warm Water, put it on in
juſt Water enough to cover, boil until tender,
or until the Bones will ſlip out; take out the largeſt
Bones, chop up the Fiſh, put in a Stew-pan with a
Pint of Water, a large Lump of Butter, one Cup of
Cream, Pepper and not much Salt; one Onion,
Teaſpoonful Muſtard, one-half Teaſpoonful of
Walnut Catſup. Stew until quite thick, garniſh
with ſliced Lemon and ſerve hot.

(Old Recipe from *Toano, Virginia.*)

Clam Chowder *

CUT in fine Dice five medium Potatoes, one
large Onion, two Slices of fried Bacon. Simmer this Mixture in the Clam Liquor with equal
Amount

Amount of Water until Potatoes are foft but un-
broken. To this Mixture add one Pint thin Cream
and bring to a Boil. Seafon with Salt and Pepper
and add finely chopped Parfley. Add twenty
finely-chopped Clams, five Minutes before ferving.

(Adapted, 1937, from old Recipe.)

Cream Chicken Soup*

CUT up one Fowl, then fimmer flowly in Water
to cover. Strain Broth and cool. Take off four
Tablefpoonfuls of the Fat and brown the Fowl in
it, then add the Broth, one chopped Onion, Salt,
and Pepper. Cook well one Cupful of Rice and add
it to the Broth and Fowl. Turn flowly over two
beaten Eggs, ftrew with Parfley, chopped fine.

(Recipe from *Courtland, Virginia,* in ufe fince 1780.)

Giblet Soup*

BOIL flowly one Pint of dried *Englifh* Peafe for
five Hours in nearly one Gallon of Water. Add
one Pound of Giblets, one Dozen of Cloves, one
fmall Piece of red Pepper, and Salt. When Peafe
are well cooked, ftrain through a Sieve, cut Giblets
into fmall Pieces, return to Soup, boil up and
ferve.   (Old Recipe, *Toano, Virginia*)

Gumbo Soup*

TAKE a Fowl of good Size, cut it up, feafon it
with Salt and Pepper, and dredge it with
Flour. Take the Soup-kettle, and put in it a
Tablefpoonful of Butter, one of Lard, and one of
Onions

Onions chopped fine. Next fry the Fowl till well-browned, and add four Quarts of boiling Water. The Pot fhould now, being well covered, be allowed to fimmer for a Couple of Hours. Then put in twenty or thirty Oyfters, a Handful of chopped Okra or Gumbo, and a very little Thyme, and let it fimmer for a half an Hour longer. Juft before ferving it up, add about half a Tablefpoonful of curry Powder. This Soup is ufually eaten with the Addition of a little *Cayenne* Pepper, and is delicious.

(Old *Williamfburg* Recipe, c-1837, from Mrs. *Elizabeth Labbé Cole's* Collection.)

A Stock for an Herb-Soup

GET Chervil, Beets, Chards, Spinach, Sellery, Leeks, and fuch like Herbs, with two or three large Crufts of Bread, fome Butter, a Bunch of Sweet-herbs, and a little Salt; put thefe, with a moderate Quantity of Water, into a Kettle, and boil them for an Hour and a half, and ftrain out the Liquor through a Sieve, and it will be a good Stock for Soups, either of Afparagus Buds, Lettuce, or any other Kind fit for Lent or Faft-Days.

(The Lady's Companion, 1753; Cook Book owned by Mifs *Anna Maria Dandridge*, 1756.)

Mullagatawny Soup *

CUT up two Chickens as for Fricaffee, place them in a Stew-pan, in which previoufly put Carrot, Onion, Celery, Parfley, Thyme, Bay-leaf, Cloves, and Mace; fill up with good Veal Broth, and when the Members of the Chicken are nearly done

done ſtrain them off into a Sieve, ſaving their Broth in a Baſin. Cool the Pieces of Chicken in Water, and then take them up on a clean Napkin, trim them neatly, and place them in a Soup-pot to put into the Soup afterward. Then cut four large Onions in Halves, taking out the Head or Root Part, and again cut theſe into Slices; place them in a Stew-pan with four Ounces of Butter, a cooked Carrot, and two Heads of cooked Celery cut ſmall, and fry theſe over a ſlow Fire until the Onion is nearly melted, and become of a fine light-brown Color, then throw in as much Flour as will ſuffice to thicken the Quantity of Soup you wiſh to make; ſtir this on the Fire two or three Minutes, and after adding a good Tableſpoonful of Curry Powder, and the ſame Quantity of Curry Paſte, proceed gradually to mix in with theſe firſt, the Broth the Chickens were boiled in, and afterward as much more Conſomme of Veal as may be found requiſite to produce the Quantity of Soup deſired. Place this on the Fire, ſtirring it the whole Time, and as ſoon as it boils, put it by the Side of the Stove to clarify itſelf in the uſual Way; then rub it through the Tammy, and pour it upon the Pieces of Chicken. Half an Hour before Dinner-time, place the Soup on the Stove, ſtir it till it boils, continue boiling gently for ten Minutes, by which Time the Chickens will be cooked; ſkim the Soup; ſee that the Seaſoning is right, and ſend to Table with two Plates of plain boiled Rice, to be paſſed with the Soup.

(Old *Williamſburg* Recipe, c-1837, from Mrs. *Elizabeth Labbé Cole's* Collection. Prov'd 1937.)

Ochra

Ochra Soup *

GET two double Handfuls of young Ochra, waſh and ſlice it thin, add two Onions chopped fine, put it into a Gallon of Water at a very early Hour in an earthen Pipkin, or very nice iron Pot; it muſt be kept ſteadily ſimmering, but not boiling: put in Pepper and Salt. At twelve o'Clock, put in a Handful of *Lima* Beans; at half-paſt one o'Clock, add three young Cimlins cleaned and cut in ſmall Pieces, a Fowl, or Knuckle of Veal, a Bit of Bacon or Pork that has been boiled, and ſix Tomatos, with the Skin taken off; when nearly done, thicken with a Spoonful of Butter, mixed with one of Flour. Have Rice boiled to eat with it.

(Mrs. *Mary Randolph's* Virginia Houſewife, 1831.)

An Onion Soup, call'd The King's Soup *

TAKE ſome Onions cut in very thin Slices, ſtew them till tender, in a ſmall Quantity of Water, then add Milk, let it all boil together, at leaſt half an Hour, with a pretty many Blades of Mace, and a quarter of a Pound of freſh Butter; a little before it is taken up, thicken it with the Yolks of two Eggs well beaten, and ſome Parſley, pick'd and chopp'd very ſmall; ſalt to your Taſte: Serve it up with Toaſt cut in Dice.

About four large Onions will do to two Quarts of Milk.

(The Lady's Companion, 1753; Cook Book owned by Miſs *Anna Maria Dandridge*, 1756.)

Another

Another Way*

SOME prefer to prepare this Soup as above directed, but add one Tablespoonful of Flour to Half of the Butter just before serving and use one whole Egg beaten well for thickening.

(Market Square Tavern Kitchen, 1937.)

Oyster Soup*

PUT one Pint of Oysters into a Sauce-pan with Pepper and Salt. Cover at once and cook until Gills of Oysters begin to curl. Heat one Pint of Milk and add one Tablespoonful of Flour and Butter which have been mixed together. Add to Oysters slowly and add Salt and Pepper. A beaten Egg added to the Soup before serving is a great Addition. Serve sprinkled with chopped Parsley.

(Market Square Tavern Kitchen, 1937.)

Black-eye Pea Soup*

WASH one Quart of Black-eye Peas well in cold Water and soak over-night. Put them to cook in four Quarts of cold Water with Salt, Pepper, one half Pound of Bacon or one Ham Bone until Peas are tender. Pass through a Sieve, rub together one Tablespoonful of Flour and one of Butter and thicken the Soup. Add one half Spoonful of Walnut Catsup Serve hot with toasted Bread cut in Dice.

(Old Richmond family Recipe.
Tested in Williamsburg, 1937.)

Dried

Dried Pea Soup*

TAKE one Quart of split Peas, or *Lima* Beans, which are better; put them in three Quarts of very soft Water with three Onions chopped up, Pepper and Salt; boil them two Hours; mash them well and pass them through a Sieve; return the Liquid into the Pot, thicken it with a large Piece of Butter and Flour, put in some Slices of nice salt Pork, and a large Teaspoonful of Celery-seed pounded; boil it till the Pork is done, and serve it up; have some toasted Bread cut into Dice and fried in Butter, which must be put in the Tureen before you pour in the Soup.

(Mrs. *Mary Randolph's* Virginia Housewife, 1831.)

Williamsburg *Split Pea Soup**

WASH and soak one Pound of dried split Peas for about three Hours. Put them on to cook in three Quarts of cold Water, with one large Onion, a Ham Bone, Pepper and Salt. Cook slowly about three Hours until Soup is thick and Peas very soft. Strain through a coarse Sieve and serve hot with toasted Bread cut in Dice.

(Mrs. *Cole's* Recipe, c-1837, adapted
Market Square Tavern Kitchen, 1937.)

Green Pea Soup*

MAKE it exactly as you do the dried pea Soup, only in Place of Celery-seed, put a Handful of Mint chopped small, and a Pint of young Peas, which must be boiled in the Soup till tender; thicken it with a quarter of a Pound of Butter, and two Spoonfuls of Flour.

(Mrs. *Mary Randolph's* Virginia Housewife, 1831.)

To

To make a Veal Glue, or Cake Soup to be carried in the Pocket

TAKE a Leg of Veal, strip it of the Skin and the Fat, then take all the muscular or fleshy Parts from the Bones; boil this Flesh gently in such a Quantity of Water, and so long a Time, till the Liquor will make a strong Jelly when it is cold: This you may try by taking out a small Spoonful now and then, and letting it cool. Here it is to be supposed, that though it will jelly presently in small Quantities, yet all the Juice of the Meat may not be extracted; however, when you find it very strong, strain the Liquor through a Sieve, and let it settle; then provide a large Stew-pan, with Water, and some _China_ Cups, or glazed Earthen-ware; fill these Cups with Jelly taken clear from the Settling, and set them in a Stew-pan of Water, and let the Water boil gently till the Jelly becomes as thick as Glue; after which, let them stand to cool, and then turn out the Glue upon a Piece of new Flannel, which will draw out the Moisture; turn them once in six or eight Hours, and put them upon a fresh Flannel, and so continue to do till they are quite dry, and keep it in a dry warm Place: This will harden so much, that it will be stiff and hard as Glue in a little Time, and may be carried in the Pocket without Inconvenience. You are to use this by boiling about a Pint of Water, and pouring it upon a Piece of the Glue or Cake, about the Bigness of a small Walnut, and stirring it with a Spoon till the Cake dissolves, which will make very strong good Broth. As for the seasoning

Part,

Part, every one may add Pepper and Salt as they like it, for there muſt be nothing of that Kind put among the Veal when you make the Glue, for any Thing of that Sort would make it mouldy. As we have obſerved above, that there is nothing of Seaſoning in this Soup, ſo there may be always added what you deſire, either of Spices or Herbs, to make it ſavoury to the Palate; but it muſt be noted, that all the Herbs that are uſed on this Occaſion, muſt be boiled tender in plain Water, and that Water muſt be uſed to pour upon the Cake Gravy inſtead of Simple Water: So may a Diſh of good Soup be made without Trouble, only allowing the Proportion of Cake Gravy anſwering to the aboveſaid Direction: Or if Gravy be wanted for Sauce, double the Quantity may be uſed that is preſcribed for Broth or Soup.

(The Lady's Companion, 1753; Cook Book owned by Miſs *Anna Maria Dandridge*, 1756.)

Pocket Soup on a new Plan*

CUT three Pounds of lean Veal from the Leg in ſmall Pieces and cook ſlowly in three Quarts of cold Water with a Bundle of Sweet-herbs, a large Onion and ſome chopped Parſley about four Hours. Strain well and add one Teaſpoonful of Gelatin for each Pint of the Broth and ſet in a very cold Place. Serve this as a cold jellied Broth. If you omit your Gelatin you may ſerve your Soup hot as a clear Broth.

(*Market Square Tavern* Kitchen, 1937.)

Snail

Snail Broth

WITH this, which is also a medicinal Broth, and very excellent in its Kind, we shall close the present Chapter; it is one of those Foods that may save much Money to the Physicians, and we should do wisely to copy the Practice of those who find it so.

Pick twenty Garden Snails out of their Shells, and pound them in a marble Mortar; take the hinder Legs of thirty Frogs, pound them with the Snails, and put them into a Pot with three Quarts of Water and a little Salt; pare and slice very thin a Dozen fine Turnips, and slice also one large Leek, first stripping off the outer Skin; put these into the Pot, and add a double Handful of pearl Barley, and twenty Grains of Saffron.

Let all boil together till there is but a Quart left, run this through a Sieve without squeezing, and let it be taken at two Messes.

It is a very agreeably-flavoured Broth, though it tastes weak. Many have recovered from the Beginning of Consumptions by this Broth alone.

(Mrs. *Martha Bradley's* British Housewife.)

Williamsburg *Savoury Jelly* ⁑

PUT three Pounds of lean Beaf and two Pounds of Fore-quarter of Veal with the Veal Bones into one Gallon of cold Water. Add three large Onions, three Carrots, three Turnips, some Sprigs of Parsley, Thyme, Marjoram, and Savoury with Salt & Pepper to taste. Cook slowly until reduced by half. Strain through a Sieve. The next Day re-move

move Fat & bring to a Boil. Add one Cup of White-wine, three Slices of Lemon, the Whites of two Eggs beaten, and their Shells. Bring to a Boil again, and boil for two Minutes. Let ſtand twenty Minutes and ſtrain through doubled Cheeſe-cloth. This may be ſerved hot as a Broth, or by adding two Tableſpoonſuls of Gelatin at the laſt, may be chilled and ſerved as ſavoury Jelly.

(Mrs. *Randolph's* Recipe, 1831, adapted *Market Square Tavern* Kitchen, 1937.)

Celery Sauce*

WASH and pare a large Bunch of Celery very clean, cut it into little Bits, and boil it ſoftly till it is tender; add half a Pint of Cream, ſome Mace, Nutmeg, and a ſmall Piece of Butter rolled in Flour; then boil it gently. This is a good Sauce for roaſted or boiled Fowls, Turkeys, Partridges, or any other Game.

(Mrs. *Mary Randolph's* Virginia Houſewife, 1831.)

To fry Cucumbers for Mutton Sauce*

YOU muſt brown ſome Butter in a Pan and cut the Cucumbers in thin Slices; drain them from the Water, then fling them into the Pan, and when they are fried brown, put in a little Pepper and Salt, a Bit of an Onion and Gravy, and let them ſtew together, and ſqueeze in ſome Juice of Lemon; ſhake them well, and put them under your Mutton.

(*E. Smith's* Compleat Houſewife, *Williamſburg*, 1742.)

Common

Common Sauce *

PLAIN Butter melted thick, with a Spoonful of Walnut Pickle or Catsup, is a very good Sauce; but you may put as many Things as you choose into Sauces.

(Mrs. *Mary Randolph's* Virginia Housewife, 1831.)

Curry Powder *

ONE Ounce Turmeric, one do. Coriander Seed, one do. Cummin Seed, one do. white Ginger, one of Nutmeg, one of Mace, and one of *Cayenne* Pepper; pound all together, and pass them through a fine Sieve; bottle and cork it well—one Teaspoonful is sufficient to season any made Dish.

(Mrs. *Mary Randolph's* Virginia Housewife, 1831.)

To make Egg Sauce *

BOIL four Eggs for ten Minutes, chop half the Whites, put them with the Yelks, and chop them both together, but not very fine; put them into a quarter of a Pound of good melted Butter, and put it in a Boat.

(Mrs. *Mary Randolph's* Virginia Housewife, 1831.)

Horse-radish Sauce *

MIX together one Teacupful grated Horse-radish, one Tablespoonful ground Mustard, one Tablespoonful Sugar, four Tablespoonfuls Vinegar, (or Olive Oil if preferred), Pepper and Salt to Taste and one Teaspoonful Turmeric.

(Recipe from an old *Williamsburg* Cook Book.)

A

A Sauce for Fiſh in Lent, *or at any Time*

TAKE a little Thyme, Horſe-radiſh, a Bit of
Onion, Lemon-peel, and whole Pepper; boil
them a little in fair Water; then put in two Anchovies, and four Spoonfuls of White-wine, then
ſtrain them out, and put the Liquor into the
ſame Pan again, with a Pound of freſh Butter;
and when 'tis melted take it off the Fire, and ſtir
in the Yolks of two Eggs well beaten, with three
Spoonfuls of White-wine; ſet it on the Fire again,
and keep it ſtirring till 'tis the Thickneſs of
Cream, and pour it hot over your Fiſh. Garniſh
with Lemon and Horſe-radiſh.

(*E. Smith's* Compleat Houſewife, *Williamſburg*, 1742.)

To make a Sauce for a Gooſe ∗

PARE, core and ſlice ſome Apples; put them in
a Sauce-pan, with as much Water as will keep
them from burning, ſet them over a very ſlow
Fire, keep them cloſely covered till reduced to a
Pulp, then put in a Lump of Butter, and Sugar to
your Taſte, beat them well, and ſend them to the
Table in a *China* Bowl.

(Mrs. *Mary Randolph's* Virginia Houſewife, 1831.)

Minced Sauce ∗

CUT Onions, Muſhrooms, and Truffles, if you
have any, very ſmall, with Capers, and Anchovies, and keep them ſeparately; put into a
Stew-pan a little Butter with your Onions; put
your Stew-pan over a briſk Fire; give it two or
three

three Tosses; then put in your Mushrooms and
Truffles strewing over them a Dust of Flour, and
moisten them with good Gravy, then put in it
your Capers and Anchovies, with a Glass of White-
wine; thicken your Sauce with a Spoonful of
Cullis. Let it be of a good Taste, and you may use
it with all Dishes with a minc'd Sauce.

(The Lady's Companion, 1753; Cook Book
owned by Miss *Anna Maria Dandridge*, 1756.)

Mushroom Sauce*

TAKE one Cup of Mushrooms and cut them in
two, put them in a Pan with three Tablespoonfuls of Butter and cook gently shaking your Pan.
Strew over this two Tablespoonfuls of Flour, add
one Cup of Cream and cook slowly for eight Minutes. Add Salt and Pepper.

(Mrs. *Randolph's* Recipe, 1831. Adapted
Market Square Tavern Kitchen, 1937.)

Poor Man's Sauce with Oil*

CHOP a Handful of Leaves of Parsley picked
from the Stalks, make it very fine, and strew
over it a little Salt; shred fine half a Dozen young
Onions, taking off two of the Skins; add these to
the Parsley, and put them into a Bason with three
Spoonfuls of Oil; add to this some Vinegar to give
it a little Sharpness, and dust in some Pepper; stir
all together, and send it up.

This eats extremely well with cold Lamb, cold
Veal, or cold Chicken; it may be eat with hot.

(Mrs. *Martha Bradley's* British Housewife.)

Parsley

Parsley and Butter Sauce *

SCALD a large Handful of Parsley in boiling Water that has some Salt in it. When tender, chop it fine and stir it into some rather thick melted Butter. There should be sufficient Parsley to make the Sauce green, and the Parsley should not be put to the melted Butter until about to be served, otherwise it will turn brown.

(Old Recipe from *Chase City, Virginia.* Adapted, 1937.)

Sauce for Roast Venison *

JELLY of Currants melted and serv'd hot, with a Lemon squeez'd into it.

(*E. Smith's* Compleat Housewife, *London*, 1739.)

Sauce for Wild Fowl

TAKE a Gill of Claret, with as much Water, some grated Bread, three Heads of Shallots, a little whole Pepper, Mace, grated Nutmeg, and Salt; let them stew over the Fire, then beat it up with Butter, and put it under the wild Fowl, which, being a little roasted, will afford Gravy to mix with this Sauce.

(Mrs. *Mary Randolph's* Virginia Housewife, 1831.)

Of

Of FLESH & FISH

F ROM Rivers and Ocean, Field and Foreft, the *Virginia* Houfewife had a varied and abundant Supply of Meat and Fifh, and the *Virginia* Gentleman, good Hunting and Fifhing. In 1739, the Botanift, *John Clayton*, wrote to a Friend in *England* of the Field Sports:

. . . To fatisfie the Gentlemen you mention who is fo defirous of knowing the Diverfion of Hunting and Shooting here and the feveral Sorts of Game pray give my Service to him and tell him, that we have all the tame domeftick Beafts and Fowls that you have in *England*, and great Variety of wild ones as Deer in great Pleanty, Bears, Buffaloes, Wolves, Foxes, Panthers, Wild Cats, Elks, Hares (fmaller than any of y's which run in Holes in the Earth and hollow Trees when preffed by the Dogs, and are much like w't you called in *England* Bufh Rabbits), Squirrels 3 or 4 Sorts, Raccoons, Oppoffums, Beavers, Otters, Mufk Rats, Pole Cats, Minks and there has been two Porcupines killed here, but they are very fcarce.

. . . Then for Fowls, wild Turkey's very numerous, Partridges (the Size and Colour like y'r Quails), wild Geefe, Swans, Brants, Cormorants, Teal Duck and Mallard, black Ducks, Plover 2 or 3 Sorts, Soris (a delicious eating Bird in Shape and Way of Living like y'r Water Rails), Heath Fowls (called here improperly Pheafants) 2 Sorts, wild Pidgeons in prodigious great Flocks, Field-
fares,

fares, Woodcocks (but what is very ſtrange they
come here only in Summer) Snipes, Herons,
Bitterns, Eagles, Larks 2 Sorts one of w'ch are
here all the Year round, are as big as Quails, the
other are ſeen only in Winter and are much like
your Lark.

As for Fiſh, freſh, ſalt Water and Shell-fiſh,
Beverley contended "no Country can boaſt of
"more Variety, greater Plenty or better of their
"ſeveral Kinds." He told of Rivers ſo teeming with
Herring that Boats could hardly get through without treading on them, and of Sturgeon that would
leap into Boats.

> Thoſe which I know of myſelf, [he ſaid,] I re-
> member by the Names. Of Herrings, Rocks,
> Sturgeons, Shads, Old-Wives, Sheep's-Heads,
> black and red Drums, Trouts, Taylors, Green-
> Fiſh, Sun-Fiſh, Baſs, Chub, Place, Flounders,
> Whitings, Fatbacks, Maids, Wives, Small-Turtle,
> Crabs, Oiſters, Muſſels, Cockles, Shrimps, Needle-
> Fiſh, Breme, Carp, Pike, Jack, Mullets, Eels,
> Conger-Eels, Perch, and Cats, &c.

The Swine, Poultry and other domeſtic Animals
brought from *England* augmented this abundant
natural Supply. The Hogs, one contemporary
Writer ſaid, ſwarmed like Vermin upon the Earth
and were permitted to run as they liked and find
their own Support in the Woods.

From theſe Hogs, the *Virginians* produced one
of their moſt famous Foodſtuffs and their moſt
popular ſtanding Diſh. Whatever elſe appeared
upon the Table, Ham, Bacon, or Jowl were always
there. *Francis Louis Michel*, a *Swiſs* who travelled
through *Virginia* in 1701-2, ſaid that all agreed
that the *Virginia* Pork was "the beſt and the moſt
"delicate."

"delicate." Another Traveller compared the Ham to the beſt *Weſtphalian* Ham.

In the conſtant Exchange of genteel Preſents which went on between *Virginia* and "Home", Ham was one of the moſt appreciated Gifts. Sir *William Gooch* (who was Lieutenant Governor of *Virginia*, 1727-1749) ſent Hams to his Brother, the Biſhop of *Norwich*, and to the Biſhops of *Saliſbury*, *London* and *Bangor*.

Nor was the *Virginia* Ham leſs eſteemed in the Colony, as the Fly-leaf of the Bible owned by the firſt *William Byrd* of *Weſtover* can teſtify, for on it was written:

> To eat ye Ham in Perfection ſteep it in half Milk and half Water for thirty-ſix Hours, and then having brought the Water to a Boil put ye Ham therein and let it ſimmer, not boil, for 4 or 5 Hours according to Size of ye Ham—for ſimmering brings ye Salt out and boiling drives it in. [c-1674.]

In the Interchange of Letters between *Virginia* and *England* and the other Colonies, Hams and Bacon were frequently the Subject of much Diſcourſe. One ſuch Letter, written from *St. Croix* to *George Flowerdewe Norton* of *Virginia* upon the Occaſion of *Norton's* Marriage is ſtill preſerved in *Williamſburg*.

St. Croix
July 11, 1785.

. . . Mrs. *Reeve* & myſelf ſincerley congratulate you & your amiable Lady (for amiable ſhe certainly muſt be if the Object of your Choice) on your Entrance into the matrimonial State—& wiſh you no more Love & Harmony, than we ourſelves have enjoy'd therein—We have four
Flitches

Flitches of Bacon now due—but fear we ſhall not
very ſoon reach that Country* where they are
demandable.

. . . Mrs. *Reeve* unites with me in ſincere
Wiſhes for your long Enjoyment of every ter-
reſtrial Bliſs & believe me with great Sincerity

Yr Affect & Obed Servt
Thomas Reeve

* DUNMOW, there was an ancient Cuſtom in
the Priory, that if any Perſon from any Part of
England would come thither, and humbly kneel
at the Church Door before the Convent, and ſol-
emnly take the enſuing Oath, he might demand
a Flitch or Gammon of Bacon, which ſhould be
freely given him.

You ſhall ſwear by the Cuſtom of our Confeſſion
That you never made any nuptial Tranſgreſſion,
Since you were married Man and Wife,
By houſehold Brawls or a contentious Strife;
Or otherwiſe, in Bed or at Board,
Offended each Other in Deed or in Word;
Or ſince the Pariſh Clerk ſaid Amen,
Wiſhed your ſelves unmarried again;
Or in a Twelvemonth and a Day
Repent not in Thought any Way;
But continued True and in Deſire
As when you joined Hands in holy Quire.
If to thoſe Conditions, without all Fear,
Of your own Accord you will freely ſwear;
A Gammon of Bacon you ſhall receive,
And bear it hence with Love and good Leave;
For this is our Cuſtom at *Dunmow* well known,
Though the Sport be ours, the Bacon's your own.

(*Bailey's* Dictionary, *London*, 1730.)

Fleſh

Fleſh & Fiſh

Beef A-la-mode

TAKE a good Buttock of Beef, interlarded with great Lard, roll'd up in ſavoury Spice, and Sweet-herbs; put it in a great Sauce-pan, and cover it cloſe and ſet in the Oven all Night. This is fit to eat cold.

(*E. Smith's* Compleat Houſewife, *Williamſburg*, 1742.)

Sirloin of Beef en Epigram

HAVING roaſted a Sirloin of Beef, take it off the Spit, and raiſe the Skin carefully off. Then cut out the lean Part of the Beef, but obſerve not to cut near the Ends nor Sides. Haſh the Meat in the following Manner: cut it into Pieces about the Size of a Crown Piece, put half a Pint of Gravy into a Toſſ-pan, an Onion chopped fine, two Spoonfuls of Catchup, ſome Pepper and Salt, ſix ſmall pickled Cucumbers cut in thin Slices, and the Gravy that comes from the Beef, with a little Butter rolled in Flour. Put in the Meat, and toſs it up for five Minutes; put it on the Sirloin, and then put the Skin over, and ſend it to Table.

(*John Farley's* London Art of Cookery, 1787.)

Beef Steak Pye

BEAT ſome Rump Steaks with a Rolling-pin, and ſeaſon them with Pepper and Salt to your Palate. Make a good Cruſt, lay in your Steaks, and

and then pour in as much Water as will half fill
the Diſh. Put on the Cruſt, and bake it well.

(*John Farley's* London Art of Cookery, 1787.
From *Brookbury, Cheſterfield* County, *Virginia.*)

Williamſburg *Beef Steak Pye* ✻

BEAT ſeveral Rump Steaks with a Rolling-pin,
cut them in Pieces and ſtrew with Flour. Fry
in Suet until brown, add ſome chopped Onion,
Salt, Pepper and a few Sprigs of Parſley. Add hot
Water to cover and ſimmer until thick. Put them
in a Baking-diſh with the Gravy, put on a top
Cruſt of rich Paſtry and bake about forty Minutes.

(Mrs. *Randolph's* Recipe, 1831. Adapted
Market Square Tavern Kitchen, 1937.)

Williamſburg *Beef Steak & Ham Pye* ✻

TAKE one Pound of nice Steaks and pound
well with Flour. Brown them in your Skillet
in a little Lard. Pour hot Water over them and
ſeaſon your Gravy well with Salt & Pepper. Arrange the Steaks in a Diſh with one half Pound of
ſliced boiled Ham, pour Gravy over, put on a Lid
of Paſtry and bake about forty Minutes.

(Mrs. *Randolph's* Recipe, 1831. Adapted
Market Square Tavern Kitchen, 1937.)

Roaſt Beef ✻

SELECT a five or ſix pound Piece of Beef fit for
roaſting. Rub over it a Piece of Suet, and in a
few ſmall Gaſhes inſert Slices of Onion or two ſmall
Cloves of Garlic. Place it on a Rack in a Dripping-
pan,

pan, put over it feveral Strips of Suet and place it in a very hot Oven to fear for about fifteen Minutes. Reduce the Heat and roaft the Beef about fifteen Minutes to the Pound or lefs if you prefer it rare. When enough, lift out the Beef, remove fome of the Drippings to make your Gravy, pour a *Yorkfhire* Pudding in the Pan and bake it quickly. Serve it up with your thickened Gravy in a feparate Difh.

(Recipe from a *Williamfburg* Cook Book. Prov'd 1937.)

Yorkfhire *Pudding**

BEAT three Eggs very light, add one and a half Cups of fweet Milk (or one Cup of Milk and a half Cup of Chicken Stock) and three Tablefpoonfuls of melted Butter. Beat in one and a half Cups of fifted Flour. If you do not bake under the Meat in a Dripping-pan, pour it into a well greafed fhallow Baking-difh and bake in a hot Oven.

(Mr. *Farley's* Recipe, 1787. Adapted *Travis* Houfe, 1938.)

Beef Rolls*

TAKE as many Beef Steaks as will fill a Difh —beat them tender then fprinkle them with the Crumbs of lite Bread. Pepper—Onions— Parfley—Thyme—roll them up and tye them with a String; fry them in Lard. The hind Quarter of Shoat inftead of Beef make nice Rolls.

(Manufcript Cook Book, prior 1839.
Morton Family of *Charlotte* County, *Virginia.*)

Englifh

Engliſh *Steak & Kidney Pie* *

REMOVE the Skin from two ſmall Beef Kidneys
and waſh in ſalted Water. Cut in two-inch
Squares and dredge with Flour. Have ready three
fourths of a Pound of Beefſteak, pound it well in
Flour and cut in ſmall Pieces. Cook ſome Bits of
Suet or other Shortening in a large Frying-pan
then brown the Steak with a finely-chopped Onion,
add the Kidneys and cook ſlowly until browned.
Add hot Water to cover and ſimmer gently. Seaſon
with a ſmall Bay-leaf, Parſley, Celery-tops, Salt
and Pepper. Simmer gently in a covered Pan for
about an Hour. The beſt Cooks then add one Cupful of raw Muſhrooms, and one half Cup of finely
diced cooked Carrots. If your Gravy needs Thickening add Flour mixed in cold Water. Pour all into
a deep Baking-diſh and cover with a Cruſt of Paſtry or of thinly-rolled Biſcuit Dough. Bake until
the Cruſt is done and ſerve it up. This old *Engliſh*
Favorite was alſo popular in the Colonies.

(Old *Virginia* Recipe. Prov'd *Blair* Kitchen, 1938.)

Brunſwick *Stew* *

CUT up two Squirrels (or a three Pound Chicken)
and put in a large Pan with three Quarts of
Water, one large ſliced Onion, one half Pound of
lean Ham cut in ſmall Pieces and ſimmer gently
for two Hours. Add three Pints of Tomatoes, one
Pint of *Lima* Beans, four large *Iriſh* Potatoes
diced, one Pint grated Corn, one Tableſpoon Salt,
one fourth Teaſpoon Pepper, a ſmall Pod of red
Pepper. Cover and ſimmer gently for one more
Hour

Hour stirring frequently to prevent Scorching. Add three Ounces of Butter and serve hot.

(Old Recipe from *Richmond, Virginia.*)

Or make it thus:*

CUT one large Chicken in eight Pieces. Cook slowly in one Gallon of cold Water two and a quarter Hours, being careful not to boil rapidly at any Time. To the Chicken and Broth add two Cups of fresh sliced Okra, two Cups of *Lima* Beans, four Cups of chopped, peeled Tomatoes and two sliced Onions. Then slowly cook for six Hours adding hot Water occasionally so that there will be between five and six Quarts of this Mixture. Then add four diced white Potatoes and four Cups of Corn. Cook one Hour. Stir to prevent Scorching. Season with two Teaspoonfuls of Salt, one-half Spoonful of Pepper and a little Sugar.

(*Market Square Tavern* Kitchen, 1937.)

Brunswick *Stew to serve Twenty**

IN a heavy *Dutch* Oven put two Pounds of diced Beef, two Veal Shanks cut up, a four-pound Chicken jointed, one half Pound of diced smoked Bacon, and one Squirrel if obtainable. Cover with cold Water, season with Salt and a Pod of red Pepper and simmer until Meat falls from Bones. Add a Quart and a half of diced *Irish* Potatoes, one and a half Pounds of *Lima* Beans, two Pounds of peeled, sliced Tomatoes. Cook until Potatoes mash up to thicken Stew. One half Hour before serving add Corn cut from one dozen Ears, one

half

half Pound of Butter, one Teaſpoon black Pepper. This requires at leaſt ſix Hours ſlow cooking. It may be made the Day before ſerving.

(Traditional *Virginia* Recipe. Prov'd 1937.)

Smothered Chicken *

SINGE a young Fowl and ſplit it down the Back. Draw it, then lay the Chicken, with Inſide downward, in a Baking-pan, breaking the Breaſt Bone to make it lie flat. Spread the Breaſt with Butter, dredge with Pepper. Put Salt and about one half Cup of Water in the Bottom of the Baking-pan, place in a hot Oven, cover with another Pan, let bake for half an Hour, baſting every ten Minutes. Remove upper Pan, turn Fowl, baſte well on Inſide, cover again and bake for another half Hour. When done place it on a hot Diſh; put Pan in which it was cooked on Top of Fire to brown, add Flour and ſtir until ſmooth and brown, then add a half Pint of Milk and ſtir until it boils. Add Salt and Pepper and ſend up your Gravy in a Boat.

(Old Recipe from *Kenbridge, Virginia.* Prov'd 1937.)

A Pilau

PUT on a good Piece of Middling of Bacon and two Fowls to boil. When done take them out and cover them over the Fire. Put into the Water in which they were boiled as much Rice as will fill yᵣ Diſh with ſome Grains of black Pepper and Allſpice if you like it—when the Rice is ſoft pour off all the Water, return the Fowls and Bacon to

the

the Pot firſt ſkinning the Bacon and let them ſtand over the Fire till you diſh them. Then lay yʳ Fowls and Bacon firſt in, and cover them with the Rice.

(Manuſcript Cook Book, c-1801, of Mrs. *Frances Bland Tucker Coalter.* Owned by Dr. *St. George Tucker Grinnan, Richmond.*)

India *Pilau*

WASH and pick clean two Pounds Rice put in a Colander and drain very dry—put one Pound Butter and one half a Pint of Water into a Stew-pan—put in the Rice. Seaſon it with beaten Cloves, Mace, grated Nutmeg, Pepper and Salt. Cover cloſe and keep in the Steam. Stir it gently and ſtir it often to keep it from burning till it is tender. In the Meantime boil two Fowls and two Pounds of Bacon. Put the Fowls into a Diſh cut the Bacon in two and lay it on each Side put the Rice over and garniſh with hard Egg and a Dozen Onions, fried whole and brown.

This is the true *India* Pilau.

(Manuſcript Cook Book, c-1801, of Mrs. *Frances Bland Tucker Coalter.* Owned by Dr. *St. George Tucker Grinnan, Richmond.*)

Chicken Pilau *

BROWN two large chopped Onions in a large Frying-pan in three Tableſpoonfuls of Butter, add three Cups of ſtewed Tomatoes, four Stalks of Celery chopped fine, a finely chopped green Pepper, three Teaſpoons Salt, ſome Pepper, three Cups of cold chopped Chicken and two Cups of boiled

boiled Rice. Cook for fifteen Minutes ſtirring to prevent Scorching. Pour into buttered Baking-diſh, cover with one Cup of well buttered Bread-crumbs and bake in moderate Oven an Hour and a quarter.

(Prov'd *Travis* Houſe, 1938.)

Chicken & Dumplins *

CUT and joint a large Chicken. Cover with Water and let boil gently until tender. Seaſon with Salt and Pepper and thicken the Gravy with two Tableſpoonfuls of Flour mixed ſmooth in a Piece of Butter the Size of an Egg. Have ready nice light Bread Dough about an Inch thick; cut with a Biſcuit-cutter. Drop into the boiling Gravy, having previouſly removed the Chicken to a hot Platter; cover and let theſe boil from one half to three quarters of an Hour.

To aſcertain whether they are done ſtick them with a Fork; if it comes out clean they are done. Lay them on the Platter with the Chicken; pour the Gravy over and ſerve.

(Old Recipe from *Highland Springs, Virginia.* Prov'd 1937.)

Croquettes *

CHOP one Pound of cold Turkey or Chicken very fine; mix with Salt and Pepper one Teaſpoon chopped Onion, three Teaſpoons chopped Parſley. Seaſon delicately with Mace and grated Nutmeg. Moiſten with three Tableſpoons of ſweet Cream, ſhape into Pear-ſhaped Balls. For the Stems inſert Cloves. Dip this in beaten Egg and then

then in grated Bread-crumbs. Cook in boiling
Lard until nice and brown.

(Recipe, c-1855, from *Wicomico Church, Virginia.*
Prov'd *Market Square Tavern* Kitchen, 1937.)

Chicken Gumbo*

JOINT a young four-pound Chicken. Roll in
Flour and fry till light brown in three Tableſpoons Butter and three Tableſpoons Lard. Put
Chicken and a Ham Bone in large Soup-kettle.
Into the Skillet in which the Chicken was fried
ſlice three medium ſized Onions and fry golden
brown. Put into the Soup-pot with three Cups
ſtewed Tomatoes, three Pints of young Okra ſliced,
three Cups ſliced Celery and two Quarts cold
Water. Simmer for four or five Hours adding one
Tableſpoon Salt and one half Teaſpoon Pepper
toward the End. The Chicken muſt drop from
Bones. Take out the Bones. Have boiled Rice
ready. Preſs Portions into ſmall buttered Cups to
mold and turn out onto Soup-plates. Pour the hot
Gumbo around it.

(Old Recipe from *Richmond, Virginia.* Prov'd 1937.)

Chicken Terrapin*

TAKE one Quart of cold diced Chicken and put
it in a Sauce-pan with one fourth of a Pound
of melted Butter, ſift over it two Tableſpoonfuls of
Flour then ſtir in one half Cup of Cream. Seaſon
with one fourth Teaſpoon of powdered Mace, one
eighth Teaſpoon of pounded Cloves, and Salt and
Pepper to your Taſte and beat thoroughly on a ſlow
Fire.

Fire. Chop the Whites of three hard-boiled Eggs
very fine and add. Mix the Yolks of the Eggs with a
few Spoonfuls of Cream and add. Add one half
Cup of Sherry and ſerve at once. Calf's Liver may
be parboiled for fifteen Minutes and is delicious
dreſſed in the ſame Manner.

(Old Recipe from *Richmond, Virginia.* Prov'd 1937.)

Chicken Pudding, a Favourite Virginia *Diſh*

BEAT ten Eggs very light, add to them a Quart
of rich Milk, with a quarter of a Pound of
Butter melted, and ſome Pepper and Salt; ſtir in
as much Flour as will make a thin good Batter;
take four young Chickens, and after cleaning them
nicely, cut off the Legs, Wings, &c. put them all
in a Sauce-pan, with ſome Salt and Water, and a
Bundle of Thyme and Parſley, boil them till nearly
done, then take the Chickens from the Water and
put it in the Batter, pour it in a deep Diſh, and
bake it; ſend nice white Gravy in a Boat.

(Mrs. *Mary Randolph's* Virginia Houſewife, 1831.)

Williamſburg *Chicken Pudding* ⁂

CUT up a four or five Pound Fowl as for Frica-
ſee, put it in your Kettle with Water to cover,
with one Onion, a few Celery Tops, ſome Sprigs of
Parſley, a Teaſpoonful of Thyme, Salt and Pepper.
Simmer gently until Fowl is tender. Take from
Broth, remove Skin and place in a ſhallow Baking-
diſh. Pour over it one Cup of ſtrained Broth.
Make a Batter of one Pint of Milk, three well-
beaten Eggs, one-fourth Cup of Flour, one-fourth
Cup

Cup melted Butter and one Teaſpoon of Salt.
Pour this over your Chicken and bake in a moderate Oven about thirty-five Minutes. Serve immediately with a Gravy made of thickened Broth
in a ſeparate Diſh.

(Mrs. *Randolph's* Recipe, 1831. Adapted
Market Square Tavern Kitchen, 1937.)

Chicken Pye

PUT yʳ Paſte in the Diſh (in the Winter make it
with full Weight of Butter, and in the Summer
with as much Butter as the Flour will take in).
Lay in two large or three ſmall Chickens cut up,
ſtrew between the Layers and at Top, a double
Handful of Bits of lean Bacon boiled or raw (if
raw yʳ Pye will require leſs Salt—Lay at Top
ſeveral large Lumps of Butter, about one fourth
of a Pound. Strew over a heaped Tableſpoon of
Salt and an even one of fine Pepper *black*). Fill
laſt of all with cold Water—Put into a *Dutch* Oven
firſt laying in the Bottom a little warm Aſhes and
let it bake gradually with the Top of very moderate Heat and put Coals under from Time to
Time, when nearly done increaſe the Fire on the
Top to brown the Paſte. It will take near two
Hours baking.

(Manuſcript Cook Book, c-1801, of Mrs. *Frances Bland
Tucker Coalter.* Owned by Dr. *St. George
Tucker Grinnan, Richmond.*)

Chicken Corn Pye *

BOIL up one Cup of Rice and butter it well
while it is hot. Put a Layer of Rice in the
Bottom of a buttered Baking-diſh, add one
Chicken

Chicken which has been cooked in a well-ſeaſoned Broth, and the Corn ſcraped from three large Ears. Pour over this one Cup of Broth, add three Table-ſpoons of Butter, Salt and Pepper. Cover with the Rice, glaze it with a beaten Egg and bake to a delicate brown.

(Old Recipe, *Henrico* County, *Virginia.* Prov'd 1937.)

Fricaſſee of Small Chickens *

TAKE off the Legs and Wings of four Chickens, ſeparate the Breaſts from the Backs, cut off the Necks and divide the Backs acroſs, clean the Gizzards nicely, put them with the Livers and other Parts of the Chicken, after being waſhed clean, into a Sauce-pan, add Pepper, Salt, and a little Mace, cover them with Water, and ſtew them till tender—then take them out, thicken half a Pint of the Water with two Tableſpoonfuls of Flour rubbed into four Ounces of Butter, add half a Pint of new Milk, boil all together a few Minutes, then add a Gill of White-wine, ſtirring it in care-fully that it may not curdle; put the Chickens in, and continue to ſhake the Pan until they are ſufficiently hot, and ſerve them up.

(Mrs. *Mary Randolph's* Virginia Houſewife, 1831. Prov'd 1937.)

Fried Chickens *

CUT them up as for the Fricaſſee, dredge them well with Flour, ſprinkle them with Salt, put them into a good Quantity of boiling Lard, and fry them a light brown; fry ſmall Pieces of Muſh and a Quantity of Parſley nicely picked, to be
served

ſerved in the Diſh with the Chickens; take half a
Pint of rich Milk, add to it a ſmall Bit of Butter,
with Pepper, Salt, and chopped Parſley; ſtew it a
little, and pour it over the Chickens, and then
garniſh with the fried Parſley.

(Mrs. *Mary Randolph's* Virginia Houſewife, 1831.)

Williamſburg *Fried Chicken**

JOINT the Chickens neatly, waſh and drain.
Soak in cold Milk for half an Hour. Dredge
them well with Flour to which Salt and Pepper
have been added. Fry in an iron Skillet in boiling
Fat almoſt deep enough to cover the Pieces of
Chicken. Turn each Piece at leaſt three Times.
Fry to a nice brown, drain on brown Paper and
ſerve with Gravy ſent up in a ſeparate Boat.

GRAVY: Brown ſome Flour in ſome of the Fat
in which the Chicken was fried. Seaſon and add
chicken Stock. Stir until thick and ready to ſerve.

(Prov'd *Travis* Houſe, 1938.)

Pullet, or Chicken Surprize

ROAST them off; if a ſmall Diſh, two Chickens,
or one Pullet, will be enough. Take the Lean
of your Pullet, or Chickens, from the Bone, cut it
in thin Slices an Inch long, and toſs it up in ſix or
ſeven Spoonfuls of Milk or Cream, with the Bigneſs of half an Egg of Butter, grated Nutmeg,
Pepper, and Salt; thicken it with a little Duſt of
Flour, to the Thickneſs of a good Cream, then boil
it up, and ſet it to cool; then cut ſix or ſeven thin
round Slices of Bacon, place them in a Patty-pan,
and

and put on each Slice ſome Forc'd-meat, then
work them up in Form of a *French* Roll, with raw
Egg in your Hand, leaving a hollow Place in the
Middle; then put in your Fowl, and cover them
with ſome of the ſame Forc'd-meat, rubbing it
ſmooth over with your Hand, and an Egg, make
them of the Height and Bigneſs of a *French* Roll;
throw a little fine grated Bread over them, bake
them three quarters of an Hour in a gentle Oven,
or under a Baking-cover, till they come to a yellow
brown, place them on your Mazarine, that they
may not touch one another, but ſo that they may
not fall flat in the Baking: But you may form
them on your Kitchen Table, with your Slices of
Bacon under them; then lift them up with your
broad Kitchen Knife, and place them on that
which you intend to bake them on. Let your
Sauce be Butter and Gravy, and ſqueez'd Lemon,
and your Garniſhing fry'd Parſley, and cut Orange.
You may put the Legs of one of your Chickens into
the Sides of one of your Loaves that you intend to
put in the Middle of your Diſh. This is proper for
a Side-diſh, for a firſt Courſe, either in Summer or
Winter, where you can have the Ingredients above
mention'd.

(The Lady's Companion, 1753; Cook Book
owned by Miſs *Anna Maria Dandridge*, 1756.)

Williamſburg *Chicken Surprize* *

TAKE the Meat of a three or four pound
Chicken which has been cooked in a Broth
ſeaſoned with Salt, Pepper, Parſley, Onion and
Celery, and cut it in ſmall Pieces. Melt two Tableſpoons

ſpoons of Butter, ſtir in one of Flour and add a Pint of thin Cream and pour over Chicken and ſet it aſide to cool. Make a Force-meat of two Cups of dry Bread-crumbs, one minc'd Onion, two Tableſpoons chopped Parſley, one half Tea-ſpoonful each of Sage & Savory, ſeaſon with Salt and Pepper and moiſten with Broth. Have ready ſix Slices of Ham, or wide Strips of Bacon and put your Force-meat on theſe and roll them up and hold together with wooden Tooth-picks. Lay theſe Rolls around the Sides of your Baking-diſh, and put your Chicken in the Center. Sprinkle the Whole with buttered Crumbs and bake in a mod-erate Oven about forty-five Minutes.

(*Market Square Tavern* Kitchen, 1937.)

Ducks to ſtew—Mrs. Walker *

TRUSS the Ducks and ſtuff them with Bread and Butter and Onion. Flour them and brown them in Lard in a Frying-pan. Have prepared in an Iron Pot Slips of Bacon, Giblets, Onion, Water, Pepper, Salt and a little Clove or Mace if you like it—Put in yʳ Ducks and let them ſtew gently but conſtantly two Hours then add the Juice of green Grapes preſſed between two pewter Plates, or Lemon-juice or Lemon-pickle. Flour yʳ Ducks each time that you turn them in the Pot. Thicken with Butter rolled in Flour—This Receipt for large Ducks. Thoſe not grown will require leſs Time.

(Manuſcript Cook Book, c-1801, of Mrs. *Frances Bland Tucker Coalter.* Owned by Dr. *St. George Tucker Grinnan,* Richmond.)

Nice

Nice brown Gravy for Ducks—Roaſt &c. ＊

MAKE a Spider quite hot. Keep it on the Fire and put into it a Tableſpoonful of Butter. Let it boil up, throw in a deſert Spoon of Sugar, ſtir them together as they boil till brown, dredge in Flour ſufficient to thicken and continue to ſtir. Add y^r Dripping and as much boiling Water in which you may firſt have boiled Sweet-herbs, Onion and Celery as will make a proper Quantity of Gravy, with Pepper and Salt. If for Ducks ſtew y^r Giblets with Onion and a Bunch of Herbs and add them with the Water they were ſtewed inſtead of the plain Water. Keep it gently ſtewing till ready to diſh.

(Manuſcript Cook Book, c-1801, of Mrs. *Frances Bland Tucker Coalter.* Owned by Dr. *St. George Tucker Grinnan, Richmond.*)

Salmi of Wild Duck ＊

PREPARE a Pair of Ducks as for roaſting; put a thin Slice of Bacon over the Breaſt of each; place them in a Pan with one-half Pint of Water, and bake in a hot Oven until nearly done, baſting frequently with Water; take from the Oven and carve the Ducks into as many Pieces as conven- ient; ſtir two Tableſpoons Butter and two of Flour together until perfectly ſmooth; put it into a Stew-pan and ſtir until a dark Brown; add the Broth; let it come to a Boil, ſtirring conſtantly; then add the Bundle of Sweet-herbs, one Table- ſpoonful Onion-juice, and one of Lemon-juice, one Tableſpoon Muſhroom Catſup, Salt, and Pepper; let all ſimmer together twenty Minutes; take out
the

the Herbs; add the Ducks and all the Gravy from the Dish on which you carve them; cover and simmer twenty Minutes longer; add one half Cup Sherry, and serve on a hot Dish. It is pretty served on a flat Dish garnished with sliced Bread cut into Triangles before frying; arrange with the Points up; scatter stoned Olives over the Top of the Dish.

(Old Recipe, *Richmond, Virginia*.)

Another Way *

CUT cold wild Duck into neat Pieces. Place Bones and Trimmings in Stew-pan with one small Onion, two Sprigs Thyme, one Bay-leaf, Salt and Pepper to Taste. Melt two Tablespoons Butter with one Tablespoon Flour. Add strained Broth and stir until it boils and thickens. Add the Duck, one Glass Claret (or any red Wine), one Teaspoon each of Orange and Lemon Juice. Serve very hot on Toast or Puff-paste. Garnish with Olives, Mushrooms or Truffles. Decorate with Slices of Orange and Lemon.

(Old Recipe from *Richmond, Virginia*, prov'd.)

To roast Wild Ducks or Teal *

WHEN the Ducks are ready dressed, put in them a small Onion, Pepper, Salt, and a Spoonful of red Wine; if the Fire be good, they will roast in twenty Minutes; make Gravy of the Necks and Gizzards, a Spoonful of red Wine, half an Anchovy, a Blade or two of Mace, one Onion, and a little *Cayenne* Pepper; boil it till it is wasted to half a Pint, strain it through a hair Sieve, and

pour

pour it on the Ducks—ferve them up with Onion
Sauce in a Boat; garnifh the Difh with Rafpings
of Bread.

(Mrs. *Mary Randolph's* Virginia Houfewife, 1831.)

A Fowl in Hafh

GET fome Fowls ready dreff'd, then take the
Flefh, and cut it very fmall; take the Car-
caffes, put them in a Stew-pan with good Broth,
an Onion cut into Slices, Parfley, and Sweet-herbs;
when it is boil'd enough, ftrain it off; then put in
it a Bit of Butter roll'd in Flour, and let it ftew a
Moment again; then put in it your Hafh of Fowls;
let your Hafh be relifhing, thicken it with three
Yolks of Eggs, or more according to the Quantity
of Hafh you make; it being thick, put in it the
Juice of a Lemon, and ferve them up hot for
Hors d'Oeuvre.

(The Lady's Companion, 1753; Cook Book owned
by Mifs *Anna Maria Dandridge*, 1756.)

Chicken Hafh *

CUT in fmall Pieces the Meat from a boiled or
roafted Chicken. Take the Carcafs and put it
in a Stew-pan with a good Broth, an Onion cut in
Slices, fome Parfley and Sweet-herbs. Simmer
flowly then ftrain. Melt four Spoonfuls of Butter
and thicken with Flour, add feveral Cups of
Broth, and the Chicken and beat well. This may
be ferved on Waffles as a Supper Difh.

(Mifs *Dandridge's* Recipe, 1753. Adapted
Market Square Tavern Kitchen, 1937.)

A

A Gooſe, Turkey, or Leg of Mutton, A-la-daube

LARD it with Bacon, and half roaſt it; then take it off the Spit, and put it in as ſmall a Pot as will boil it, put to it a Quart of White-wine, ſtrong Broth, a Pint of Vinegar, whole Spice, Bay-leaves, ſweet Marjoram, Winter-ſavoury, and green Onions. When it is ready lay it in the Diſh, make Sauce with ſome of the Liquor, Muſhrooms, dic'd Lemon, two or three Anchovies; thicken it with brown Butter, and garniſh it with ſliced Lemon.

(*E. Smith's* Compleat Houſewife, *Williamſburg*, 1742.)

Wild Gooſe *

PUT a ſmall Onion, a Slice of Pork, Pepper, Salt, and a Spoonful of red Wine inſide the Gooſe. Lay it in a Pan with Water enough to make Gravy. Dredge with Flour and baſte with Butter frequently. Cook quickly and ſerve with Gravy made from the thickened Stock.

(Old Recipe from *Toano, Virginia.*)

Baked Ham *

MOST Perſons boil Ham. It is much better baked, if baked right. Soak it overnight in clear Water, and wipe it dry. Next ſpread it all over with a thin Batter and then put it into a deep Diſh with a Rack under it to keep it out of the Gravy. When it is fully cruſted upon the Fleſh Side ſet it aſide to cool. It ſhould bake from four to ſix Hours.

After

After removing the Skin sprinkle over with two Tablespoons of Sugar, some black Pepper and powdered Crackers. Put in a Pan and return to the Oven to brown; then take up and stick Cloves through the Fat and dust with powdered Cinnamon.

(Old Recipe, c-1851, *Wicomico Church, Virginia*.)

Spiced Ham*

WASH a ten-pound Ham in cold Water, put in a large Boiler nearly filled with cold Water. Add two Blades of Mace, a dozen Cloves, half a Dozen Peppercorns and a Bay-leaf. Set over a slow Fire. Let heat gradually. Let simmer for one and a half Hours then boil gently fifteen Minutes to every Pound. When done let cool in Water in which it was cooked. Then take up and skin. Brush the Fat over with dried Bread-crumbs in which is mixed four Spoonfuls of brown Sugar. Set in a moderate Oven to brown. Baste with a Pint of White-wine to which has been added a Tablespoonful each of Celery-seed, Cloves, and Ginger. When browned, take up, stick whole Cloves over thickly. Set away twenty-four Hours before using.

(Old Recipe, *Chase City, Virginia*.)

Baked Spiced Ham*

SELECT a nicely cured Ham. Soak overnight in cold Water. Wipe off and put on in enough Water to cover. Simmer for three Hours. Let cool in the Water it was cooked in. Take out and trim. Put into Baking-pan, stick with Cloves and cover with

with brown Sugar. Bake in a moderate Oven for
two Hours. Baſte with white Wine. Serve with a
ſavoury Salad.

(Old Recipe from *Charlotte Court Houſe.* Said to have
been uſed by *Jefferſon's* Family at *Monticello.*)

How to cook an old Virginia *Ham**

SELECT a three to five Year old Ham weighing
twelve to eighteen Pounds. Trim and waſh
carefully and ſoak Overnight. Change Water and
add one Cup of Apple Vinegar and one Cup of
brown Sugar. Cover with Water. Boil very ſlowly
five or ſix Hours, or until end Bone is looſe. Leave
the Ham in the Water in which it was cooked until
the Water is cold then ſkin. Stuff and bake in the
following Manner; gaſh Fat on Top of Ham in
Gaſhes one Inch apart, ſtuff with Bread-crumbs
mixed with Chow-chow Pickle, a little of the Ham
Stock, and Butter. Pat ſmooth and put on Top
Cucumber Pickle cut in Rings. Put Ham in Baking-
pan and bake to a nice Brown.

(*Eggleſton* Family Recipe, 1840.)

*Boiled Ham**

THE Day before you wiſh to boil a Ham, ſcrape,
waſh and wipe dry and put in the Sun. At
Night put it into Water and ſoak until next
Morning. Then lay it with the Skin down in a
Boiler of cold Water, and boil ſlowly for five
Hours. If the Ham is large, boil for ſix Hours.
When tender, ſet the Boiler aſide, with the Ham
and Liquor untouched, until cold. Then take off
Skin,

Skin, sprinkle black Pepper over thickly, and sift over it Crackers first browned and pounded. For special Occasions, place at equal Distances over the Ham scraped Horse-radish in Lozenge Shape and edge with curled Parsley. This Mode keeps the Ham juicy.

(Old Recipe, *Toano, Virginia.*)

Ham and Egg Pudding (*A Spring Dish*)＊

TAKE some Slices of boiled Ham (both Fat and Lean) and sprinkle with Pepper, lay them across a deep Dish that has been buttered. Make a Pudding Batter of six Eggs beaten very light, a light Pint of Flour, a Pint of Milk, a small Piece of Butter, and Salt and Pepper to the Taste. Pour this Pudding Batter over the Ham and bake quickly.

(Recipe from an old *Williamsburg* Cook Book.)

Jugged Hare or Rabbit ＊

CUT into Joints one Hare or two Rabbits. Dust with Flour and fry until brown. Put into Stew-pan and add—one Onion, one Turnip, two Celery Stalks, small Bunch of Parsley, small Slice of Lemon-rind, two Cloves, two Bay-leaves, one Blade of Mace, three Peppercorns, one half Teaspoon Salt. Fill Stew-pan with boiling Broth and simmer for three Hours. When cooked, take out Pieces of Meat and keep hot. Make Force-meat Balls of the following—four Tablespoons Bread-crumbs, one and a half Tablespoons ground Suet, one Teaspoon Parsley, one half Teaspoon each of Thyme and Marjoram, pinch of powdered Mace,

one

one half Teaſpoon grated Lemon, Salt and Pepper to Taſte, four Tableſpoons chopped Ham or Veal. Mix well, moiſten with Broth and add one Egg, well beaten. Roll in Flour and cook in boiling Broth for fifteen Minutes. Skim out and set aſide with Meat to keep hot. Thicken Gravy with Flour, pounded Livers and one Tableſpoon red Currant Jelly, Juice of one half Lemon, two wine Glaſſes of red Wine (preferably Port). Parboil and ſkin one Cup of Cheſtnuts. Heat all together very thoroughly with Meat, Force-meat and ſerve.

(Old Recipe, c-1780, *Richmond, Virginia.*)

Kidney Stew *

SOAK overnight in cold, ſalted Water ſix Lamb Kidneys. Drain—parboil in Water to cover, three Times. Waſh in cold Water, remove all Fat, cut in Cubes, add three Potatoes and one Onion which have been cubed, cover with Water and cook thirty Minutes. Add Cream, Butter and chopped Parſley, Salt and Pepper to Taſte. Serve on Waffles.

(Traditional *Virginia* Recipe. Adapted 1937.)

A Fricaſy of Lamb

CUT an hind Quarter of Lamb into thin Slices, ſeaſon it with ſavoury Spices, Sweet-herbs, and a Shalot; then fry them, and toſs them up in ſtrong Broth, White-wine, Oyſters, Balls, and Palates, a little brown Butter to thicken it, or a Bit of Butter roll'd up in Flour.

(*E. Smith's* Compleat Houſewiſe, *Williamſburg,* 1742.)

Loin

Loin or Neck of Lamb *

HAVING cut your Lamb into Chops, rub both Sides of them with the Yolk of an Egg, and sprinkle some Crumbs of Bread over them, mixed with a little Parsley, Thyme, Marjoram, Winter Savory, and a little Lemon-peel, all chopped very fine. Fry them in Butter till they are of a nice light Brown, and garnish with fried Parsley.

(*John Farley's* London Art of Cookery, 1787. Prov'd *Market Square Tavern* Kitchen, 1937.)

Calf's Liver *

LARD it with Bacon, (spit it first) and roast it. Serve it up with good Gravy.

(*John Farley's* London Art of Cookery, 1787. Prov'd *Market Square Tavern* Kitchen, 1937.)

Mutton *

WHEN you intend to hash your Mutton, you must cut it in Slices, and put a Pint of Gravy or Broth into a Tossing-pan, with a Spoonful of Mushroom Catchup, and one of Browning. Add to it a sliced Onion, and a little Pepper and Salt. Put it over the Fire, and thicken it with Butter and Flour. When it boils, put in your Mutton; keep shaking it till it be perfectly hot, and then serve it up in a Soup-dish.

Another Method to hash Mutton, is cut it as thin as you can, strew a little Flour over it, have ready some Gravy, in which have been boiled Sweet-herbs, with some Onions, Pepper, and Salt.

Put

Put in your Meat, and with it a ſmall Piece of
Butter rolled in Flour, a little Salt, a Shalot cut
fine, and a few Capers cut fine. Toſs all together
for a Minute or two, and have ready ſome Bread
toaſted, and cut into thin Sippets. Lay them round
the Diſh, pour in your Haſh, and garniſh with
Pickles and Horſe-radiſh. To toaſt the Sippets may
be conſidered as an Improvement.

(*John Farley's* London Art of Cookery, 1787.)

A Leg of Mutton A-la-royal

LARD your Mutton and Slices of Veal with
Bacon roll'd in Spice and Sweet-herbs, then,
bringing them to a Brown with melted Lard, boil
the Leg of Mutton in ſtrong Broth, with all Sort of
Sweet-herbs, and an Onion ſtuck with Cloves;
when it is ready, lay it on the Diſh, lay round the
Collops; then pour on it a Ragoo and garniſh with
Lemon and Orange.

(*E. Smith's* Compleat Houſewife, *Williamſburg,* 1742.)

To fry Mutton Cutlets

CUT a Neck of Mutton Bone by Bone, and beat
it flat with your Cleaver; have ready Seaſoning, with grated Bread, a little Thyme rubb'd
to Powder, ſhred Parſley, with grated Nutmeg,
and ſome Lemon-peel minc'd; then beat up two
Eggs with Salt, flour your Cutlets on both Sides,
and dip them in the Eggs, ſprinkle them with
Seaſoning on both Sides; put ſome Butter in a
Frying-pan, and when it is hot lay in your Cutlets,
and

and fry them brown on both Sides; for Sauce take
Gravy, or strong Broth, an Onion, some Spice, a
Bit of Bacon, and a Bay-leaf, and boil them well
together; then beat it up with Anchovy, or some
Oysters, and a quarter of a Pint of red Wine, and
pour over your Cutlets, garnish with pickled
Walnuts cut in Quarters, Barberries, Samphire,
pickled Cucumbers, and slic'd Lemon.

(The Lady's Companion, 1753; Cook Book owned
by Miss Anna Maria Dandridge, 1756.)

Mutton Chops dressed with Tomatoes ❊

PLACE in a Pan Tomatoes peeled and chopped;
season with Butter, Pepper, Sugar and Salt.
Take from your Gridirons some nicely broiled
Mutton Chops; put in a Pan, cover close and
simmer for fifteen Minutes. Lay the Chops on a
hot Dish, put on a little Butter, Pepper and Salt.
With a Spoon cover each Chop with Tomatoes.
Sift pounded Crackers over and serve.

(Old Recipe, Toano, Virginia.)

Oxford John ❊

CUT a stale Leg of Mutton into as thin Collops
as you can, and take out all the fat Sinews.
Season them with a little Salt, Pepper, and Mace,
and strew among them a little shred Parsley,
Thyme, and two or three Shalots. Put a good
Lump of Butter into a Stew-pan, and as soon as
it be hot, put in all your Collops. Keep stirring
them with a wooden Spoon till they be three Parts
done, and then add half a Pint of Gravy, a little
Juice

Juice of Lemon, and thicken it with Flour and
Butter. Let them fimmer four or five Minutes,
and they will be quite enough; but if you let them
boil, or have them ready before you want them,
they will grow hard. Throw fried Pieces of Bread,
cut in Dices, over and round them, and ferve them
up hot.   (*John Farley's* London Art of Cookery, 1787.
Prov'd *Market Square Tavern* Kitchen, 1937.)

To roaſt Partridges or any ſmall Birds *

LARD them with Slips of Bacon, put them on a
Skewer, tie it to the Spit at both Ends, dredge
and baſte them, let them roaſt ten Minutes, take
the grated Crumb of half a Loaf of Bread, with a
Piece of Butter the Size of a Walnut, put it in a
Stew-pan, and fhake it over a gentle Fire till it is
of a light brown, lay it between your Birds, and
pour over them a little melted Butter.

(Mrs. *Mary Randolph's* Virginia Houfewife, 1831.)

Pigeon Pye *

TAKE four Pigeons nicely cleaned and fimmer
gently until done in Water with an Onion,
fome Parfley and a few Celery-feeds. Seafon with
Pepper and Salt and put infide of every one a large
Piece of Butter and the Yolk of a hard-boiled Egg.
Have ready a Paſte, allowing one Pound of Butter
to two Pounds of Flour. Roll it out rather thick
and line with it the Bottom and Sides of a large
deep Difh. Put in the Pigeons and lay on the Top
fome Bits of Butter rolled in Flour. Pour in nearly
enough Water to fill the Difh. Cover the Pye with

a

a Lid of Paste rolled out thick and neatly notched. Ornament with Paste Leaves and Flowers, and bake until Crust is enough.

(Old Recipe, c-1848, from *Atlee, Virginia.*)

Squab Pie *

AFTER the Squabs are picked as for roasting, put them in a Sauce-pan with a close Cover. Cover with boiling Water and boil slowly till tender, with a little Salt and an Onion and Cloves. Then take them out, drain and dry, and put in each Squab a Teaspoonful of Butter, a little Pepper, Salt, minced Parsley and Thyme. Then put into the Cavity of each Squab, a hard-boiled Egg. Lay them in a large, round, earthen Baking-dish, three or four Inches deep. Strain over them the Liquor in which they were simmered. Add a Tablespoonful of Butter and a Teacup of Milk or Cream. Sift in two Tablespoonfuls of Cracker-crumbs not browned, a Tablespoonful of minced Parsley and Thyme, and a little Salt. Put in a few Slips of Pastry. Cover with a rich Crust and bake.

The same Recipe will answer for Robins, except that the Eggs must be chopped, instead of being placed whole in the Bird.

(Recipe from *Lynchburg, Virginia.*)

Leg of Pork with Pease Pudding

BOIL a small Leg of Pork that has been sufficiently salted, score the Top and serve it up; the Pudding must be in a separate Dish, get small delicate Pease, wash them well, and tie them in a Cloth,

Cloth, allowing a little Room for ſwelling, boil
them with the Pork, then maſh and ſeaſon them,
tie them up again and finiſh boiling it; take care
not to break the Pudding in turning it out.

(Mrs. *Mary Randolph's* Virginia Houſewife, 1831.)

*To roaſt Quails**

GET Quails, truſs them, ſtuff their Bellies with
Beef-ſewet and Sweet-herbs, chopp'd well together; ſpit them on a ſmall Spit, and when they
grow warm, baſte firſt with Water and Salt, but
afterwards with Butter, and drudge them with
Flour. For Sauce, diſſolve an Anchovy in Gravy,
into which put two or three Shalots, ſlic'd and
boil'd; add the Juice of two or three *Seville*
Oranges and one Lemon; diſh them in this Sauce,
and garniſh with Lemon-peel and grated Manchet:
Be ſure to ſerve them up hot.

(The Lady's Companion, 1753; Cook Book
owned by Miſs *Anne Maria Dandridge*, 1756.)

*Roaſted Quail**

TAKE as many Quail as you have Gueſts, remove Feathers and Entrails without ſplitting
as you would a Fowl for roaſting. Fill Cavity with
a large Oyſter or two ſmall ones. Sprinkle the
Oyſters with Pepper and Salt and a few Bread-
crumbs. Put Birds in a Baking-pan with ſome
Water and Butter, bake in a moderate Oven,
baſting frequently, until well brown and done.
Serve on Toaſt with the Gravy poured over each
one.   (Old Recipe, 1863, *Phenix, Virginia*.)

Roaſt

Roaſt Quail*

PLUCK and draw the Birds, rub a little Butter over them, tie a Strip of Bacon over the Breaſts, ſet them in the Oven for twenty or twenty-five Minutes.

(Old Recipe from *Wicomico Church, Virginia*.)

Stewed Rabbit*

CUT up the Rabbit and waſh it. Put it in a Stew-pan and ſeaſon with Salt and Pepper. Pour in half a Pint of Water, and when this has nearly ſtewed away, add half a Pint of *Port* Wine, two or three Blades of Mace, and a Tableſpoonful of Flour mixed with a quarter of a Pound of Butter. Let it ſtew gently till quite tender, and then ſerve hot.

(Old Recipe, *Toano, Virginia*.)

Excellent Recipe for Sauſage*

GRIND twelve Pounds of the Lean of the Chine of Pork and ſix Pounds of the Fat. Add to it five Tableſpoonfuls of Salt, ſix of Sage, two of Thyme, five of black Pepper, three of ſweet Marjoram and mix all together well.

(Traditional *Virginia* Recipe. Prov'd *Brookbury*, 1938.)

Sauſages*

TAKE ſix Apples, and ſlice four of them as thick as a Crown-piece; cut the other two in Quarters, and fry them with the Sauſages till they be brown.

brown. Lay the Saufages in the Middle of the
Difh, and the Apples round them. Garnifh with
the quartered Apples. Saufages fried, and ftewed
Cabbage, make a good Difh. Heat cold Peafe-
pudding in the Pan, lay it in the Difh, and the
Saufages round; heap the Pudding in the Middle
and lay the Saufages all round up edge-ways,
except one in the Middle at length.

(*John Farley's* London Art of Cookery, 1787,
from *Brookbury, Chefterfield* County, *Virginia.*)

Saufage and Fried Apples *

SHAPE the Saufage Meat in fmall Cakes and
cook flowly in an iron Frying-pan until the Middle is well done. Do not cook too faft, nor let the
Outfide get too hard. Pour off moft of the Fat.
Have ready good cooking Apples which have been
cored and fliced (without peeling) in Slices about
one fourth Inch thick. Put thefe in the Pan and
cover your Pan for a While. Turn the Apples carefully to avoid breaking. Sprinkle well with brown
Sugar and cook flowly, well-covered, until the
Apples are almoft tender. Remove the Cover and
cook until the Apples are well glazed. Thefe may
be feafoned with powdered Cinnamon and Cloves
if defired. Place the Apples in the Center of a hot
Platter and arrange the Saufage around the Edge.

(Old *Williamfburg* Recipe. Prov'd *Blair* Kitchen, 1938.)

To

To Cook Sora, Ortolans, and Other Small Birds *

AFTER they are ſplit open in the Back and dreſſed, lay them in weak Salt and Water for a ſhort Time. Then lay them on a Board and roll with a Rolling-pin to flatten the Breaſt-bone. Put Butter, Pepper, and Salt on them. Lay them on a Gridiron and broil ſlowly. When juſt done, add more Butter and Pepper, lay in a flat tin Bucket, which ſet over a Veſſel of boiling Water to keep the Birds hot, juicy, and tender till wanted.— Mrs. *T.*

(Old Recipe from a *Williamſburg* Cook Book.)

Another Way to Cook Small Birds *

THEY ſhould be carefully cleaned, buttered, ſprinkled with Pepper and Salt, and broiled. When they are ſerved, butter them again. If you like, ſerve each Bird on a Piece of Toaſt, and pour over them a Sauce of red Wine, Muſhroom Catſup, Salt, *Cayenne* Pepper, and Celery.

(Old Recipe from a *Williamſburg* Cook Book.)

Barbecued Squirrel *

PUT ſome Slices of fat Bacon in an Oven. Lay the Squirrels on them and lay two Slices of Bacon on the Top. Put them in the Oven and let them cook until done. Lay them on a Diſh and ſet near a Fire. Take out the Bacon, ſprinkle one Spoonful of Flour in the Gravy and let it brown. Then

Then pour in one Teacup of Water, one Tableſpoonful of Butter and ſome Tomato or Walnut
Catſup. Let it cool and pour over the Squirrel.

(Old Recipe from *Toano, Virginia.*)

To broil Steaks*

FIRST have a very clear briſk Fire: let your
Gridiron be very clean; put it on the Fire,
and take a Chaffing-diſh with a few hot Coals out
of the Fire. Put the Diſh on it which is to lay your
Steaks on, then take fine Rump Steaks about half
an Inch thick; put a little Pepper and Salt on
them, lay them on the Gridiron, and (if you like
it) take a Shalot or two, or a fine Onion and cut it
fine; put it into your Diſh. Don't turn your Steaks
till one Side is done, then when you turn the other
Side there will ſoon be fine Gravy lie on the Top
of the Steak, which you muſt be careful not to
loſe. When the Steaks are enough, take them carefully off into your Diſh, that none of the Gravy be
loſt; then have ready a hot Diſh and Cover, and
carry them hot to Table, with the Cover on.

(Mrs. *Hannah Glaſſe's* Art of Cookery, 1774.)

Fried Sweetbreads—Muſhroom Sauce*

SOAK Sweetbreads for one half Hour in cold,
ſalted Water to cover. Remove from Water
and boil gently in freſh Water for twenty-five
Minutes. When thoroughly cooled cut in Slices
one half Inch thick. Dip in beaten Egg which has
been

been feafoned with Salt and Pepper. Roll in Bread-
crumbs, fry in deep Fat until a golden brown.
Serve on Toaft with Mufhroom Sauce. (See Recipe
on Page 28).

(*Market Square Tavern* Kitchen, 1937.)

To make a Pie of Sweetbreads and Oyfters

BOIL the Sweetbreads tender, ftew the Oyfters,
feafon them with Pepper and Salt, and thicken
with Cream, Butter, the Yelks of Eggs, and Flour,
put a Puff-pafte at the Bottom and around the
Sides of a deep Difh, take the Oyfters up with an
Egg-fpoon, lay them in the Bottom, and cover
them with the Sweetbreads, fill the Difh with
Gravy, put a Pafte on the Top, and bake it. This
is the moft delicate Pie that can be made. The
Sweetbread of Veal is the moft delicious Part, and
may be broiled, fried, or dreffed in any Way, and is
always good.

(Mrs. *Mary Randolph's* Virginia Houfewife, 1831.)

Williamfburg *Oyfter and Sweetbread Pie*✳

PREPARE one Pint of Sweetbreads as for fried
Sweetbreads then cut them in Cubes. Heat one
Pint of Oyfters through and drain off all Liquor.
Add well feafoned Cream Sauce to Oyfters and
Sweetbreads, cover with rich Pie Cruft (not too
thin). Brufh Top with Cream and bake for forty
Minutes.

(*Market Square Tavern* Kitchen, 1937.)

Or

Or do it thus*

BAKE your creamed Sweetbreads and Oysters in a covered Baking-dish and serve them up with a Pastry Lid which has been cut round with a large Cutter, well-pricked and baked on a Tin Sheet.

(Prov'd at *Travis* House, 1938.)

Tongue a la Terrapin*

TAKE a freshly boiled Tongue, split it and stick some Cloves in; cut up a small Onion, put in some Blades of Mace and a little browned Flour in Butter. Have Water enough in a Stew-pan to cover the Tongue; mix in the Ingredients before putting in the Tongue. Add three hard-boiled Eggs chopped up fine. Send to Table hot, garnished with hard-boiled Eggs cut in Rings.

(Old Recipe, *Toano, Virginia.*)

Roast Turkey*

PUT the Gizzard, Heart and Liver in cold Water and boil till tender. When done, chop fine and add stale Bread, grated, Salt and Pepper, Sweet-herbs, two Eggs well beaten.

Fill the Turkey with this Dressing, sew the Openings, drawing the Skin tightly together. Put a little Butter over the Turkey and lay it upon the Grate of your Meat-pan. Cover the Bottom of the Pan well with boiling Water. In half an Hour, baste the Turkey by pouring over it the Gravy that has begun to form in the Pan. Repeat
this

this Basting every fifteen Minutes. In an Oven of average Temperature, a twelve-Pound Turkey will require at least three Hours' cooking.—Mrs. *A. D.*

(Old Recipe from a *Williamsburg* Cook Book.)

Oyster Stuffing for Turkey ✳

TO a Pint of Cracker-crumbs add a Pint of solid Oyster-meats, moisten the Whole with new Milk or sweet Cream, adding Butter, Salt, and Pepper to Taste; the Stuffing ought to be prepared some Time before needed.

(Old *Williamsburg* Recipe, c-1837, from Mrs. *Elizabeth Labbé Cole's* Collection.)

Sausage Stuffing for a Turkey ✳

SOAK one large Loaf of stale Bread in Milk enough to moisten, add Salt, Pepper, one half Teaspoon of Thyme, the Same of Marjoram, three large Sprigs of chopped Parsley, one finely chopped Onion, two Stalks of Celery cut fine, twelve Olives stoned and cut small, and one Pound of Sausage which has been slightly cooked in a Skillet. Knead this all very well together then add one Pound of roasted Chestnuts cut in two. Stuff your Turkey, sew it and truss it well. Cook in a moderate Oven and baste frequently. This will fill a ten or twelve pound Turkey.

(Old *Morgan* Family Recipe.)

Wild Turkey ✳

IF the Turkey is old, after it is dressed wash it inside thoroughly with Soda and Water. Rinse it and plunge it into a Pot of boiling Water for five Minutes.

Minutes. Make a Stuffing of Bits of Pork, Beef, or any other cold Meat, plenty of chopped Celery, stewed Giblets, hard-boiled Eggs, pounded Cracker, Pepper, and Salt, and a heaping Spoonful of Butter. Work this well and fill the Turkey. With another large Spoonful of Butter grease the Bird, and then sprinkle Salt and Pepper over it. Lay in a Pan, with a Pint of Broth in which Meat has been boiled. Place in a hot Oven. When it begins to brown, dredge with Flour and baste, turning often, so that each Part may be equally browned. Put a buttered Sheet of Paper over the Breast, to prevent Dryness. When thoroughly done, lay on a Dish, brown some Crackers, pound and sift over it, and serve with Celery or Oyster Sauce.

(Recipe from an old *Williamsburg* Cook Book.)

Turkey Hash *

CUT up the Meat very fine. Stew the Bones in a little Water, strain, then stir into this Water the Meat, adding a large Tablespoonful Butter mixed with Flour, a Cup of Cream, Salt and Pepper, a little chopped Parsley, Thyme or Celery (or else a very few Celery-seeds). Stew all together.

(Recipe from an old *Williamsburg* Cook Book.)

Veal Rolls *

TAKE ten or twelve little thin Slices of Veal, lay on them some Force-meat according to your Fancy, roll them up, and tie them just across the Middle with coarse Thread, put them on a Bird-spit, rub them over with the Yolks of Eggs,
flour

flour them, and baste them with Butter. Half an
Hour will do them. Lay them into a Dish, and
have ready some good Gravy, with a few Truffles
and Morels, and some Mushrooms. Garnish with
Lemon.

(Mrs. *Hannah Glasse's* Art of Cookery, 1774.)

Williamsburg *Veal Partridges* ✲

TAKE twelve very thin Slices of Veal Cutlet
and have ready two Cups of Force-meat made
of stale Bread-crumbs, a small Onion chopped fine
and browned in Butter, Salt, Pepper, one half
Teaspoon each of Thyme, Marjoram, and Basil,
moistened with Milk. Lay your Force-meat on a
Piece of Veal and roll it up and skewer together
with two wooden Tooth-picks stuck through di-
agonally to cross each other. Roll in Flour and
brown in Fat. As they brown place them in a
Baking-dish. Thicken the Fat in the Pan with
Flour, add hot Water. Pour over the Veal, cover
your Baking-dish and bake in a slow Oven forty
Minutes. Serve with steamed wild Rice.

(*Market Square Tavern* Kitchen, 1937.)

Venison Pastey ✲

CUT the Venison into small Pieces; place them
in a Sauce-pan with one Ounce of Butter, and
brown them well; then one Ounce of Flour, which
should be browned; stir until perfectly smooth; add
one Quart of Broth, one large Onion, a Bundle of
Sweet-herbs, Salt, Pepper, and a little Nutmeg;
place on the Stove where it will simmer for one
Hour;

Hour; when done, add two Teaspoons of Walnut Catsup, one half Cup of *Madeira* Wine. By this Time the Gravy will be thick. Butter a deep Baking-dish and put the Stew in it, first taking out the Onion and Herbs; cover it with a Top of Puff-pastry; make Slits in the Top of the Pastry. Serve hot. If preferred, this Stew may be served over Toast or Waffles instead of being baked in a Dish as above directed.

(Recipe from an old *Williamsburg* Cook Book.)

Scotch *Collops* ❋

TAKE Veal, cut it thin, beat it well with a Rolling-pin and grate some Nutmeg over them, dip them in the Yolk of an Egg, and fry them in a little Butter till they are of a fine brown then pour the Butter from them, and have ready half a Pint of Gravy, a little Piece of Butter rolled in Flour, a Glass of White-wine, the Yolk of an Egg and a little Cream mixed together. Stir it all together and when it is of a fine Thickness dish it up. It does very well without Cream if you have none and very well without Gravy, only put in just as much warm Water and either red or white Wine.

(Manuscript Cook Book, c-1825, of Miss *Margaret Prentis* of *Williamsburg.* Owned by *Robert H. Webb*, Esq., *Charlottesville.*)

To fry cold Veal

CUT it in Pieces and dip them into the Yolk of an Egg and then in Crumbs of Bread with a few Sweet-herbs, and spread Lemon Peel in it. Grate a little Nutmeg over them and fry them in fresh Butter.

The

The Butter muſt be hot, juſt enough to fry them in. In the meantime make a little Gravy of the Bone of the Veal, when the Meat is fried take it out with a Fork and lay it in a Diſh before the Fire then ſhake a little Flour into the Pan and ſtir it round, then put in the Gravy, ſqueeze in a little Lemon and pour it over the Veal.—Garniſh with Lemon.

(Manuſcript Cook Book, c-1825, of Miſs *Margaret Prentis* of *Williamſburg.* Owned by *Robert H. Webb*, Eſq., *Charlotteſville.*)

To make an Egg as big as Twenty

PART the Yolks from the Whites of twenty Eggs, ſtrain the Yolks by themſelves, and the Whites by themſelves, boil the Yolks in a Bladder, in the Form either of an Egg or Ball; when they are boiled hard, put the Ball of Yolks into another Bladder, and the Whites round about it, and bind it up oval or round, and boil it. Theſe Eggs are uſed in grand Sallads.

If you pleaſe you may add to the Yolks of the Eggs, Ambergreeſe, Muſk, grated Biſcuits, candy'd Piſtachoes and Sugar; and to the Whites, Muſk, Almond-paſte, beaten Ginger, and the Juice of Oranges, and ſerve them up with Butter, Almond-milk, Sugar, and Juice of Orange.

(The Lady's Companion, 1753; Cook Book. owned by Miſs *Anna Maria Dandridge*, 1756.)

Williamſburg *Stuffed Eggs* ⁂

TAKE a Dozen hard-boiled Eggs, ſplit them in two and maſh up the Yolks. Saute three large Muſhrooms and one Tableſpoon of minced Onion in in Butter. Add to the Yolks one Tableſpoon chopped Parſley, one Tableſpoon fine Bread-crumbs, a Pinch of Savory, a Teaſpoon of prepared Muſtard, one Tableſpoon Lemon-juice, Salt, Pepper and the Muſhroom and Onion. Fill the Whites of the Eggs with it and lay them in a Baking-diſh in which you have placed a Layer of Force-meat made with Chicken or Veal. Bake them in a ſlow Oven until they are brown and ſerve them hot with a Muſhroom Sauce, or a Cream-ſauce ſeaſoned with White-wine.

(Miſs *Dandridge's* Recipe, 1756. Adapted *Market Square Tavern* Kitchen, 1937.)

To make a Welch *Rabbit*⁎

TOAST the Bread on both Sides, then toaſt the Cheeſe on one Side, lay it on the Toaſt, and with a hot Iron brown the other Side. You may rub it over with Muſtard.

(Mrs. *Hannah Glaſſe's* Art of Cookery, 1774.)

To make an Engliſh *Rabbit*⁎

TOAST a Slice of Bread brown on both Sides, then lay it in a Plate before the Fire, pour a Glaſs of red Wine over it, and let it ſoak the Wine up; then cut ſome Cheeſe very thin, and lay it very thick over the Bread, and put it in a Tin Oven before the Fire, and it will be toaſted and browned preſently. Serve it away hot.

(Mrs. *Hannah Glaſſe's* Art of Cookery, 1774.)

Devilled

Devilled Crabs*

BLEND together two Tablespoons Flour with two Tablespoons Butter. Add one Cup Cream, stirring constantly. Mix with Yolks of four hard-boiled Eggs chopped fine, two Teaspoons chopped Parsley and one Teaspoon Walnut Catsup. Add one Pound Crab-flakes, season to Taste. Put them back in the well-cleaned Shells, sprinkle with buttered Bread-crumbs and bake in a moderate Oven until brown.

(Recipe from *Richmond, Virginia.*)

Another Way*

TO the Meat of one Dozen Crabs, boiled fifteen Minutes and picked free from Shell, add three Tablespoonfuls stale Bread-crumbs, two Tablespoonfuls Cream, Yolks of three Eggs, a little chopped Parsley, one Tablespoonful Butter, Salt and Pepper to Taste. Put in Shells and bake in a quick Oven.

(Old Recipe, *Toano, Virginia.*)

Scalloped Crabs*

TO one Pound of well-cleaned Crab-meat add a Sauce made as follows:

Blend four Tablespoons of Flour and Butter and add one Pint of rich Milk. Cook over a slow Fire, stirring constantly, until thick. Remove. Add one Teaspoonful of *Worcestershire* Sauce, one half Teaspoonful of Salt, a few Dashes of Pepper Sauce and one third of a Cup of dry Sherry. Beat in two Egg Yolks.

Mix lightly with Crab and place in buttered Scallop

Scallop Shells, ſprinkle with Crumbs, dot with Butter, and bake in moderate Oven until light brown. Serve with a ſmall, thin Slice of Lemon on each.

(*Williamſburg* Recipe, c-1830.
Prov'd *Blair* Kitchen, 1938.)

Soft Shell Crabs *

WASH and dry thoroughly. Remove the Eyes and Sandbag. After removing Subſtance under Flaps on each Side and the Piece called the Apron, waſh and dry thoroughly. Dip in Eggs which have been beaten well and ſeaſoned with Salt and Pepper. Roll in Bread-crumbs. Fry in hot Fat until well browned on both Sides. Serve with a good Sauce.

(*Market Square Tavern* Kitchen, 1937.)

To boil Flounders or Plaice *

PUT Salt, whole Spice, White-wine, and a Bunch of Sweet-herbs into your Water; when it boils put in a little Vinegar, for that will make the Fiſh criſp; let it boil apace before you put in your Fiſh; let them boil till they ſwim, then take them up, and drain them; take a little of the Liquor, put it into ſome Butter, two or three Anchovies, and ſome Capers; ſet it over the Fire, and beat it up thick, then pour it over the Fiſh, with Parſley, Capers, Orange and Lemon.

(The Lady's Companion, 1753; Cook Book owned by Miſs *Anna Maria Dandridge*, 1756.)

To

To pickle Herring or Mackerel

CUT off the Heads and Tails of your Fiſh, gut them, waſh them, and dry them well; then take two Ounces and a Half of Salt-petre, three quarters of an Ounce of *Jamaica* Pepper, and a quarter and half quarter of white Pepper, and pound them ſmall; an Ounce of ſweet Marjoram and Thyme chopp'd ſmall; mix all together, and put ſome within and without the Fiſh; lay them in an earthen Pan, the Roes at Top, and cover them with White-wine Vinegar, then ſet them into an Oven, not too hot, for two Hours. This is for Fifteen; and after this Rule do as many as you pleaſe.

(The Lady's Companion, 1753; Cook Book owned by Miſs *Anna Maria Dandridge,* 1756.)

To fry Oyſters ✳

BEAT Eggs, with a little Salt, grated Nutmeg, and thicken it like thick Batter, with grated white Bread and fine Flour; then dip the Oyſters in it, and fry them brown with Beef-dripping.

(E. *Smith's* Compleat Houſewife, *Williamſburg,* 1742.)

Batter to fry Oyſters in ✳

SIX Eggs beaten very light; add to them ſix Tableſpoonfuls ſifted Flour, and one and a half Pint rich Milk, and one-fourth Teaſpoonful grated Nutmeg; beat all together to a ſmooth Paſte.

(Old *Williamſburg* Recipe, c-1837, from Mrs. *Elizabeth Labbé Cole's* Collection)

Fried

Fried Oysters *

DRAIN Liquor from one Quart of large Oysters.
Prepare three Eggs, well-beaten, to which
has been added two Tablespoons Milk, one half
Teaspoon Salt, one fourth Teaspoon Pepper. First
dip Oyster in beaten Egg, then in Bread-crumbs.
Fry in deep Fat until golden brown. Serve immediately.

(Prov'd *Market Square Tavern* Kitchen, 1937)

Oyster Loaves

TAKE a Quart of middling Oysters, and wash
them in their own Liquor; then strain them
through a Flannel, and put them on the Fire to
warm; then take three quarters of a Pint of Gravy
and put to the Oysters, with a Blade of Mace, a
little white Pepper, a little Horse-raddish and a
Piece of lean Bacon, and half a Lemon; then stew
them leisurely. Take three Penny Loaves, and pick
out the Crumb clean; then take a Pound of Butter,
and set on the Fire in a Sauce-pan that will hold
the Loaves, and when it is melted, take it off the
Fire, and let it settle; then pour off the Clear, and
set it on the Fire again with the Loaves in it, and
turn them about till you find them crisp; then put
a Pound of Butter in a Frying-pan, and with a
dredging Box dust in Flower till you find it of a
reasonable Thickness, then mix that and the
Oysters together; and when stewed enough take
out the Bacon, and put the Oysters into the
Loaves; then put them into a Dish, and garnish
the Loaves with the Oysters you cannot get in,
and

and with Slices of Lemon; and when you have thickened the Liquor, squeeze in Lemon to your Taste; or you may fry the Oysters with Batter to garnish the Loaves.

(*E. Smith's* Compleat Housewife, *London*, 1739.)

Panned Oysters *

PUT in a Sauce-pan, over the Fire, enough Butter to cover the Bottom when melted. When hot, pour in one Quart of nice Oysters, shake the Pan until the Oysters curl. Serve hot on Toast. Some of the Liquor may be added to the Oysters in the Pan.

(Old *Maryland* Recipe from a *Virginia* Cook Book.)

Pickled Oysters *

TAKE one Gallon Oysters and cook them in their own Liquor till nearly done. Then skim out the Oysters and add to the Liquor one Teaspoonful whole black Pepper, one Teaspoonful Allspice, one Teaspoonful Mace, a little red Pepper and half a Pint of strong Vinegar. Let it boil a few Minutes and then pour over the Oysters. When nearly cool, slice in them a large fresh Lemon.

(Old Recipe from *Lynchburg, Virginia,*
in a *Williamsburg* Cook Book.)

Oysters Pickled *

COOK Oysters with a little Salt. Then strain through a Sifter, throw the Oysters in Ice-water, strain the Liquor. To every two Cups of Liquor

Liquor add one Cup of good Vinegar, some whole Peppercorns and a little Mace; boil until seasoned. Let it be very cold before adding the Oysters. Add sliced Lemon before serving.

(Old *Nelson* Family Recipe.)

Scalloped Oysters *

HAVING opened your Oysters into a Bason, and washed them out of their own Liquor, put some into your Scollop-shells, and strew over them a few Crumbs of Bread. Lay a Slice of Butter on them, then more Oysters, Bread, and Butter successively, till your Shell be as full as you intend it. Put them into a *Dutch* Oven to brown, and serve them up in the Shells in which they are scolloped.

(*John Farley's* London Art of Cookery, 1787, from *Brookbury*, *Chesterfield* County, *Virginia*. Prov'd 1937.)

Oyster Soup

TAKE two Quarts of fine Oysters, strain the Liquor and if there is not Liquor sufficient to make your Soup, put as much Water—one Onion, two Blades of Mace, boil these well together, throw in your Oysters and give them a Boil, have ready a Piece of Butter say from a quarter to half a Pound, with Flour sufficient to thicken, rub them up together. Season with Pepper and Salt to your Taste. When just ready to dish throw in at least half a Pint of rich Cream, then give one more Boil,

Boil, ſend up to Table. The Oyſters will be plump and the Soup very nice.

[Note: This Recipe is on a Slip of Paper pinned to a Page of the Cook Book and is ſigned

"with much love
Mrs. *B.* recipes"]

(Manuſcript Cook Book, c-1801, of Mrs.
Frances Bland Tucker Coalter. Owned by
Dr. *St. George Tucker Grinnan, Richmond.*)

Stewed Oyſters ✳

HAVE the Veſſel hot, then take the Oyſters out of their own Liquor with a Fork, and put them in the Veſſel, ſtirring them ſo as to prevent Burning or Scorching. Cook quickly, when half done add to each Quart of Oyſters, a Piece of freſh Butter the Size of a large Egg, half Pint of Cream or rich Milk, the Yolks of two Eggs well beaten up, Pepper and Salt to Taſte and ſerve hot.

(Old Recipe from *Matthews Court Houſe, Virginia.*)

Stuffed Oyſters ✳

PUT together in a Pan two Dozen Oyſters, drained and chopped fine; two Slices of Bread, crumbled; half an Onion, ſome chopped Celery, one Tableſpoon Parsley chopped, a little *Cayenne* Pepper, one Teaſpoonful Walnut Catchup, Butter the Size of an Egg, Juice and grated Rind of one Lemon. Cook on Top of Stove ſtirring conſtantly for thirty Minutes. Add two beaten Eggs. Put Mixture in Oyſter Shells. Cover with buttered Crumbs, and brown in Oven. Serve with thin Slices of Lemon.

(Old Recipe, adapted 1937.)

To

To bake Shad

THE Shad is a very indifferent Fish unless it be large and fat; when you get a good One, prepare it nicely, put some Force-meat inside, and lay it at full length in a Pan with a Pint of Water, a Gill of red Wine, one of Mushroom Catsup, a little Pepper, Vinegar, Salt, a few Cloves of Garlic, and six Cloves: stew it gently till the Gravy is sufficiently reduced; there should always be a Fish-slice with Holes to lay the Fish on, for the Convenience of dishing without breaking it; when the Fish is taken up, slip it carefully into the Dish; thicken the Gravy with Butter and brown Flour, and pour over it.

(Mrs. *Mary Randolph's* Virginia Housewife, 1831.)

Baked Shad*

CLEAN Shad, being careful not to break Roe, if there is any. Make a plain Stuffing of Bread-crumbs, Butter, Salt and Pepper as for Fowls, and stuff the Body of the Fish with it, sewing it up with a soft Thread; lard one Side of the Fish and score it with a sharp Knife, making the Scores about one Inch apart, and put a Strip of salt Pork in each Gash. Butter a Tin Sheet, dredge with Salt, Pepper and Flour, cover the Bottom of the Pan with boiling Water and put into a hot Oven. Bake fifteen Minutes for every Pound of Fish, basting each ten Minutes with the Gravy in the Pan. When done lift out carefully and

and slide in Center of the Dish to be served. Garnish with sliced Lemon, fried Potato Balls and Parsley.

(Old Recipe, *Richmond, Virginia.*)

Another Way *

OPEN the Shad down the Back, wash well and salt it; wipe dry and rub inside and out with a little *Cayenne* Pepper. Prepare a Stuffing of Bread, seasoned with Pepper, Salt, Thyme or Parsley, Celery-seed, a little chopped Onion, Piece of Butter the Size of a Walnut. Tie up the Fish and put in a Baking-pan with one Pint Water and Butter the Size of an Egg. Sprinkle with Flour, baste well and bake slowly an Hour and a half.

(Old Recipe from *Toano, Virginia.*)

To butter Shrimps *

STEW a Quart of Shrimps in Half a Pint of White-wine, a Nutmeg grated, and a good Piece of Butter; when the Butter is melted, and they are not through, beat the Yolks of four Eggs with a little White-wine, and pour it in, and shake it well, till it is of the Thickness you like; then dish it on Sippets, and garnish with sliced Lemon.

(Mrs. *E. Smith's* Compleat Housewife, *London*, 1739. Prov'd 1937.)

To bake Sturgeon *

GET a Piece of Sturgeon with the Skin on, the Piece next to the Tail, scrape it well, cut out the Gristle, and boil it about twenty Minutes to take

take out the Oil; take it up, pull off the large
Scales, and when cold, ftuff it with Force-meat
made of Bread-crumbs, Butter, chopped Parfley,
Pepper and Salt, put it in a *Dutch* Oven juft large
enough to hold it, with a Pint and a half of Water,
a Gill of red Wine, one of Mufhroom Catfup, fome
Salt and Pepper, ftew it gently till the Gravy is
reduced to the Quantity neceffary to pour over it;
take up your Sturgeon carefully, thicken the Gravy
with a Spoonful of Butter rubbed into a large One
of brown Flour, fee that it is perfectly fmooth
when you put it in the Difh.

(Mrs. *Mary Randolph's* Virginia Houfewife, 1831.)

To fry Trouts *

YOU muft, with a Knife, gently fcrape off all the
Slime from your Fifh, wafh them in Salt and
Water, gut them, and wipe them very clean with
a Linnen Cloth; that done, ftrew Flour over them,
and fry them in fweet Butter, till they are brown
and crifp; then take them out of the Frying-pan,
and lay them on a Pewter Difh, well-heated before
the Fire; pour off the Butter they were fry'd in,
into the Greafe Pot, and not over the Trouts:
Afterwards, good Store of Parfley and young Sage
being fry'd crifp in other fweet Butter, take out
the Herbs, and lay them on your Fifh. In the mean-
while, fome Butter being beaten up with three or
four Spoonfuls of fcalding hot Spring-water, in
which an Anchovy has been diffolved, pour it on
the Trouts, and let them be ferved up. Garnifh
with the Leaves of Strawberries, Parfley, &c.

After this Manner, Grailings, Perches, fmall
Pikes

Pikes or Jacks, Roaches and Gudgeons may be
fry'd, their Scales being first scraped off: And you
may thus fry small Eels, when they are flea'd,
gutted, wiped clean, and cut into Pieces of four or
five Inches long; several Pieces of Salmon, or a
Chine of it, may likewise be dressed in the same
Manner.

(The Lady's Companion, 1753; Cook Book
owned by Miss *Anna Maria Dandridge*, 1756.
Recipe prov'd 1937.)

Turtle Soup ✻

KILL the Turtle at Daylight in Summer, the
Night before in Winter, and hang it up to
bleed. After Breakfast, scald it well and scrape the
outer Skin off the Shell; open it carefully, so as
not to break the Gall. Break both Shells to Pieces
and put them into the Pot. Lay the Fins, the
Eggs and some of the more delicate Parts by—
put the Rest into the Pot with a Quantity of Water
to suit the Size of your Family. Add two Onions,
Parsley, Thyme, Salt, Pepper, Cloves and Allspice
to suit your Taste.

About half an Hour before Dinner thicken the
Soup with brown Flour and Butter rubbed together. An Hour before Dinner, take the Parts
laid by, roll them in brown Flour, fry them in
Butter, put them and the Eggs in the Soup; just
before Dinner add a Glass of Claret or *Madeira*
Wine.

(Recipe from an old *Williamsburg* Cook Book.)

Turtle

Turtle or Terrapin Stew

AFTER they are well cleaned, parboil the Meat, then pick it to Pieces. Seaſon highly with Pepper, Salt, *Cayenne* Pepper, hard-boiled Egg, Spices, Lemon, and Champagne or other Wine. Stew until well done.

(Old Recipe, *Cheſterfield* County, *Virginia*.)

Of BREAD

"AND as they brew, ſo do they bake daily, "Bread or Cakes, eating too much hot and "new Bread, which cannot be wholſom, tho' it be "pleaſanter than what has been baked a Day or "two."

Theſe Words, written by the Reverend *Hugh Jones* in 1724, in *The Preſent State of Virginia*, reflected an early Apprehenſion for the good Digeſtion of the *Virginians*, who then as now would ſcorn to eat any Bread ſo old it had even grown cool. And it may be remarked, by one who has had Opportunity for cloſe Obſervation, that the Digeſtion of thoſe addicted to this and ſimilar Apprehenſions, cannot compare in Soundneſs with that of the *Virginians* who have been for Generations eſtabliſhed in this Habit.

The moſt characteriſtic hot Breads are thoſe which

which are made from *Indian* Corn. As early as the
Year 1608, the Coloniſts had gathered *Indian* Corn
of their own planting and had learned to make
Bread of it in the *Indian* Manner, by mixing Corn
Meal and Water, ſhaping it into Cakes, or Pones,
which were baked in hot Aſhes, or on Hoes. Of Corn
Pone, the Hiſtorian, *Beverley*, wrote in 1705:

> The Bread in Gentlemen's Houſes is generally
> made of Wheat, but ſome rather chooſe the Pone,
> which is the Bread made of *Indian* Meal. Many
> of the poorer Sort of People ſo little regard the
> *Engliſh* Grain, that though they might have it
> with the leaſt Trouble in the World, yet they don't
> mind to ſow the Ground, becauſe they won't be
> at the Trouble of making a Fence particularly for
> it. And therefore their conſtant Bread is Pone,
> not ſo called from the *Latin*, *Panis*, but from the
> *Indian* Name *Oppone*.

Although Pone (or Hoe Cakes and Aſh Cakes as
they were alſo called) became the "conſtant Bread"
of the Slaves and the poorer People, excellent Breads
were developed from *Indian* Meal during the ſeven-
teenth and eighteenth Centuries, which remain in
ſtaunch Favour today among all Claſſes of *Virginians*. There are the Batter Breads (by ſome,
eſpecially thoſe in the more ſouthern Colonies,
called Spoon Breads) Egg Breads, and Corn Breads
for which proper Recipes are given in this Chapter.

Of prime Importance in the Making of theſe
Breads is the Selection of a proper Meal. Only the
native Corn, ground ſlowly in a Water Griſt Mill
may be uſed and under no Circumſtances ſhould
a Cook ſo far depart from the good Judgment of
Generations

Generations of *Virginia* Houſewives as to permit
Sugar in any Variety of Corn Bread.

Biſcuits, Muffins, *Sally Lunn*, Rolls, Waffles,
and other Breads made of Wheat Flour are alſo
ſerved "hot and new"; and to thoſe who enjoy
Virginia Hoſpitality for the firſt Time they are
uſually ſerved with the Inſtruction "Take two,
"and butter them while they're hot." So ſeductive is
the Cuſtom, that it may be obſerved that it is a rare
Viſitor to whom the Inſtruction muſt be repeated.

All Sorts of BREADS

Apoquiniminics — *Mrs*. Skipwith

INTO one Quart of Flour rub one Spoonful Butter and two Eggs, Whites and Yolks. Put in as
much ſweet Milk as will make it the Conſiſtence of
Paſte—Roll them [thin, and cut into round Cakes]
and bake on a Gridiron.—Dip them in Butter
melted in a Plate.   (Manuſcript Cook Book, c-1801,
                      of Mrs. *Frances Bland Tucker Coalter*.
         Owned by Dr. *St. George Tucker Grinnan, Richmond*.)

Beaten Biſcuits ＊

TAKE one Quart of Flour, Lard the Size of a
Hen's Egg, one Teaſpoonful of Salt. Make into
a moderately ſtiff Dough with ſweet Milk. Beat for
half an Hour. Make out with the Hand or cut with
                                        the

the Biscuit Cutter. Stick with a Fork and bake in a hot Oven, yet not sufficiently hot to blister the Biscuit.

(Recipe from *Lynchburg, Virginia.*
From an old *Williamsburg* Cook Book.)

Beaten Biscuit *

ONE Quart of Flour, one Teacup of Lard (if you prefer it use Lard and Butter mixed), one Teaspoon of Salt, one Cup of sweet Milk. Make a stiff Dough, then beat it fifteen or twenty Minutes until it blisters. Roll and cut in small round Biscuits. Bake in a moderately hot Oven.

(*Read* Family Recipe.)

Cheese Biscuit *

SIFT one Cup of Flour with one fourth Teaspoon of Salt, cut in one third of a Cup of Butter. Add one Cup of grated Cheese. Work lightly into a stiff Paste. Roll out one half Inch thick and cut with very small Cutter and prick Tops with Fork. Bake in a moderate Oven about twelve Minutes, but do not brown. These burn very easily.

(Old *Williamsburg* Recipe. Prov'd *Blair* Kitchen, 1938.)

Breakfast Puffs *

HEAT greased iron or other heavy Muffin Pans in the Oven until very hot. Fill two-thirds full with a Batter made as follows: Sift one Cup of Flour with one fourth Teaspoon of Salt. Mix together two well-beaten Eggs, seven-eighths of a Cup of Milk and one Tablespoonful of melted Butter.

ter. Stir ſlowly into Flour but do not overmix. Bake in a hot Oven for about twenty Minutes and dry them in a moderate Oven for about fifteen. Serve at once.

(Old Recipe, *Toano, Virginia.* Prov'd *Blair* Kitchen, 1938.)

To Make Bread*

SCALD three Cups of Milk and pour them in a large Bowl in which you have three fourths of a Cup of Sugar, two Teaſpoons of Salt and one Tableſpoonful of Butter. Cool and add one Yeaſt Cake diſſolved in one half Cup lukewarm Water, and ſift in three Quarts of Flour (enough to make a ſtiff Dough). Knead ſmooth, ſet to riſe in a warm Place, when it has doubled in Bulk turn onto floured Board and knead lightly. Shape into Loaves. Place in Pans and ſet to riſe again. Bake in moderate Oven about one Hour.

(Mrs. *Cole's* Recipe, c-1837. Adapted *Market Square Tavern* Kitchen, 1937.)

Buns—Miſs Bowdoin

TAKE eight Eggs, one Pound Sugar, two Pounds Flour, one half Pound freſh Butter. Work half the Flour with the Butter till very light. Beat the Eggs light with the Sugar and the Balance of the Flour. Mix all together with a Glaſs of Wine, half a Nutmeg, and a Teaſpoonful of beaten Mace. Bake them in a quick Oven, either in Shapes or (which I like beſt) by dropping the Batter in Spoonfuls on the Bottom of the *Dutch* Oven.

(Manuſcript Cook Book, c-1801, of Mrs. *Frances Bland Tucker Coalter.* Owned by Dr. *St. George Tucker Grinnan, Richmond.*)

Williamſburg

Williamſburg *Buns* ❊

SCALD one Cup of Milk, add one half Cup of
melted Butter, two Teaſpoonfuls of Salt and
one half Cup of Sugar. Cool to lukewarm. Add two
Yeaſt Cakes which have been diſſolved in one fourth
Cup of warm Water. Add three beaten Eggs to
Liquids, then beat in well four and a half Cups of
Flour. (One Teaſpoonful each of Nutmeg and
Mace and a Wine-glaſs of Sherry may be added.)
Let the Dough riſe until double in Bulk, turn it out
and knead lightly. Fill Muffin Pans two-thirds full
and let riſe until light (about twenty Minutes).
Bruſh with melted Butter and bake in a moder-
ately hot Oven about twenty Minutes. Makes
about three Dozen ſmall Buns which are very nice
for Tea.

(Miſs *Bowdoin's* Recipe, c-1801.
Adapted *Blair* Kitchen, 1938.)

Coach Wheels ❊

ROLL out your Dough in a long narrow Strip.
Rub with ſoft Butter, ſprinkle with brown
Sugar and Cinnamon. Roll up into a Roll as round
as your Buns are to be. Slice three quarters Inch
thick with a floured Knife, and place almoſt touch-
ing in a well-buttered Pan. Let them riſe until light
and bake in a moderate Oven.

(*Richmond* Recipe.
Prov'd *Blair* Kitchen, 1938.)

Madiſon *Cakes* ❊

COOK two medium-ſized *Iriſh* Potatoes in one
and one fourth Cups of boiling Water, ſtrain off
the Water into a Cup. Maſh the Potatoes well, and
meaſure

meafure one Cupful of Potato Water (adding cold Water if not enough). When lukewarm, diffolve one Yeaft Cake in it. To mafhed Potatoes add four Tablefpoonfuls of Butter, two Teafpoonfuls of Salt, two Tablefpoons of Sugar, and two beaten Eggs. Add Yeaft Mixture then one and one half Quarts of fifted Flour. Knead until fmooth and fpongy. Put in a greafed Crock and let rife four or five Hours until light. Roll one Inch thick and cut up into Rolls. Set them far apart on your buttered Sheet, let rife until light and bake twenty Minutes in a moderate Oven.

(Old *Virginia* Recipe. Prov'd 1937.)

Crumpets ✻

TAKE a Quart of Dough from your Bread at a very early Hour in the Morning; break three frefh Eggs, feparating the Yelks from the Whites—whip them both to a Froth, mix them with the Dough, and add gradually milk-warm Water, till you make a Batter the Thicknefs of Buckwheat Cakes: beat it well, and fet it to rife till near Breakfaft Time; have the Griddle ready, pour on the Batter to look quite round: they do not require turning.

(Mrs. *Mary Randolph's* Virginia Houfewife, 1831.)

Huckleberry Muffins ✻

SIFT together two Cups of Flour, four Tablefpoonfuls of Sugar, four Teafpoons of baking Powder, one half Teafpoon of Salt. Add one Cup of well-cleaned Huckleberries. Beat an Egg and
add

add to it one Cup of Milk and pour into Flour. Then add four Tableſpoons of melted Butter. Half fill buttered Muffin Tins and bake in a moderate Oven.

(*Williamſburg* Family Recipe, Adapted 1938.)

Rice Muffins *

SIFT together three Cups of Flour, two Tableſpoons of Sugar, three Teaſpoons of baking Powder and one Teaſpoon of Salt. Stir in three fourths of a Cup of Milk, then add one and a half Cups of cooked Rice which is mixed with one Cup of Milk. Add three beaten Eggs, and one fourth of a Cup of melted Butter. Bake in well-greaſed Tins in a hot Oven. This will make twenty-four Muffins.

(Old Recipe from *Diſputanta, Virginia.* Prov'd *Williamſburg*, 1937.)

Martha Waſhington's *Potato Light Rolls* *

BOIL and maſh two good ſized *Iriſh* Potatoes and while ſtill hot add two Tableſpoons of Butter, one Tableſpoon of Lard, two Tableſpoons of Sugar, one Teaſpoon Salt, and one and a half Cupfuls of Water in which the Potatoes were boiled, and one Cupful of tepid Milk. Beat all well, adding gradually four Cups ſifted Flour and when lukewarm ſtir in a Yeaſt Cake diſſolved in one fourth Cup of tepid Water. Beat very hard, then turn out on a Board, adding more Flour as required and knead well. Set away in a warm ſheltered Place for ſix Hours. Do not knead again. Roll, cut into Rounds, let ſtand until very light, and bake in a hot Oven.

(Old Recipe, *Chaſe City, Virginia.*)

Sour

Sour Milk Griddle Cakes *

DISSOLVE one and a half Teaſpoons of Soda in ſour Milk. Add one and one half Cups of Flour, one Tableſpoonful of Sugar and one half Teaſpoon of Salt which have been ſifted together. Add two unbeaten Eggs and beat well. Add one Tableſpoon of melted Butter. Drop on hot Griddle. Brown on both Sides. This Recipe may be varied by uſing half Corn Meal and half Flour or half Hominy Grits and half Flour.

(*Virginia* Recipe, adapted and prov'd 1937.)

Sally Lunn *

BEAT four Eggs well; then melt a large Table-ſpoonful of Butter, put it in a Teacup of warm Water, and pour it to the Eggs with a Tea-ſpoon of Salt and a Teacup of Yeaſt (this means Potato Yeaſt); beat in a Quart of Flour making the Batter ſtiff enough for a Spoon to ſtand in. Put it to riſe before the Fire the Night before. Beat it over in the Morning, greaſe your Cake-mould and put it in Time enough to riſe before baking. Should you want it for Supper, make it up at 10:00 o'Clock in the Morning in the Winter and 12: o'Clock in the Summer.

(Recipe, c-1770, of Governor *Spotſwood's* Grand-daughter. From *Charlotte Court Houſ:, Virginia.*)

Williamſburg *Sally Lunn* *

PUT one Yeaſt Cake in one Cup of warm Milk. Cream together one half Cup of Butter and one third of a Cup of Sugar, add three beaten Eggs and mix

mix well. Sift in one Quart of Flour, alternately
with the Milk and Yeaſt. Let riſe in a warm Place
then beat well. Pour into one well-buttered *Sally
Lunn* Mold or two ſmaller Molds. Let riſe again
before baking in a moderate Oven.

(*Barlow* Family Recipe, *Williamſburg.*
Prov'd *Market Square Tavern* Kitchen, 1937.)

Sally Lunn Muffins ✷

SCALD one and one fourth Cups Milk and let
cool until luke-warm. Add two heaping Teaspoons Sugar and two Yeaſt Cakes to diſſolve.
Then add two Eggs, well beaten, two Tableſpoons
Cream, four Tableſpoons melted Butter, three and
one third Cups of Flour, one Teaſpoon Salt. Beat
hard and let riſe again, about two Hours in all.
Put in greaſed Muffin Tins and let riſe again for an
Hour. Bake in moderate Oven.

(Traditional *Virginia* Recipe.
Prov'd *Market Square Tavern* Kitchen, 1937.)

Williamſburg *Sweet Potato Buns* ✷

MASH two boiled ſweet Potatoes while hot
with three Tableſpoons of Butter. When
cool add one well-beaten Egg, one Teaſpoon of
Salt, three Tableſpoons of Sugar, then one half of
a Yeaſt Cake diſſolved in half a Cup of warm Water.
Then ſift in four Cups of Flour alternately with
about one Cup of warm Water (or enough to make
a ſoft Dough). Knead until ſmooth, let it riſe in a
warm Place until double in Bulk. Put in well-
buttered

buttered Muffin Pans, let riſe again and bake in a
moderate Oven. Juſt before removing from Oven
rub the Tops with melted Butter.

(Mrs. *Randolph's* Recipe, 1831.
Adapted *Market Square Tavern* Kitchen, 1937.)

Sweet Potato Biſcuits *

SIFT together two Cups of Flour, one half Teaſpoon of Soda, and one Teaſpoon of Salt. Work
in four level Tableſpoons of Lard. Mix one Cup of
maſhed ſweet Potatoes with one half Cup of ſour
Milk and mix to a ſoft Dough. Roll thin, cut and
bake in a hot Oven.

(Old Recipe from *Diſputanta, Virginia*.
Adapted *Market Square Tavern* Kitchen, 1937.)

Waffles *

TAKE one and a half Cups Buttermilk, two
Eggs, one-half Teaſpoon Salt, one-half Teaſpoon Sugar, one Tableſpoon of Butter, one Teaſpoon Baking-powder, one half Teaſpoon Soda,
one Pint of Flour. Melt Butter, beat Eggs, add
Salt and Sugar, then Buttermilk. Sift Flour, Soda,
and Powder into the Milk and Egg Mixture. Laſtly
add melted Butter. If Batter is too ſtiff, add a Bit
of cold Water. Have Waffle Iron well greaſed and
ſmoking hot.

(Old Recipe from *Phenix, Virginia*.)

Old

*The Market Square Tavern Kitchen
at Williamsburg.*

PLATE II.   E. JONES.

Old Virginia *Aſh Cake* *

ADD a Teaſpoonful of Salt to a Quart of ſifted Corn Meal. Make up with boiling Water and knead well. Make into round, flat Cakes. Sweep a clean Place on the hotteſt Part of the Hearth. Put the Cake on it and cover it with hot Wood Aſhes.

Waſh and wipe it dry before eating it. Sometimes a Cabbage Leaf is placed under it, and one over it, before baking, in which Caſe it need not be waſhed.

(*Shepperſon* Family Recipe, *Charlotte* County. Prov'd *Highland* County, *Virginia*, 1938.)

Batter Bread *

TAKE ſix Spoonfuls of Flour and three of Corn Meal, with a little Salt—ſift them, and make a thin Batter with four Eggs, and a ſufficient Quantity of rich Milk; bake it in little Tin Moulds in a quick Oven.

(Mrs. *Mary Randolph's* Virginia Houſewife, 1831.)

Another Batter Bread *

ADD two well-beaten Eggs to one and three fourths Cups of cooked Rice or fine Hominy. Add two and one half Cups of ſweet Milk then ſift in one Cup of Meal, one Teaſpoon of Salt and add one Tableſpoon of melted Butter. Beat very thoroughly and bake in hot well-buttered Baking-diſh for forty Minutes in a very hot Oven.

(Old Recipe, *Richmond, Virginia.* Prov'd *Market Square Tavern* Kitchen, 1937.)

Batter

Batter Cakes*

BOIL two Cups of ſmall Hominy very ſoft; add an equalQuantity ofCornMeal with a little Salt, and a large Spoonful of Butter; make it in a thin Batter with three Eggs, and a ſufficient Quantity of Milk—beat all together ſome Time, and bake them on a Griddle, or in Waffle Irons. When Eggs cannot be procured, Yeaſt makes a good Subſtitute; put a Spoonful in the Batter, and let it ſtand an Hour to riſe.

(Mrs. *Mary Randolph's* Virginia Houſewife, 1831.)

Old Virginia *Batter Cakes*

BEAT two Eggs very light in a Bowl. Add one Teacup of Clabber, one of Water, one of Corn Meal, a Teacup of Flour, one-half Teaſpoonful of Salt. Juſt before baking, ſift in half a Teaſpoonful of Soda and ſtir well. It is better to greaſe the Griddle with fat Bacon than with Lard.

The above Proportions will make enough Batter Cakes for two or three Perſons.

(Recipe from a *Williamſburg* Family Cook Book.)

Williamſburg *Corn Meal Bread**

POUR one Cup of boiling Water over one Cup of Meal, add one Cup of ſweet Milk, one Teaſpoon of Salt, one beaten Egg, and two Tableſpoons of melted Butter, one half Cake of Yeaſt diſſolved in one fourth Cup of warm Water. Let riſe one Hour, bake in buttered Muffin Tins in quick Oven about twenty Minutes.   (Mrs. *Randolph's* Recipe, 1831.
Adapted *Market Square Tavern* Kitchen, 1937.)

Spoon

Spoon Bread *

STIR one Cup of Corn Meal into one Pint of boiling Water, which contains one half Teaspoon of Salt. Stir one Minute, remove from Fire and add two Tablespoons of Butter. Beat well, add four beaten Eggs and beat in one Cup of cold Milk. Beat again and pour into hot buttered Baking-dish. Bake twenty-five Minutes in hot Oven and serve from Baking-dish.

(Traditional *Virginia* Recipe. Prov'd
Market Square Tavern Kitchen, 1937.)

Another Way *

PUT one Pint of Milk on the Fire and when it comes to a Boil stir in two Tablespoons of Corn Meal. Let cook until very thick stirring constantly. Cool, add three beaten Eggs, two Tablespoons of Flour, one half Teaspoon of Salt, one Tablespoon melted Butter. Bake in a buttered Dish for thirty-five Minutes in a moderate Oven.

(Old Recipe, *Petersburg, Virginia.*
From a *Williamsburg* Family Cook Book.)

Hoe Cakes *

SCALD one Pint of *Indian* Meal with enough boiling Water to make a stiff Batter (about three Cups). Add one Teaspoon of Salt. Drop on hot greased Tin and bake in hot Oven thirty Minutes. (Some Cooks prefer to spread their Batter one half Inch thick in their Dripping-pan and serve the Cake up hot by cutting it in Squares.)

(*Virginia* Recipe, c-1776.)

Corn

Corn Sticks *

BEAT together three Cups of Meal, three Cups of Milk, two Eggs, two Tablespoons of melted Lard, one and a half Teaspoons of Salt and three Teaspoons of baking Powder. Bake in hot greased Bread-stick Pans in hot Oven for twenty Minutes.

(**King's Arms** Recipe, *Williamsburg*.)

Cracklin Bread *

TAKE one Quart sifted Corn Meal and a Teacup of Cracklins. Rub the latter in the Meal as fine as you can. Add a Teaspoonful of Salt and make up with warm Water into a stiff Dough. Make into Pones, and eat hot.

(Old Recipe, *Lynchburg, Virginia*.
From a *Williamsburg* Family Cook Book.)

Soft Egg Bread *

MIX one Cup of Meal with one Quart of Butter-milk or Clabber. Add three beaten Eggs and one half Teaspoon of Salt. Bake in slow Oven in well-buttered Pudding-dish until a Silver Knife thrust into it comes out clean.

(Old Recipe, *Toano, Virginia*.)

Of GARDEN STUFF

CAPTAIN *Newport*, in 1607, said that *Virginia* was Nature's Nurse to all Vegetables—a Land where *West Indies* Plants would thrive and all *English* Garden-feeds prosper well. After the Lapse of a Century, a native Inhabitant reported of the *Virginians:*

> They live in so happy a Climate, and have so fertile a Soil, that no Body is poor enough to beg, or want Food, though they have Abundance of People that are lazy enough to deserve it.

The Kitchen Gardens of the Town Houses in *Williamsburg*, and of the great Plantation Houses were not Products of Nature's Nurse and Laziness. It required constant and careful Effort from the Householder to get a proper Supply of Seeds and to superintend the Planting, Cultivating and Harvesting of the Kitchen Garden.

Seeds could be propagated by the Gardener, bought in the Shops in *Williamsburg*, or ordered from *London* Seedsmen. Again and again, the Letters from *Virginia* carried Complaints and Injunctions like the following, found in the Papers of the Counting House of *John Norton & Sons*, Merchants of *London* and *Virginia:*

> The Seedsmen I can't but complain of for sending such a Parcel of Trumpery, several of the Articles

Articles are Weeds in this Country & many of the Seeds are not good.

I did not receive your Letter of the *1ſt* of Decr. pr. Capt. *Grieg* 'till Yeſterday, with the Physick, Garden-ſeeds & Biſcuit; which however are not yet landed, ſo that by the Length of the Paſſage, the Seeds are but of little Uſe for this Year's Crop.

The few Buſhels of Eggſhell Wheat imported laſt Spring proved good for Nothing; I ſuppoſe not one Grain in a Hundred vegitated; ſo that my Friend is greatly diſappointed. If you can prevail with the Captain to bring my Seeds in his Cabbin, it will be the moſt likely Means of preſerving them.

In a Letter dated September 7th, 1771, *Robert Carter Nicholas* of *Williamsburg* (Treaſurer of the Colony of *Virginia*) ſent the following Liſt to *John Norton & Sons:*

Garden Seeds to be ſent as early as poſſible in the Cabbin if it can be done.

2 Galls. earlieſt Peaſe
4 do midling
2 do of the lateſt Sort
1 Gal *Windſor* Beans
2 qts beſt *French* Beans
8 oz. orange Carrot
4 oz. ſwelling Parſnip
1 lb. earlieſt Turnip
4 lb. hardieſt Winter do.
4 oz. Turnip Radiſh. 1 pt. Salmon do.
1 oz. white Caſs Lettuce 1 oz. *Silecia* do.
1 oz. *Dutch* Cabbage do.
1 qt. round Spinage—1 qt. prickly do.
1 oz. beſt Endive. 1 oz. beſt Cellery 1 oz. *Roman* Mellon 1 oz. Cantaloupes
1 oz. Celleriack. 1 oz. ſollid Cellery

1 pt.

1 pt. water Creſſes. 1 pt. white Muſtard—1 do. corn Sallad—2 qts Rape Seed

2 oz. early Colliflower—Seed—2 oz. latter do.

2 oz. earlieſt ſugar Loaf Cabbage 1 oz. red Cabbage. 2 oz. green Savoy—2 oz. yellow do.

1 oz. green Brocoli—1 oz. red do. 1 oz. purple do. 1 oz. white do. 1 oz. prickly Cucumber—1 oz. earlieſt do.—1 oz. green & white Turkey Cucumber.

N. B. if theſe Seeds are not quite freſh & good it will not be worth while to ſend them; many of thoſe laſt ſent faild to my great Diſappointment.

It was a Citizen of *Williamſburg, John Randolph,* the Attorney General of the Colony, who wrote the earlieſt *American* Book on Kitchen Gardening, baſing his Obſervations upon his own Garden in the City.

It was firſt publiſhed about 1766, and was republiſhed ſeveral Times, becauſe of its Uſe in adapting *Engliſh* Agriculture to Conditions in *Virginia.* One of the later Publiſhers wrote of Mr. *Randolph's* Work:

The annexed little TREATISE was written many Years ago, by a learned and eminent CITIZEN OF VIRGINIA, who delighted in directing under his own Eye the Cultivation of his Garden, and who printed it for the Uſe of Friends, by whom it has been long and highly prized for the uſeful Information it conveys in a ſmall Compaſs, and without the Introduction of a uſeleſs Word.

The Reſidence of the Author, and his Garden, from which he drew his Obſervations, were in *Williamſburg, Virginia.*

Thoſe who conſult the Treatiſe, will know from this Hint, how to make a proper Allowance according to Variance in Climate, for the Seaſons and Times of ſowing, planting, &c.   Garden

Garden Stuff & Salads

To make a Sallad of Anchovies ✳

WASH them in Water or Wine till the Liquor
be clear; then dry them with a Linnen Cloth;
take off the Tails and Fins, ſlip them from the Bones,
and having laid them in a Plate, garniſh them with
young Onions, Parſley, Slices of Lemon and Beet-
roots; then beat up ſome ſweet Oil with Lemon-
juice, and pour it on the Anchovies.

(The Lady's Companion, 1753; Cook Book
owned by *Miſs Anna Maria Dandridge* 1756.)

Aſparagus forced in French *Rolls*

CUT a Piece out of the Cruſt of the Tops of
three *French* Rolls, and take out all their
Crumb; but be careful that the Cruſts fit again in
the Places from whence they were taken. Fry the
Rolls brown in freſh Butter. Then take a Pint of
Cream, the Yolks of ſix Eggs beat fine, and a little
Salt and Nutmeg. Stir them well together over a
ſlow Fire till it begins to be thick. Have ready an
Hundred of ſmall Graſs boiled, and ſave Tops
enough to ſtick the Rolls with. Cut the Reſt of the
Tops ſmall, put them into the Cream and fill the
Loaves with them. Before you fry the Rolls, make
Holes thick in the Top-cruſts, to ſtick the Graſs in.

Then

Then lay on the Pieces of Crust, and stick the Grass
in, that it may look as if it were growing. At a
second Course, this makes a pretty side Dish.

(*John Farley's* London Art of Cookery, 1787.
From *Brookbury, Chesterfield* County, *Virginia*.)

French *Beans* ⁕

STRING your Beans, cut them in Two, and then
acrofs; but if you wish to do them in a nice
Manner, cut them into Four, and then acrofs, so
that each Bean will then be in eight Pieces. Put
them into Salt and Water, and when the Pan boils,
put them in with a little Salt. They will be soon
done, which may be known by their becoming
tender; but take Care that you do not suffer them
to lose their fine green Colour. Lay them in a Plate,
and send them up with Butter in a Boat.

(*John Farley's* London Art of Cookery, 1787.
Prov'd *Market Square Tavern* Kitchen, 1937.)

To dress Brockala ⁕

STRIP all the little Branches off til you come to
the top One, then with a Knife peel off all the
hard outside Skin, which is on the Stalks and little
Branches, and throw them into Water. Have a
Stew-pan of Water with some Salt in it: when it
boils put in the Brockala, and when the Stalks are
tender it is enough, then send it to Table with
Butter in a Cup. The *French* eat Oil and Vinegar
with it.

(Mrs. *Hannah Glasse's* Art of Cookery, 1774.
Prov'd *Market Square Tavern* Kitchen, 1937.)

Brocoli

Brocoli *

THE Kind which bears Flowers around the
Joints of the Stalks muſt be cut into conveni-
ent Lengths for the Diſh; ſcrape the Skin from the
Stalk, and pick out any Leaves or Flowers that require to be removed; tie it up in Bunches and boil
it as Aſparagus; ſerve it up hot, with melted Butter
poured over it. The Brocoli that heads at the Top
like Cauliflowers muſt be dreſſed in the ſame Manner as the Cauliflower.

(Mrs. *Mary Randolph's* Virginia Houſewife, 1831.)

Lima *Beans and Sweet Corn* *

FOR a Change I cook theſe together, cutting the
Corn from the Cob and cooking with the Beans
until tender and about dry. Seaſon with Butter,
Cream and Pepper, Salt being added when they
are put on to boil.

(*Williamſburg* Recipe, c-1837. From Manuſcript
Collection of Mrs. *Elizabeth Labbé Cole.*)

Cabbage *

PICK Cabbages very clean, and waſh them thoroughly; then look them carefully over again;
quarter them if they are very large; put them into
a Sauce-pan with plenty of boiling Water; if any
Skum riſes, take it off, put a large Spoonful of Salt
into the Sauce-pan, and boil them till the Stalks
feel tender. A young Cabbage will take about
twenty Minutes, or half an Hour; when full grown,
nearly an Hour; ſee that they are well covered with
Water all the Time, and that no Dirt or Smoke
ariſes from ſtirring the Fire. With careful Management,

ment, they will look as beautiful when dreſſed as they did when growing. It will much ameliorate the Flavour of ſtrong old Cabbages, to boil them in two Waters, i.e. when they are half done, to take them out, and put them into another Sauce-Pan of boiling Water.

(Mrs. *Mary Randolph's* Virginia Houſewife, 1831.)

Williamſburg *Stuffed Cabbage*❊

TAKE the Inſide of the Cabbage and chop it fine, if you have any freſh Meat chop it up with ſome chopped fat Bacon, Crumbs of Bread. Mix it all up together with one or two Eggs, Butter, Pepper, Salt, then put it all in the outſide Part of the Cabbage. Put in a Cloth and boil it until done, ſerve it up with melted Butter.

(*Williamſburg* Recipe, c-1837. From Manuſcript Collection of Mrs. *Elizabeth Labbé Cole*.)

Purple Cabbage❊

SPLIT the Cabbage, and ſprinkle them well with Salt, pack them in a Jar one Night then drain them, pack them in a Puter Baſon, add Pepper, Allſpice, Gingir, Cloves, Horſe-raddiſh, Mace, Muſtard-ſeed. Cover them with Winegar and ſimmer them over hot Embers untill they are tender.

(Manuſcript Cook Book, prior to 1839. *Morton* Family of *Charlotte* County, *Virginia*.)

To Stew Cucumbers

PARE your Cucumbers and ſlice them thick and put them to drain, then lay them on a coarſe Cloth till they are dry, flour them and fry them brown

brown in Butter, then put to them some Gravy, a
little Claret, ſome Pepper, Cloves, and Mace and
let them ſtew a little then roll a bit of Butter in
Flour and toſs them up.

(Manuſcript Cook Book, c-1825, of Miſs *Margaret
Prentis* of *Williamſburg.* Owned by *Robert H.
Webb,* Eſq., *Charlotteſville.*)

Chicken Salad and Dreſſing *

CUT one well boiled Hen into Dice, add an
equal Quantity of Celery cut into ſmall Pieces
the Whites of four boiled Eggs chopped rather fine.
Mix theſe Ingredients well together, juſt before the
Salad is to be made, then ſerve the Dreſſing with
it.

DRESSING*: Yolks of four Eggs, one Gill of
good Vinegar (or Juice of Lemon if that is preferred),
one Gill of Olive Oil, one and one-half Teaſpoonfuls
of Salt, one-quarter Teaſpoonful of *Cayenne* Pepper,
one large Tableſpoon of mixed Muſtard, a little
Sugar to give a piquant Zeſt to the Vinegar. Beat
the Yolks of four Eggs to a light Cream, then ſtir
the Vinegar gradually into them, beating hard all
the Time. Stir the Mixture over the Fire until it
thickens, then remove, and beat gradually into it
the Sugar, Salt and Pepper and Oil. Do not fail to
beat it well. When very ſmooth ſet it upon Ice to
become well chilled.

(Recipe from *Cape Charles, Virginia.*
Manuſcript in *Barlow* Family Cook Book, *Williamſburg.*)

Cold

Cold Slaw *

CUT up a Quantity of Cabbage, and ſprinkle upon it a Teaſpoonful Salt. For a large Diſh uſe two Eggs, a Piece of Butter the Size of an Egg, one-half Cupful Water, one-half Teacupful Vinegar; beat the Eggs very light; add the Water, Vinegar, and Butter, with a little Pepper and Muſtard, and pour while hot over the Cabbage.

(Mrs. *Cole's* Recipe, c-1837. Prov'd *Market Square Tavern* Kitchen, 1937.)

To dreſs Parſnips *

BOIL them tender, ſcrape them clean, then ſcrape all the ſoft Part into a Sauce-pan; leave out the Strings, and put as much Milk or Cream as may be neceſſary, ſtir them over the Fire till they are thick, add a good Piece of Butter and a little Salt and when the Butter is melted ſend them to Table.

(Manuſcript Cook Book, c-1825, of Miſs *Margaret Prentis* of *Williamſburg.* Owned by *Robert H. Webb,* Eſq., *Charlotteſville.*)

Corn Fritters *

GRATE the Corn from three Dozen Ears, add to it three Tableſpoonfuls of Flour, and gradually mix with ſix Eggs, beaten well. Beat all hard together, and add Salt to the Taſte. Drop in oval Shapes, three Inches long, into a Pan, in which fry them brown, in equal Parts of Lard and Butter.

(Old Recipe, *Bedford* County, *Virginia.* From a *Williamſburg* Family Cook Book, Prov'd, 1937.)

Williamſburg

Williamſburg *Corn Fritters* *

TAKE two Cups of Corn. Make a Batter by ſifting one and two thirds Cups of Flour with three fourths of a Teaſpoon Salt, and two and one half Teaſpoons baking Powder. Beat two Eggs, add one third Cup of Milk and beat into the dry Ingredients. Add Corn and ſtir into the Batter. Drop by Spoonfuls into hot Fat.

(Old *Williamſburg* Family Recipe. Prov'd.)

Corn Pudding *

TAKE ſix large, tender, milky Ears of Corn. Split the Corn down the Center of each Row; cut off the Top and then ſcrape the Cob well. Beat two Eggs and ſtir them into the Corn. Add one fourth Cup of Flour, one Teaſpoon of Salt and one half Teaſpoon of black Pepper. Stir in one Pint of freſh Milk and mix all together thoroughly. Put in a cold buttered Pan about four Inches deep. Cover the Top with two heaping Tableſpoonfuls of Butter cut in ſmall Pieces. Bake in a moderately hot Oven about one Hour. Serve hot.

(Traditional *Virginia* Recipe.
From *Morgan* Family. Prov'd 1937.)

Squaſh or Cimlin *

GATHER young Squaſhes, peel, and cut them in Two; take out the Seeds, and boil them till tender; put them into a Colander, drain off the Water, and rub them with a wooden Spoon through the Colander; then put them into a Stew-

pan,

pan, with a Cup full of Cream, a small Piece of Butter, some Pepper and Salt—stew them, stirring very frequently until dry. This is the most delicate Way of preparing Squashes.

(Mrs. *Mary Randolph's* Virginia Housewife, 1831. Prov'd *Market Square Tavern* Kitchen, 1937.)

Cymlings Fried with Bacon *

FRY some Slices of fat Bacon in a Pan. Remove the Bacon and keep hot. Fry in the Drippings some Cymlings that have been boiled tender and cut in Slices. While frying, mash fine with a large Spoon and add Pepper and Salt. Fry brown and serve with the Bacon.

(Old Recipe, *Toano, Virginia*.)

Oyster Salad *

DRAIN the Liquor from one-half Gallon fresh Oysters and throw them into some hot Vinegar on the Fire; let them remain until they are plump, not cooked. Then put them at once into clear, cold Water. Drain the Water from them and set them away in a cool Place, and prepare your

DRESSING: Mash the Yolks of four hard-boiled Eggs as fine as you can and rub into it two Teaspoonfuls Salt, two Teaspoonfuls black Pepper and two Teaspoonfuls made Mustard, then rub two large Spoonfuls Salad Oil or melted Butter in, a few Drops at a Time. When it is all smooth, add one raw Egg, well beaten, and then one Teacup good Vinegar, a Spoonful at a time. Set aside. Mix Oysters, Celery (nearly as much Celery as Oysters) cut

cut up into small Dice, and two good sized pickled
Cucumbers, cut up fine, tossing up well with a Silver
Fork. Sprinkle in Salt to your Taste. Then pour
Dressing over all.

(Old Recipe, *Lynchburg, Virginia.*
From a *Williamsburg* Family Cook Book.)

Green Peas *

TO have them in Perfection, they must be quite
young, gathered early in the Morning, kept in
a cool Place, and not shelled until they are to be
dressed; put Salt in the Water, and when it boils,
put in the Peas; boil them quick, twenty or thirty
Minutes, according to their Age; just before they
are taken up, add a little Mint chopped very fine;
drain all the Water from the Peas, put in a Bit of
Butter, and serve them up quite hot.

(Mrs. *Mary Randolph's* Virginia Housewife, 1831.
Recipe prov'd 1937.)

Black-eye Peas *

SHELL early in the Morning, keep in Water
until an Hour before Dinner, then put into
boiling Water, covering close while cooking. Add a
little Salt just before taking from Fire. Drain and
serve with a large Spoonful fresh Butter.

(Old Recipe, *Toano, Virginia.*)

Mrs. B's *Pumpkin Fritters* *

THE Pumpkin must be well boiled, left from
Dinner. Take four Spoonfuls Pumpkin, two
Eggs, one half Pint to more of Milk (or Cream if
you wish) one or more Tablespoonfuls of brown
Sugar.

Sugar. Thicken with Wheat Flour about the Thick-
ness of Batter for Waffles well beaten and light.
Fry in boiling Lard two or three Spoonfuls for each
Fritter. Tried and found good.

(Manuscript Cook Book, c-1801, of Mrs. *Frances
Bland Tucker Coalter.* Owned by Dr. *St.
George Tucker Grinnan, Richmond.*)

Spinach *

HAVING picked your Spinach very clean, and
washed it in five or six Waters, put it into a
Sauce-pan that will just hold it, throw a little Salt
over it, and cover it close. Put in no Water, but
take Care to shake the Pan often. Put your Sauce-
pan on a clear and quick Fire, and as soon as you
find your Greens are shrunk and fallen to the Bottom, and the Liquor that comes out of them boils
up, it is a Proof your Spinach is enough. Throw
them into a clean Sieve to drain, and just give them
a gentle Squeeze. Lay them in a Plate, and send
them up with Butter in a Boat, but never pour any
over them. (*John Farley's* London Art of Cookery, 1787.
From *Brookbury, Chesterfield* County, *Virginia.*)

Baked Tomatoes *

PEEL the Tomatoes. Cut in small Pieces, season
with a little Sugar, Salt, Pepper, and finely
minced Onion. Grease a Baking-dish and line it
with thin Slices of buttered Bread. Pour the Tomatoes in the Dish, crumbing up a little Bread on
them. Dot the Top with Butter and bake.

(Recipe from a *Williamsburg* Family Cook Book.)

Escalloped

Escalloped Tomatoes *

MIX two and one half Cups of Tomatoes, two Slices of Bread broken in Pieces, one half Cup of finely chopped Celery, one Tablespoon of finely minced Onion, one Teaspoon of Salt, one fourth Teaspoon of black Pepper and three Tablespoons of Sugar. Pour into buttered deep Baking-dish and cover well with small Pieces of Butter. Bake in a slow Oven at least an Hour, stirring occasionally at first. (Old Recipe, adapted *Market Square Tavern* Kitchen, 1937.)

Turnip Tops *

PARE the Shoots which grow out (in the Spring) from the old Turnip Roots. Put them in cold Water an Hour before they are dressed; the more Water they are boiled in, the better they will look; if boiled in a small Quantity of Water, they will taste bitter; when the Water boils, put in a small Handful of Salt, and then your Vegetables; they are still better boiled with Bacon in the *Virginia* Style: if fresh and young, they will be done in about twenty Minutes—drain them on the Back of a Sieve, and put them under the Bacon.

(Mrs. *Mary Randolph's* Virginia Housewife, 1831.)

Jowl and Turnip Salad *

THIS is an old *Virginia* Dish, and much used in the Spring of the Year. The Jowl must be washed clean and boiled for three Hours. Put in the Salad and boil half an Hour. If you boil it too long it will turn yellow. The Jowl and Salad should always be served with poached Eggs.

(Old Recipe from *Toana, Virginia*.)

Salmagundi

Salmagundi ✻

TURN a Bowl on the Diſh, and put on it in regular Rings, beginning at the Bottom, the following Ingredients, all minced: Anchovies with the Bones taken out, the white Meat of Fowls without the Skin, hard-boiled Eggs, the Yelks and Whites chopped ſeparately, Parſley, the Lean of old Ham ſcraped, the inner Stalks of Celery; put a Row of Capers round the Bottom of the Bowl, and diſpoſe the others in a fanciful Manner; put a little Pyramid of Butter on the Top, and have a ſmall Glaſs with Egg mixed as for Sallad, to eat with the Salmagundi.

(Mrs. *Mary Randolph's* Virginia Houſewife, 1831.)

Cooking Salſify ✻

PREPARE it, by boiling in Milk untill the Slices are tender, adding Pepper & Salt and a good Slice Butter. When ready to ſerve, ſtir in two or three well beaten Eggs, taking Care not to let it boil afterwards. This is very nice poured over Slices of Toaſt.

(Manuſcript Cook Book, c-1839. *Morton* Family of *Charlotte* County, *Virginia*.)

To Roaſt Potatoes ✻

WASH and dry your Potatoes (all of a Size) and put them in a tin *Dutch* Oven, or Cheeſe Toaſter; take Care not to put them too near the Fire, or they will get burned on the Outſide before they are warmed through. Large Potatoes will require two Hours to roaſt them. To ſave Time and Trouble, ſome Cooks half-boil them firſt.

(Mrs. *Mary Randolph's* Virginia Houſewife, 1831.)

Potato

Potato Balls *

MIX mashed Potatoes with the Yelk of an Egg, roll them into Balls, flour them, or cover them with Egg and Bread Crumbs, fry them in clean Dripping, or brown them in a *Dutch* Oven. They are an agreeable Vegetable Relish, and a Supper Dish. (Mrs. *Mary Randolph's* Virginia Housewife, 1831.)

To Dress Salad *

TO have this delicate Dish in perfection, the Lettuce, Pepper-grass, Chervil, Cress, &c., should be gathered early in the Morning, nicely picked, washed, and laid in cold Water, which will be improved by adding Ice; just before Dinner is ready to be served, drain the Water from your Salad, cut it into a Bowl, giving the proper Proportions of each Plant; prepare the following Mixture to pour over it: boil two fresh Eggs ten Minutes, put them in Water to cool, then take the Yelks in a Soup-plate, pour on them a Tablespoonful of cold Water, rub them with a wooden Spoon until they are perfectly dissolved; then add two Spoonfuls of Oil: when well mixed, put in a Teaspoonful of Salt, one of powdered Sugar, and one of made Mustard; when all these are united and quite smooth, stir in two Tablespoonfuls of common, and two of Tarragon Vinegar; put it over the Salad, and garnish the Top with the Whites of the Eggs cut into Rings and lay around the Edge of the Bowl young Scallions, they being the most delicate of the Onion Tribe. (Mrs. *Mary Randolph's* Recipe, 1831. Prov'd *Market Square Tavern* Kitchen, 1937.)

Salad

Salad Dreſſing (Boiled) *

YOLK of one Egg well beaten, add one Teaſpoonful dry Muſtard, ſmall Teaſpoonful Salt, Speck
of *Cayenne* Pepper, one Tableſpoonful Sugar, one
Tableſpoonful melted Butter, three Tableſpoonfuls
hot Vinegar, laſtly, White of Egg beaten ſtiff. Cook
on very ſlow Fire until thick as Cream.

(Old *Williamſburg* Recipe, *Barlow* Family Manuſcript.)

Sour Cream Dreſſing for Salad *

MIX the Yolks of four Eggs with two Tableſpoonfuls of cold Water and four of Vinegar.
Add one Teaſpoonful of dry *Engliſh* Muſtard
which has been made into a Paſte with a little
Water and one Teaſpoonful of Sugar. Cook over a
very ſlow Fire, ſtirring ſteadily until it thickens.
Cool. Add one Teaſpoonful of Salt and one Cupful
of sour Cream which has been whipped.

(Old *Morgan* Family Recipe. Prov'd, *Blair* Kitchen, 1938.)

To make a Sallad with Freſh Salmon *

TAKE some ſoufed Salmon, and mince it ſmall,
with Apples and Onions, put to it Oil, Vinegar
and Pepper, and ſerve it up, garniſhing your Diſh
with Slices of Lemon and Capers.

(The Lady's Companion, 1753; Cook Book
owned by Miſs *Anna Maria Dandridge*, 1756.)

Of

👑 👑 👑 👑 👑 👑 👑 👑 👑 👑 👑 👑

Of PASTRY

THE *Virginia* Houſewife made Cheeſecakes, Pies and Tarts from the Recipes ſhe found in her *Engliſh* Cook Books and from favorite Family Recipes, but beſt of all her Recipes were thoſe which ſhe developed in *Virginia*. The ſweet Potato, the Pecan, the Fox Grape and other native Products offered Opportunities for ingenious Adaptation. The following Recipes repreſent ſome of the *Engliſh* Favorites, but are chiefly thoſe developed in *Virginia*.

Paſtries & Cheeſecakes

Pie Cruſt ⁂

SIFT together four Cups of Flour and one Teaſpoon of Salt. Cut into this with Silver Knives one Cup of chilled Lard. Add juſt enough Ice-water to hold together, handle very lightly and roll out on a Board.

(Old Recipe. Adapted *Market Square Tavern* Kitchen, 1937.)

To

To make Puff Paſte

SIFT a Quart of Flour, leave out a Little for rolling the Paſte, make up the Remainder with
cold Water into a ſtiff Paſte, knead it well, and roll
it out ſeveral Times; waſh the Salt from a Pound
of Butter, divide it into four Parts, put one of them
on the Paſte in little Bits, fold it up, and continue
to roll it till the Butter is well mixed; then put another Portion of Butter, roll it in the ſame Manner;
do this till all the Butter is mingled with the Paſte;
touch it very lightly with the Hands in Making—
bake it in a moderate Oven, that will permit it to
riſe, but will not make it brown. Good Paſte muſt
look white, and as light as a Feather.

(Mrs. *Mary Randolph's* Virginia Houſewife, 1831.)

Williamſburg *Puff Paſte* ⁑

SET aſide two Tableſpoons of Butter, and ſhape
Remainder of a Pound of ſweet Butter into a
circular Piece one-half Inch thick, put on floured
Board. Work the two Tableſpoons Butter into one
Pound of Flour. Moiſten to a Dough with Ice-
water, turn on floured Board, knead five Minutes
—let ſtand a few Minutes covered with a Towel.
Roll lightly one-fourth Inch thick keeping Paſte
a little wider than long—Corners ſhould be ſquare.
Place Butter on Centre of lower Half of Paſte.
Cover Butter by folding upper Half of Paſte over
it. Preſs Edges firmly—ſo as to keep in as much
Air as poſſible. Fold right Side of Paſte over en-
cloſed Butter, the left Side under encloſed Butter.
Turn

Turn Paſte one-fourth Way round, lift, and roll one-fourth Inch thick, having Paſte longer than wide, lifting often to prevent Paſte from Sticking. Add Flour to prevent Paſte from ſticking to Board. Fold from Ends toward Centre, making three Layers. Repeat four Times turning Paſte one-fourth Way round each Time before rolling. After fourth Rolling fold from Ends to Centre and double, making four Layers. Put in Place to chill. Cut round or fancy Shapes, prick on Top with Fork. Bake in quick Oven on brown Paper.

(Recipe prov'd *Market Square Tavern* Kitchen, 1937.)

Apple Pie *

HAVING put a good Puff-paſte Cruſt round the Edge of your Diſh, pare and quarter your Apples, and take out the Cores. Then lay a thick Row of Apples, and throw in Half the Sugar you intend to put into your Pie. Mince a little Lemon-peel fine, ſpread it over the Sugar and Apples, and ſqueeze a little Lemon over them. Then ſcatter a few Cloves over it, and lay on the Reſt of your Apples and Sugar. Sweeten to your Palate, and ſqueeze a little more Lemon. Boil the Peeling of the Apples and Cores in ſome fair Water, with a Blade of Mace, till it has a pleaſing Taſte. Strain it, and boil the Syrup with a little Sugar, till there be but a ſmall Quantity left. Then pour it into your Pie, put on your upper Cruſt, and bake it. If you chooſe it, you may put a little Quince or Marmalade. In the ſame Manner you may make a *Pear Pie*; but in that you muſt omit the Quince. You
may

may butter them when they come out of the Oven, or beat up the Yolks of two Eggs, and half a Pint of Cream, with a little Nutmeg, fweetened with Sugar. Put it over a flow Fire, and keep ftirring it till it begins to boil; then take off the Lid, and pour in the Cream. Cut the Cruft in little three-corner Pieces, and ftick them about the Pie.

(*John Farley's* London Art of Cookery, 1787. From *Brookbury, Chefterfield* County, *Virginia*.)

Deep Diſh Apple Pie*

PARE and flice five Pounds of Apples in thin Slices, place in Baking-pan, fprinkle with Sugar and dot with Bits of Butter. Continue Layers and ftrew with Nutmeg before covering with Pie-cruft. Bake forty Minutes or until brown and Apples are thoroughly foft.

(Old Recipe. Adapted *Market Square Tavern* Kitchen, 1937.)

Bell Fritters

PUT a Piece of Butter the Size of an Egg into a Pint of Water; let it boil a few Minutes— thicken it very fmoothly with a Pint of Flour; let it remain a fhort Time on the Fire, ftir it all the Time that it may not ftick to the Pan, pour it in a wooden Bowl, add five or six Eggs, breaking one and beating it in—then another, and fo on till they are all in, and the Dough quite light—put a Pint of Lard in a Pan, let it boil, make the Fritters fmall and fry them to a fine amber Colour.

(Mrs. *Mary Randolph's* Virginia Houfewife, 1831.)

Caramel

Caramel Pie*

BEAT five Eggs very light, gradually beat in two Cups of brown Sugar. Then add one Cup of melted Butter and one Cup of *Damson* Plum Preserves or of Fox-grape Preserves. Mix well, pour into a Pie-plate lined with a good Paſtry and bake three Quarters of an Hour in a moderate Oven.

(Old Recipe from *Charlotte Court Houſe, Virginia.* Prov'd, *Market Square Tavern* Kitchen, 1937.)

To make Lemon Cheeſecakes

TAKE two large Lemons, grate off the Peel of both and ſqueeze out the Juice of one; add to it half a Pound of fine Sugar; twelve Yolks of Eggs, eight Whites well beaten; then melt half a Pound of Butter in four or five Spoonfuls of Cream; then ſtir it all together, and ſet it over the Fire, ſtirring it 'till it begins to be pretty thick; then take it off, and when 'tis cold, fill your Patty-pans little more than half full; put a fine Paſte very thin at the Bottom of the Patty-pans; half an Hour, with a quick Oven, will bake them.

(*E. Smith's* Compleat Houſewife, *Williamſburg,* 1742.)

Court Cheeſecakes

BOIL a Bit of Butter in a little Water and a little Salt; thicken it with as much Flour as it will take, ſtirring it on the Fire conſtantly until it becomes quite a Paſte; then mix the Eggs with it one

by

by one, to make it almoſt as liquid as a thick Batter; and mix ſome good Cream Cheeſe with it; bake it in good Puff-paſte, coloured with Yolks of Eggs: ſerve hot or cold.

(Court and Country Confectioner. *London*, 1770. From *Tucker* Houſe, *Williamſburg*.)

Lemon Cheeſecakes

TAKE the Peel of two large Lemons, boil it very tender then pound it well in a Mortar with a Quarter of a Pound, or more of Loaf-sugar, the Yolks of ſix Eggs, half a Pound of freſh Butter, mix all well together and fill your Patty-pans half full.

Orange Cheeſecakes are done the ſame Way, only the Peel muſt be boiled in two or three Waters to take the Bitterneſs out.

(Manuſcript Cook Book, c-1825, of Miſs *Margaret Prentis* of *Williamſburg*. Owned by *Robert H. Webb*, Eſq., *Charlotteſville*.)

Cheſs Cakes*

CREAM one half Pound of Butter and one half Pound of Sugar well together. Beat the Yolks of ſix Eggs until light in Color and add to the Butter and Sugar. Put in a Pinch of Salt and ſtir in one third of a Cup of white Wine. Bake in ſmall Paſtry Shells rolled thin in Muffin Tins. Fill the Shells about three-fourths full. Bake in a moderately hot Oven. Serve cold. Will keep for ſeveral Days in a cool Place.

(Traditional *Virginia* Recipe, *Morgan* Family. Prov'd, *Market Square Tavern* Kitchen, 1937.)

Cheſs

Chess Pie*

TAKE one fourth of a Pound of Butter and mix well with one Cup of Sugar and one Tablespoon of Flour. Beat eight Egg Yolks very light and slowly beat in them one Cup of Sugar. Combine. Add one Cup of Milk slowly, and last, the Juice of one Lemon. Pour into two Pie-pans lined with rich Pastry and bake in a slow Oven about one Hour or until firm.

(Mrs. *Frances Bland Tucker Coalter's* Recipe, c-1801
Adapted *Travis* House, 1938.)

Cheese Pie*

SEPARATE four Eggs. Beat Yolks with one and a half Cups of Sugar. Add Juice and grated Rind of one Lemon. Beat thoroughly. Rub one Pound Cottage Cheese through Colander. Whip Whites of Eggs stiff, and fold in well. Line large, deep Pie-tin with rather thick Pastry. Pour in the Mixture. Sprinkle with Nuts and bake in moderate Oven about thirty Minutes.

(Mrs. *E. Smith's* Recipe, 1742.
Adapted *Market Square Tavern* Kitchen, 1937.)

Crullers*

MIX six Tablespoons of Sugar well with two of Butter. Add four Egg Yolks, and four Tablespoons of thick sour Cream. Sift in four Tablespoons of Flour mixed with one Teaspoon of Salt and one half Teaspoon of Soda. Roll out on a floured Board and cut in small Shapes. Fry in deep, hot Fat.

(Recipe from *Woodstock, Virginia,* c-1829.)

Plain

Plain Cuſtard Pie *

FOUR Eggs, one Quart Milk, four Tableſpoons white Sugar; flavor with Nutmeg, or other Spice to Taſte. Bake without top Cruſt; the ſame Mixture cooked in a Diſh ſet in boiling Water makes a good boiled Cuſtard Pudding. Bake in moderate Oven about forty-five Minutes.

(*Williamſburg* Recipe, c-1837.
From Collection of Mrs. *Elizabeth Labbé Cole.*)

Damſon Pie *

TAKE the Yolks of five Eggs and beat them well, then add ſlowly three fourths of a Cup of Sugar, beating well. Beat another three fourths of a Cup of Sugar into a half a Cup of Butter. Combine, adding one eighth of a Teaſpoon of Salt and one Tableſpoon of Flour. Add one Cup of *Damſon* Plum Preſerves, and laſt the beaten Whites of the Eggs. Bake in Paſtry-ſhells in a moderate Oven until ſet (about thirty-five Minutes). This makes ten ſmall Pies.

(Traditional *Virginia* Recipe, *Morgan* Family.
Prov'd *Market Square Tavern* Kitchen, 1937.)

Lemon Cheſs Pie *

MIX well one Teacup of Sugar with two Tableſpoons of Butter. Beat the Yolks of four Eggs very light, and beat in well. Add the grated Rind of two Lemons and the Juice of one. Beat the Whites of the Eggs ſtiff, and fold in lightly. Pour into lightly baked Pie Shell, and bake in moderately ſlow Oven until ſet and light golden brown.

(Old *Buckingham* County Recipe of *Gracie Maſon.*)

Lemon

Lemon Pies*

TAKE three large fresh Lemons; grate off the Rind; pare off every Bit of the white Skin of the Lemon (as it toughens while cooking); then cut the Lemon into very thin Slices with a sharp Knife, and take out the Seeds; two Cupfuls of Sugar, three Tablespoonfuls of Water, and two of sifted Flour. Put into the Pie a Layer of Lemon, then one of Sugar, then one of the grated Rind, and, lastly, of Flour, and so on till the Ingredients are used; sprinkle the Water over all, and cover with Upper-crust. Be sure to have the Under-crust lap over the Upper, and pinch it well, as the Syrup will cook all out if Care is not taken when finishing the Edge of Crust. Bake in moderate Oven. This Quantity makes one medium-size Pie.

(Mrs. *Cole's* Recipe, c-1837.   Prov'd *Market Square Tavern* Kitchen, 1937.)

Maids of Honor*

BEAT four Eggs well, adding gradually a Cup of Sugar in which you have mixed well four Tablespoons of Flour. Add five Tablespoons of melted Butter and one Cup of ground Almonds or Almond Paste moistened with a little Sherry and season with Nutmeg. Line Patty-pans with rich Pastry, and spread on the Bottom of each a Tablespoon of Strawberry or Raspberry Preserves. Put the Filling on Top and bake in a moderate Oven twenty-five Minutes.

(Early *English* and *Virginia* Recipe. Adapted *Market Square Tavern* Kitchen, 1937.)

Molasses

Molaſſes Pie *

FOUR Eggs—beat the Whites ſeparate—one
Teacupful of brown Sugar, half a Nutmeg, two
Tableſpoonfuls of Butter; beat them well together;
ſtir in one Teacupful and a half of Molaſſes, and
then add the Whites of Eggs. Bake on Paſtry.

(Mrs. *Cole's* Recipe, c-1837. Prov'd
Market Square Tavern Kitchen, 1937.)

Another Way *

BEAT ſix Eggs very light with two Cups of
Sugar, add one fourth of a Cup of Molaſſes,
three Tableſpoons of melted Butter, one Teaſpoon
of Cinnamon, one of Allſpice and mix well. Add
one Pint of Milk. Pour into a large Pie-tin lined
with rich Paſtry and bake ſlowly.

(Recipe from *Cheſterfield, Virginia,* c-1800.)

Moonſhines *

MIX and ſift together into one beaten Egg and
one half Cup of Milk, one third Cup of Sugar
one and a third Cups of Flour, two Teaſpoons of
baking Powder, one fourth Teaſpoon of Salt, one
half Teaſpoon of Nutmeg, one Teaſpoon of melted
Butter. Drop into boiling Fat, drain on brown
Paper. Split and put Currant Jelly between. Roll
in Confectioner's Sugar.

(Mrs. *Cole's* Recipe, c-1837. Adapted
Market Square Tavern Kitchen, 1937.)

Orange

Orange Pie*

PUT two Tableſpoons of Butter in three-fourths of a Cup of Sugar and mix well. Add three well-beaten Egg Yolks, then the Juice and grated Rind of one-half of an Orange and one-half of a Lemon, Nutmeg to Taſte. Pour into Pie-pan lined with good Paſtry and bake in moderate Oven about forty-five Minutes. Beat the Egg Whites ſtiff, and ſlowly ſift in three Tableſpoons of powdered Sugar, ſpread on your Pie and bake very ſlowly until ſlightly browned.

(Old *Williamſburg* Recipe, c-1837.
Adapted *Market Square Tavern* Kitchen, 1937.)

A Bon Chretien Pear Pye
(Call'd a la Bonne Femme)

SLIT in two ſome *bon chretien* Pears, take out the Core, pare them. Put into an earthen Pot ſome of the Parings, put the Apple over them, add a Stick of Cinnamon and ſome Sugar, and a Glass of red Wine, with a little Water; and cover the Same with the Reſt of the Parings. Cover your Pot with ſome Paſte round, and let your Pears be doing ſlowly during five or ſix Hours, with Fire under and over; then put ſome Paſte in the Bottom of a Baking-pan, as large as the dainty Diſh you deſign to ſerve up, making round it a Cruſt the Breadth of a Thumb; and let the Paſte be not too thick. Put the Pan in the Oven, and when baked, glaze the Paſte. Your Pears being done, place them in the Pan, with their Liquor, which muſt be of a lively red, ſtrain it
through

through a Sieve, and pour it over them. If your
Liquor is too thin, set it over again to thicken, then
pour it over your Pears. Serve it up either hot or
cold.

(Court & Country Confectioner. *London*, 1770.
From *Tucker* House, *Williamsburg*.)

Pecan Pie *

BEAT three Eggs very light, then slowly beat in
three-fourths of a Cup of Sugar, one-fourth
of a Pound of melted Butter and one Cup of brown
Corn Syrup. Pour into uncooked Pie-crust and cook
very slowly forty Minutes until almost set, cover
the Top with halves of Pecans, return to Oven and
increase Heat and cook for another ten or fifteen
Minutes in a moderate Oven.

(Traditional *Virginia* Recipe. Prov'd
Market Square Tavern Kitchen, 1937.)

Potato Pies *

POTATOES (Sweet) well cooked, boiled or
baked. When cold, slice them about one fourth
of an Inch thick. A Layer of Potatoes placed on the
Pastry in the Pan. Then a Layer of Sugar, finely
beaten Allspice sprinkled over it. Considerable
Butter over this if desired to be rich. According to
Taste. Then Potatoes, Allspice, Sugar and Butter
again: and keep alternating thus until Pie is of desired Thickness, then fill the Plate with White-wine,
cover the Whole with Pastry, cook it well and send
me a Piece. Eat hot. For Mrs. *Cote*, with Mrs. *Pey-
ton's* Compliments.

(Mrs. *Cole's* Recipe, c-1837. Prov'd
Market Square Tavern Kitchen, 1937.)

Sweet

Sweet Potato Pie *

MASH five Cups of ſweet Potatoes well. Add one Cup of Milk, three well-beaten Eggs, two Cups of Sugar, and one Teaſpoon of Cinnamon. Bake in a Pie-pan lined with good Paſtry about one-half Hour in a moderate Oven. Makes two Pies.

(Traditional *Virginia* Recipe. Adapted.)

Pumpkin Pye *

TAKE one Quart of Milk, two beaten Eggs, one Teaſpoon Salt, one of Ginger, one of Cinnamon, one half Cup of Sugar, three Tableſpoons of Molaſſes and one Pint of maſhed, ſteamed Pumpkin. Beat well together. Pour into partially baked Pie-cruſts. This will make two Pies.

(Recipe from *Wicomico* Church, c-1829.
Prov'd *Market Square Tavern* Kitchen, 1937.)

Williamſburg *Snow Balls* *

PARE and core ſix large Apples, and fill the Holes with Orange Marmalade. Make a Paſte by mixing together one-fourth of a Cup of Butter, one-half Cup of brown Sugar, four Teaſpoons of Cinnamon, one Teaſpoon Allſpice and one Teaſpoon Nutmeg. Spread an Apple with the Paſte then wrap each Apple in a good Paſtry. Bake in a ſlow Oven about one Hour. Serve hot with Rum Hard-ſauce.

(Mr. *Farley's* Recipe, 1787. Adapted
Market Square Tavern Kitchen, 1937.)

Of

Of Preserving & Pickling

PICKLES, Preserves, Jellies, Sweetmeats, Conserves and Relishes were such staple Table Delicacies in colonial *Virginia* that one can rarely examine the Inventory of any Person of Substance without finding Preserving-kettles, stone and earthen Jars, Jelly Glasses, Pickle Dishes, Corner Dishes and an Abundance of Utensils for making or serving them.

Ships coming into *Virginia's* Rivers and Harbours from *England* and the northern *Colonies* almost invariably brought in large Supplies of earthen and stone Ware. This Trade was of great Interest to the *British* Potteries and the Lords of Trade and Plantations observed carefully any Sign of colonial Manufacturing that might diminish it. The royal Governors were required to reply to elaborate Questionnaries sent them each Year by these Commissioners.

In 1732, Governor *Gooch* reported to them, "a "poor Potter at *Yorke* makes Vessels of Earthen-"ware, but this is of so little Consequence that I "believe it hath occasion'd little or no Diminution "in the Quantity of Earthen-ware that hath been "commonly imported." Each Year he reported deprecatingly of the poor Potter at *York;* until in the year 1743, in Reply to the Question, "What Manu-"factories have you?", he answered "None, as the "poor old Potter is dead."

Preserves

Preferves & Pickles

*Apricots in Brandy**

TAKE freshly gathered Apricots not too ripe; to Half their Weight of loaf Sugar, add as much Water as will cover the Fruit; boil and skim it: then put in the Apricots, and let them remain five or six Minutes; take them up without Syrup, and lay them on Dishes to cool; boil the Syrup till reduced one Half; when the Apricots are cold, put them in Bottles, and cover them with equal Quantities of Syrup and *French* Brandy. If the Apricots be clingstone, they will require more scalding.

(Mrs. *Mary Randolph's* Virginia Housewife, 1831.)

*To Pickle Beet Root**

BOIL them till tender, take the Skins off, cut them in Slices and gimp them in the Shape of Wheels, Flowers, or what you please; put them in a Jar and take as much Vinegar as you think will cover them, boil it with a little Mace, Ginger, and Horse-radish, pour it hot on the Root, it makes pretty Garnish for Fish or other Things.

(Court & Country Confectioner. *London*, 1770. Recipe prov'd *Market Square Tavern* Kitchen, 1937.)

*Spiced Cantaloupe**

USE ripe Cantaloupes. Pare and slice in desired Size and Shape and place in crockery Jar. Cover with Vinegar and let stand twelve to fifteen Hours.

Hours. Drain off Vinegar and to each Gallon of Cantaloupe use five Pounds of Sugar, whole Cloves and Cinnamon Sticks and small Amount of Mace to Taste, add to the Vinegar which has been drained off. Boil fifteen Minutes. Then add Cantaloupe and continue to boil about twenty Minutes or until Cantaloupe is clear. Remove the Cantaloupe and continue to boil the Syrup ten Minutes longer. Again add the Fruit to the Syrup and boil five Minutes. Remove and place in Jars.

(Miss *Margaret Prentis'* Recipe, c-1825, Adapted 1938.)

Cherries in Brandy *

GET the short stemmed bright red Cherries in Bunches—make a Syrup, with equal Quantities of Sugar and Cherries; scald the Cherries, but do not let the Skins crack, which they will do if the Fruit be too ripe. Put them in Bottles, and cover them with equal Quantities of Syrup and *French* Brandy. (Mrs. *Mary Randolph's* Virginia Housewife, 1831.)

Brandy Cherries *

SELECT the nicest Cherries, trim them, leaving a short Stem to each Cherry that the Juice may be retained. Wash & wipe them gently & put them in large-mouthed Bottles. Have ready a good Syrup (a Pint of Water to a Pound of Sugar) & when it is nearly cold add one Pint & a Half of *French* Brandy to every Pint of Syrup mix it thoroughly & pour it cold over yr. Cherries. Seal the Bottles well. (Manuscript Cook Book, *Charlottesville,* 1836. Owned by Mrs. *Virginia Grasty Griffin.*)

Celery

Celery Vinegar*

POUND two Gills of Celery-feed, put it into a
Bottle and fill it with ftrong Vinegar; fhake it
every Day for a Fortnight, then ftrain it, and keep
it for Ufe. It will impart a pleafant Flavour of Celery to anything with which it is ufed. A very delicious Flavour of THYME may be obtained, by
gathering it when in full Perfection; it muft be
picked from the Stalks, a large Handful of it put
into a Jar, and a Quart of Vinegar or Brandy
poured on it; cover it very clofe—next Day, take
all the Thyme out, put in as much more; do this a
third Time; then ftrain it, bottle and feal it fe-
curely. This is greatly preferable to the dried
Thyme commonly ufed, during the Seafon when it
cannot be obtained in a frefh State. MINT may be
prepared in the fame Way. The Flavour of both
thefe Herbs muft be preferved by Care in the Preparation: if permitted to ftand more than twenty
Hours in the Liquor they are infufed in, a coarfe
and bitter Tafte will be extracted, particularly
from Mint.

(Mrs. *Mary Randolph's* Virginia Houfewife, 1831.)

Englifh *Chop Pickle*

CHOP fine one large Cabbage, one half Gallon
of green Tomato, one half Gallon of firm Cucumbers. Sprinkle with Salt and let ftand Overnight. Wafh off Salt and add fix finely chopped red
Peppers, fix finely chopped green Peppers, four
Tablefpoons of Celery-feed, eight Tablefpoons of
Muftard-feed. One Teafpoon each of Allfpice, Ginger,

ger, Turmeric, Cloves, and if deſired one Pound of finely chopped Raiſins. Heat four Pounds of brown Sugar until diſſolved in three Quarts of good Vinegar. While warm but not hot pour over your Reliſh and put it away in covered Stone Crocks.

(Old Recipe from *Toano, Virginia*.
Prov'd *Travis* Houſe, 1938.)

Pickled Figs *

BRING to a boil one Quart of Vinegar, five Sticks Cinnamon, one Tableſpoon each whole Cloves, Allſpice, and Celery-ſeed. Drop in Figs waſhed and dried. Cook twenty Minutes.

(Traditional *Virginia* Recipe.)

Gerkins

TAKE a large earthen Pan with Spring-water in it, and to every Gallon of Water put two Pounds of Salt. Mix them well together, and throw in five hundred Gerkins. In two Hours take them out, and put them to drain. Let them be drained very dry, and then put them into a Jar. Put into a Pot a Gallon of the beſt white-wine Vinegar, half an Ounce of Cloves and Mace, an Ounce of Allſpice, the ſame Quantity of Muſtard-ſeed, a Stick of Horſe-radiſh cut in Slices, ſix Bay-leaves, two or three Races of Ginger, a Nutmeg cut in Pieces, and a Handful of Salt. Boil up all together in the Pot, and pour it over the Gerkins. Cover them cloſe down, and let them ſtand twenty-four Hours. Then put them in your Pot, and let them ſimmer over the Fire till they be green; but be careful not
to

to let them boil, as that will fpoil them. Then put them into your Jar, and cover them clofe down till they be cold. Then tie them over with a Bladder and a Leather, and put them in a cold, dry Place.

(*John Farley's* London Art of Cookery, 1787.
From *Brookbury, Chefterfield* County, *Virginia*.)

Green Gages

TAKE any Quantity of Green-gages, prick them with a Pin, put them in a Pan with Water, and fet them on the Fire; when you fee the Water is beginning to boil, take them off and leave them in the fame Water to cool till the next Day, when you are to fet them again on a very gentle Fire, that they may turn green. When you fee they are green enough, you put them in a Sieve to drain; then you take the firft Degree of clarified Sugar, in which you add three Parts Water, then the Plums, and fet the Whole on a flow Fire to make them throw off their Water; after which, you put them in a Pan for two Days, and then you add clarified Sugar, and proceed as for Preferves.

(Court & Country Confectioner. *London,* 1770.
From *Tucker* Houfe, *Williamfburg*.)

Conferve of Lemons *

WASH and dry yᵣ Lemons, pare off the yellow Rinds clear of the White and beat them in a Marble Mortar with nearly double their Weight of white Sugar. Pack clofely in a Jar or Glafs and cover the Top with the Balance of the Sugar. One

even

even Teaspoonful added to six Bottles Toddy gives an agreeable Flavour. This Conserve is delightful in all sweet Dishes when you have not fresh Fruit.

(Manuscript Cook Book, c-1801,
of Mrs. *Frances Bland Tucker Coalter.*
Owned by Dr. *St. George Tucker Grinnan, Richmond.*)

To make Lemon Wafers*

TO the Juice of two or three Lemons, with the Rind of one of them grated or cut very fine, put of double refined Sugar, pounded and sifted, enough to make it of a Consistency like thick Cream. Set it over a Lamp in a Silver Bason or Plate, stirring it as it heats, and when hot (but not boiling) dip in your Wafer Paper (cut in what Form and Size you please) one Bit at a Time, and when both Sides are wetted, lay them on Glasses, or glazed Plates at a Distance from the Fire to dry. N. B. It will be two or three Days before they are dry.

(Wines & Cookery. *English* Manuscript Book, c-1740
Owned by Colonial *Williamsburg.*)

To make Melon Mangoes*

TAKE small Melons, not quite ripe, cut a Slip down the Side, and take out the Inside very clean; beat Mustard-seeds, and shred Garlick, and mix with the Seeds, and put in your Mangoes; put the Pieces you cut out into their Places again, and tie them up, and put them into your Pot, and boil some Vinegar (as much as you think will cover them) with whole Pepper, and some Salt, and *Jamaica* Pepper, and pour in scalding hot over your

Mangoes,

Mangoes, and cover them clofe to keep in the
Steam; and fo do every Day for nine Times to-
gether, and when they are cold cover them with
Leather.

(*E. Smith's* Compleat Houfewife, *Williamsburg,* 1742.)

To pickle Nafturtium Buds

GATHER your little Knobs quickly after your
Bloffoms are off; put them in cold Water and
Salt for three Days, fhifting them once a Day; then
make a Pickle (but do not boil it at all) of fome
White-wine, fome White-wine Vinegar, Efchalot,
Horfe-radifh, Pepper, Salt, Cloves and Mace whole
and Nutmeg quartered; then put in your Seeds
and ftop them close; they are to be eaten as
Capers.   (*E. Smith's* Compleat Houfewife, *London,* 1739.)

To pickle Nafturtiums

GATHER the Berries when full grown but
young, put them in a Pot, pour boiling Salt
and Water on, and let them ftand three or four
Days; then drain off the Water, and cover them
with cold Vinegar; add a few Blades of Mace, and
whole Grains of black Pepper.

(Mrs. *Mary Randolph's* Virginia Houfewife, 1831.)

To pickle Onions*

GET white Onions that are not too large, cut
the Stem clofe to the Root with a fharp Knife,
put them in a Pot, pour on boiling Salt and Water
to cover them, ftop the Pot clofely, let them ftand
a Fortnight, changing the Salt and Water every
three

three Days; they muſt be ſtirred daily, or thoſe that float will become ſoft; at the End of this Time, take off the Skin and outer Shell, put them in plain cold Vinegar with a little Turmeric. If the Vinegar be not very pale, the Onion will not be of a good Colour. (Mrs. *Mary Randolph's* Virginia Houſewife, 1831.)

Orange Marmalade*

PEEL one Dozen Oranges. Throw the Peel in a Bucket of Water, take out the Seed, cut up the Pulp fine with a Pair of old Sciſſors. Then take the Peel, cut it in thin Strips and throw it into freſh Water. Pare and ſlice Pippins (or any other nice Apples). Weigh ſix Pounds of them, ſtew with a little Water till perfectly done, and ſet away. Next Day, run this Pulp through a Colander into a Preſerving-kettle. Add ſix Pounds Sugar and boil ſlowly, conſtantly ſcraping from the Bottom.

Take the Orange-peel (which ſhould have been left in ſoak all Night), boil till perfectly ſoft and free from Bitterneſs, changing the Water three Times while boiling. In another Preſerving-kettle, ſimmer this with the Orange Pulp and two Pounds Sugar. When both are nearly done, turn the Oranges into the Apples and cook them very thick. Store in covered Jars.

(Traditional Recipe, *Lynchburg, Virginia.* From a *Williamſburg* Family Cook Book.)

Candied Orange or Lemon Peel*

TAKE large Pieces of Orange-peel or Lemon-peel and cover them well in cold Water. Bring ſlowly to a Boil and boil very gently for a few Minutes

utes until ſlightly tender. Drain, and put them in
cold Water. Scrape out the looſe white Pulp with a
ſilver Spoon and cut the Peel in long narrow Strips.
Return the Peel to cold Water, bring ſlowly to a
Boil, then drain and blanch. Repeat four Times.
Make a boiling Syrup of one fourth Cup Water and
one half Cup Sugar for the Peeling from two Pieces
of Fruit. Add the Peel and boil it ſlowly until all
the Syrup is gone—do not burn. Cool the Peel, roll
it in coarſe Sugar and ſpread it out to dry.

(Recipe from Wines and Cookery, c-1740.
Adapted *Blair* Kitchen, 1938.)

Peaches in Brandy *

GET yellow ſoft Peaches, perfectly free from
Defect and newly gathered, but not too ripe;
place them in a Pot, and cover them with cold,
weak Lye; turn over thoſe that float frequently,
that the Lye may act equally on them; at the End
of an Hour take them out, wipe them carefully
with a ſoft Cloth to get off the Down and Skin, and
lay them in cold Water; make a Syrup as for the
Apricots, and proceed in the ſame Manner, only
ſcald the Peaches more.

(Mrs. *Mary Randolph's* Virginia Houſewife, 1831.)

Brandy Peaches—Mrs. Madiſon *

PEEL your Peaches & put them in a Stone Pot,
ſet the Pot into a Veſſel of Water and let it boil
until a Straw will pierce the Fruit, then make a
Syrup of Brandy & Sugar, one Pound of Sugar to a
Quart

Quart of Brandy, put in your Peaches. They will
be fit for use in a Month. Brown Sugar will do very
well. (Better without peeling.)—*St. G. T.*

(Recipe found in letter written February 6 [1804],
by *St. George Tucker*, of *Williamsburg*, to his
Daughter, Mrs. *Frances Coalter*.)

Brandy Peaches—Mrs. Skipwith *

MAKE a rich Syrup. Have Lye boiling hot, put
in a few Peaches at a Time & let them remain
just long enough to take off the Fur. Wipe or rub
them as they are taken out with a coarse Towel, &
drop them in cold Water—then put the Peaches in
Syrup, & let them boil gently till a Straw will pierce
the Fruit—when sufficiently done put them in a
Jar & whilst the Syrup is hot, mix equal Quantities
of Brandy with it, & pour it hot, over the Peaches.

(Manuscript Cook Book, *Charlottesville*, 1836.
Owned by Mrs. *Virginia Grafty Griffin*.)

Peach Chips *

SLICE them thin, and boil them till clear in a
Syrup made with Half their Weight of Sugar;
lay them on Dishes in the Sun, and turn them till
dry; pack them in Pots with powdered Sugar sifted
over each Layer; should there be Syrup left, continue the Process with other Peaches. They are
very nice when done with pure Honey instead of
Sugar.

(Mrs. *Mary Randolph's* Virginia Housewife, 1831.)

Peach

Peach Mangoes*

TAKE large plum Peaches, ſufficient Quantity to fill the Jar. Peel nicely and take out the Stones. Have ready the Stuffing in Proportion to the Peaches. Mince fine ſome ſoft Peaches, preſerved Orange-peel, preſerved Ginger, Coriander-seed, Celery-ſeed, a ſmall Quantity of Mace, Cinnamon, candied Strawberries, if you have them, and pickled Cherries. Sew the Peaches up after ſtuffing them and fill the Jar. Then to every Pound of Sugar add one-half Pint of Vinegar, allowing the above Quantity to two Pounds of Fruit. Make a Syrup of the Sugar and Vinegar, and pour on the Peaches, boiling hot. Repeat this for three Mornings; the fourth Morning put them all on together, and boil a ſhort Time; add a few Spices, Cinnamon, and Ginger to the Syrup when you make it. They will be ready for Uſe in a few Weeks.

(Recipe from a *Williamſburg* Family Cook Book.)

Peach Marmalade*

TAKE the ripeſt ſoft Peaches (the yellow ones make the prettieſt Marmalade), pare them, and take out the Stones; put them in the Pan with one Pound of dry, light-coloured brown Sugar to two of Peaches: when they are juicy, they do not require Water; with a Silver or Wooden Spoon, chop them with the Sugar; continue to do this, and let them boil gently till they are a tranſparent Pulp, that will be a Jelly when cold. Puffs made of this Marmalade are very delicious.

(Mrs. *Mary Randolph's* Virginia Houſewife, 1831.)

Sweet

Sweet Pickled Peaches*

PUT four Pounds of Sugar into a Preserving-
kettle with one Quart of Vinegar and Spices.
Boil them for five Minutes after the Sugar is dissolved. Pare seven Pounds of Peaches and stick a
Clove into each one. Place a few at a Time in the
boiling Syrup and cook them until they look clear,
but are not softened enough to fall apart. When all
are cooked, continue to boil the Syrup until it is
reduced nearly one half, and pour it over the
Peaches.

(Old Recipe from *Richmond, Virginia.*)

Pear Marmalade*

SLOWLY boil Pears until soft. Chill and put
through Sieve. To each two Pounds of Pears
add one Pound of Sugar. Boil this to a Jelly.

(Traditional *Virginia* Recipe. Prov'd
Market Square Tavern Kitchen, 1937.)

To pickle Peppers

GATHER the large bell Pepper when quite
young, leave the Seeds in and the Stem on,
cut a Slit in one Side between the large Veins, to
let the Water in; pour boiling Salt and Water on,
changing it every Day for three Weeks—you must
keep them closely stopped; if, at the End of this
Time, they be a good green, put them in Pots, and
cover them with cold Vinegar and a little Turmeric; those that are not sufficiently green, must
be continued under the same Process till they are
so. Be careful not to cut through the large Veins,
as the Heat will instantly diffuse itself through the
Pod.

(Mrs. *Mary Randolph's* Virginia Housewife, 1831.)

Pepper

Pepper Vinegar

GET one Dozen Pods of Pepper when ripe, take out the Stems, and cut them in Two; put them in a Kettle with three Pints of Vinegar, boil it away to one Quart, and ſtrain it through a Sieve. A little of this is excellent in Gravy of every Kind, and gives a Flavour greatly ſuperior to black Pepper; it is alſo very fine when added to each of the various Catſups for Fiſh Sauce.

(Mrs. *Mary Randolph's* Virginia Houſewife, 1831.)

Quinces*

SELECT the fineſt and moſt perfect Quinces, lay them on Shelves, but do not let them touch each other; keep them till they look yellow and have a fragrant Smell; put as many in the Preſerving-pan as can lie conveniently, cover them with Water, and ſcald them well: then take out the Cores, and put them in Water; cover the Pan and boil them ſome Time; ſtrain the Water, add to it the Weight of the Quinces in pounded Loaf Sugar, diſſolve and ſkim it, pare the Quinces, put them in the Pan, and ſhould there not be Syrup enough to cover them, add more Water—ſtew them till quite tranſparent. They will be light coloured if kept covered during the Proceſs, and red if the Cover be taken off. Fill the Space the Cores occupied with Quince Jelly, before they are put into the Pots— and cover them with Syrup.

(Mrs. *Mary Randolph's* Virginia Houſewife, 1831.)

Moiſt

*Moist Quinces**

TAKE any Quantity of Quinces; cut them into four Quarters; take well off the Heart and the Skin, and put them in a Pan of Water which you have on the Fire; boil them thus till a Skewer can get into them easily. Then take them off and put them upon a Cloth to drain their Water away; while this is doing, you set your Preserving-pan on the Fire, with the Quantity of Sugar of the first Degree which is necessary, and put your Quinces in it; boil the Whole well, till you see the Sugar becomes very red. Then to know the proper Time of its being done, take a little Syrup with a Spoon in a Saucer, and let it cool; if it turns into a Jelly, you must directly take away your Quinces from the Fire, and put them immediately quite hot into very dry Pots, for should you let them be cold before you pot them, they would jelly, and you could no more make them fill all the Parts of the Pots without some Air along with them. Take Care that your Syrup should always well cover your Fruit, as I have said before.

(Court & Country Confectioner. *London*, 1770. From *Tucker* House, *Williamsburg*.)

*Quince Marmalade**

BOIL the Quinces in Water until soft, let them cool, and rub all the Pulp through a Sieve: put two Pounds of it to one of Sugar, pound a little Cochineal, sift it through fine Muslin, and mix it with the Quince to give a Colour; pick out the

Seeds,

Seeds, tie them in a Muslin Bag, and boil them with the Marmalade; when it is a thick Jelly, take out the Seeds, and put it in Pots.

(Mrs. *Mary Randolph's* Virginia Housewife, 1831.)

Conserve of Red Roses

BEAT one Pound of red Rose-leaves in a Mortar. Add this to two Pounds of refined Sugar. Make a Conserve.

After the same Manner are prepared the Conserves of Orange-peel, Rosemary Flowers, Sea-wormwood, of the Leaves of Wood Sorrel, etc.

(Old Recipe, *Wicomico* Church, *Virginia*.)

Tomato Pickle*

CUT up one-half Peck of Onions, one Peck of Tomatoes and add one and one-half Cups of Salt. Let stand for twelve Hours, boil in Vinegar and Water, drain off and boil for two Hours. Add three Pounds Sugar, two Tablespoons of Celery-seed, two Tablespoons ground Mustard, one Table-spoon black Pepper, one Ounce Mace, one and one-half Ounce Alspice, one Ounce Cloves. Cover with good Vinegar and boil slowly for two Hours.

(Old *Barlow* Family Recipe, *Williamsburg, Virginia*.)

To make Walnut Catsup

GATHER the Walnuts as for pickling, and keep them in Salt Water the same Time; then pound them in a marble Mortar—to every Dozen Walnuts, put a Quart of Vinegar; stir them well every Day for a Week, then put them in a Bag,

and

and press all the Liquor through; to each Quart,
put a Teaspoonful of pounded Cloves, and one of
Mace, with six Cloves of Garlic—boil it fifteen or
twenty Minutes, and bottle it.

(Mrs. *Mary Randolph's* Virginia Housewife, 1831.)

To Pickle English *Walnuts*

THE Walnuts should be gathered when the Nut
is so young that you can run a Pin into it easily;
pour boiling Salt and Water on, and let them be
covered with it nine Days, changing it every third
Day—take them out, and put them on Dishes in
the Air for a few Minutes, taking Care to turn
them over; this will make them black much sooner
—put them in a Pot, strew over some whole Pepper, Cloves, a little Garlic, Mustard-feed, and
Horse-radish scraped and dried; cover them with
strong, cold Vinegar.

(Mrs. *Mary Randolph's* Virginia Housewife, 1831.)

Sweet *Watermelon Pickle**

TRIM the Rinds nicely, being careful to cut off
the hard Coating with the outer green. Weigh
ten Pounds Rind and throw in a Kettle and cover
with soft Water. Let this boil gently for half an
Hour, take it off and lay it on Dishes to drain. Next
Morning put one Quart of Vinegar, three Pounds
brown Sugar, one Ounce Cinnamon, one Ounce
Mace, the White of one Egg well beaten, and put
on Top of the Liquid (to clear it as you would
Jelly), three Teaspoonfuls Turmeric, all together
and

and boil for a few Minutes. Skim off what riſes as Scum with the Egg. Throw in the Rind and boil for twenty Minutes. The Peel of two freſh Lemons will give a nice Flavor, though not at all neceſſary.

(Old Recipe, *Toano, Virginia*.)

Watermelon Rind Pickle *

PARE the Rind of a Melon, cutting away all pink Meat inſide. Then place it in an earthen Crock of ſalt Water, ſalt enough to float an Egg. Let the Rind remain a Week in this, or longer if you wiſh. Make a Brine by filling the Crock with Water and placing a Lump of Alum or two Teaſpoons of powdered Alum. Let the Rind remain in this two Days, then ſoak the Rind in cold Water for a Day and Night, then cook it in cold Water until clear, ſqueeze the Water out and let it ſtand for a Night, and then make a Syrup of Vinegar and Sugar and mixed Spices, cooking the Rind awhile in it.   (Old Recipe, *Norfolk, Virginia*.)

Williamſburg *Watermelon Pickle* *

PARE the Rind of a Watermelon, cutting away the pink Part. Cut them in ſmall Pieces with a fluted Cutter and let ſtand over Night in equal Parts of Vinegar and Water to cover. Put it on to boil in this Vinegar, cook until tender and drain well. Make a Syrup of five Pounds of Sugar, one Quart of Vinegar and put in a Spice Bag containing ſeveral Blades of Mace, two Ounces of Cloves, and
one

one Ounce of whole Cinnamon. Boil for ten Minutes. Put Rind in and cook a few Minutes, then remove it to hot Jars. Boil the Syrup down until it is thick and pour it over the Rind and ſeal hot.

(Traditional *Virginia* Recipe. Adapted *Market Square Tavern* Kitchen, 1937)

To make Vinegar for Pickles*

TO every Peck of very ripe Gooſeberries of any Sort, put two Gallons of Water, cruſh the Fruit well with your Hands, and mix it well with the Water; let it work three Weeks, ſtirring it four or five Times a Day, then ſtrain the Liquor, put a Pound of brown Sugar, a Pound of Treacle, and a Spoonful of freſh Barm; let it work three or four Days, turn it in iron-hooped Barrels, let it ſtand a Year or more, it is the beſt Vinegar for Uſe.

(Court & Country Confectioner *London*, 1770. From *Tucker* Houſe, *Williamſburg*.)

Favorite

❀❀❀❀❀❀❀❀❀❀❀❀❀❀❀❀❀❀❀❀❀❀❀❀❀❀

Favorite *Williamsburg* Garden Herbs

Common Name	Botanical Name	Use
Agrimony	*Agrimonia Eupatoria*	Flavoring
		Medicine
Angelica	*Archangelica officinalis*	Culinary
		Medicine
Anise	*Pimpinella Anisum*	Flavoring
		(Seeds)
		Medicine
		(Seeds)
		Culinary
		(Seeds)
		Seasoning
		Garnishing
Apple Mint	*Mentha rotundifolia*	Flavoring
Balm of Gilead	*Cedronella triphylla*	Medicine
		Scent
Basil	*Ocimum basilicum*	Seasoning
		Scent
Bay	*Laurus nobilis*	Seasoning
Beebalm	*Monarda didyma*	Medicine
		Scent
Bergamot	*Monarda fistulosa*	Medicine
Betony	*Stachys Betonica*	Medicine
Bloodroot	*Sanguinaria canadensis*	Medicine
Borage	*Borago officinalis*	Cordials
		Salads
Calamint	*Calamintha Acinos*	Scent
		Medicine
Caraway	*Carum carvi*	Flavoring
		(Seeds)
Catnip	*Nepeta cataria*	Medicine

Celery

Rosemary | Sage | Mint | Thyme | Marjoram | Chives

*The Blair Kitchen and Herb Garden
at Williamsburg.*

PLATE III.   E. JONES.

Currant Squares*

HEAT until warm, but not hot, one Cupful of Cream on a very low Fire, ſtir in one half Cupful of melted Butter, add one Cup of Sugar, then three well beaten Eggs. Add one ſmall Yeaſt Cake diſſolved in a little Milk-warm Water. Sift in four Cups of Flour, one Tableſpoon of powdered Mace, one Teaſpoon of Salt. Beat well for at leaſt fifteen Minutes. Pour into ſhallow buttered Baking-pans and let riſe until double in Bulk. Bake in a quick Oven, ſprinkle with powdered Sugar and Cinnamon juſt before removing from Oven. Cool a little and cut into Squares.

(Old *Henrico* County Recipe.
Prov'd *Market Square Tavern* Kitchen, 1937.)

Cookies of 1812*

CREAM one Cup of Butter with two Cups of fine Sugar. Beat the Yolks of four Eggs very light, then combine with the well-beaten Whites and add to creamed Mixture. Sift in two Cups of Flour, one Teaſpoon of Cream of Tartar, one half Teaſpoon of Nutmeg. Add two Tableſpoons of ſweet Milk, one half Teaſpoon of Soda in a little warm Water, one Teaſpoon of Vanilla. Mix well, adding more Flour if neceſſary to make Dough ſtiff enough to roll out thin. Bake in moderate Oven, a delicate brown. This Dough may be made into ſmall Rolls, chilled Overnight and ſliced into ſmall Cakes for baking.

(Traditional *Virginia* Recipe.
Adapted *Market Square Tavern* Kitchen, 1937.)

Dough

COMMON NAME	BOTANICAL	USE
Celery	*Apium graveolens*	Salads
		Seaſoning
Chamomile	*Anthemis nobilis*	Medicine
		Scent
Chervil	*Anthriſcus Cerefolium*	Seaſoning
		Salads
Chicory	*Cichorium intybus*	Salads
		Flavoring
Chives	*Allium ſchœnopraſum*	Seaſoning
Clary	*Salvia Sclarea*	Medicine
		(Salves)
		Seaſoning
Common Balm	*Meliſſa officinalis*	Flavoring
Coriander	*Coriandrum ſativum*	Confectionery
		Cordials
		(Seeds)
		Seaſoning
		(Seeds)
		Flavoring
		(Seeds)
Fennel	*Foeniculum vulgare*	Seaſoning
		Flavoring
		Scent
Feverfew	*Chryſanthemum parthenium*	Medicine
Garden	*Valeriana officinalis*	Scent
Heliotrope		Medicine
Garlic	*Allium ſativum*	Seaſoning
Hoarhound	*Marrubium vulgare*	Culinary
		Medicine
Horſe Mint	*Mentha longifolia*	Scent
		Medicine
Horſe radiſh	*Radicula Armoracia*	Reliſh
		Seaſoning
		Medicine
Hyſſop	*Hyſſopus officinalis*	Seaſoning
		Medicine
Lavendar	*Lavandula vera*	Reliſh
		Scent
		Lemon

COMMON NAME	BOTANICAL NAME	USE
Lemon (Bergamot) Mint	*Mentha citrata*	Relish Flavoring Scent
Monkshood	*Aconitum Napellus*	Medicine
Mandrake	*Podophyllum peltatum*	Medicine
Mustard	*Brassica nigra*	Seeds Condiment Medicine
Mustard	*Brassica japonica*	Salads
Nasturtium	*Tropaeolum majus*	Garnishes Relish (Seeds) Salads
Parsley	*Petroselinum hortense*	Seasoning Garnish Medicine
Pennyroyal	*Mentha Pulegium*	Medicine Seasoning
Peppermint	*Mentha piperita*	Medicine Flavoring Scent
Peppers	*Capsicum*	Condiment Medicine Seasoning
Periwinkle	*Vinca minor*	Medicine
Rhubarb	*Rheum Rhaponticum*	Medicine (Root) Food (Stalks)
Rosemary	*Rosmarinus officinalis*	Scent Seasoning
Rue	*Ruta graveolens*	Medicine Seasoning Flavoring Scent
Saffron	A form of *Crocus sativus*	Seasoning Medicine Scent
Sage	*Salvia officinalis*	Medicine Seasoning Scent

Savory,

COMMON NAME	BOTANICAL NAME	USE
Savory, Summer	*Satureja hortensis*	Seasoning
Self Heal	*Prunella vulgaris*	Medicine
Shallot	*Allium ascalonicum*	Seasoning
Sorrel	*Rumex Acetosa*	Culinary
		Medicine
		Salads
		Drinks
Spearmint	*Mentha spicata*	Medicine
		Flavoring
Sweet Marjoram	*Origanum Majorana*	Seasoning
		Scent
Tansy	*Tanacetum vulgare*	Flavoring
		Medicine
Tarragon	*Artemisia Dracunculus*	Seasoning
Thyme	*Thymus citriodorus*	Seasoning
Thyme	*Thymus Serpyllum*	Seasoning
Thyme	*Thymus vulgaris*	Seasoning
		Scent
Turmeric	*Curcuma longa*	Condiment
		Flavoring
		Medicine
		Dyes
Violet	*Viola odorata*	Scent
		Confectionery
Winter Savory	*Satureja montana*	Seasoning
		Scent

Confectionery

CONFECTIONERY

IT ſeems to have been the Fate of moſt Cookery Books to have found their Way to the Kitchen from the Library—and there to have had a Period of ſuch ſtrenuous Uſe that they ended their Days with Batter-beſpattered Pages and broken Backs. The Life of a Book might be prolonged by binding the Pages of an earlier Cookery Book with a newer one, perhaps ſewing in extra Pages for the Houſe-wife to uſe for Writing or Pinning in her own favor-ite Recipes.

However, in the Library of *St. George Tucker*, Eſquire, of *Williamſburg*, there is one neat leather-bound Volume, called the "Confectioner" which ſeems worn and uſed, but entirely unſtained by even a ſingle Drip of Syrup. One Explanation might be that in his well-managed Houſehold the Recipes went out to the Kitchen on ſmall Slips of Paper and the Cookery Book was replaced on the Library Shelf. Another Solution to this Puzzle, in *St. George Tucker's* own Hand, is a ſhort Verſe which he penned in *May*, 1781, to his Friend, Mr. *Lomax* who had failed to avail himſelf of an Invita-tion to viſit him at *Matoax*:

> Though you expected naught to eat,
> We could have given you some Meat.
> Veal that had ſucked two well-fed Cows.
> Lamb that was fattened in a Houſe.

Bacon

Bacon well-fed on *Indian* Corn.
And Chicken crammed both Night & Morn.
Sturgeon likewiſe adorned the Board.
Of Pears we had a monſtrous Hoard.
Half ate, and half untouched remained
For scanty Meſſes we diſdained.
Next Strawberries in View appear.
And Apple Tarts bring up the Rear.
Theſe Dainties too were one half left,
Madeira filled each Chink & Cleft.
We ate, we drank, we went to Bed,
And ſlept as though we all were Dead.

Where, in ſuch a Bill of Fare could one find Room for even a ſingle *Savoy* Biſcuit, a Coffee-cream Bomboon, a Petticoat Tail, a Wig, or a Quire of Paper Pancakes?

All Sorts of Confectionery

To fricaſy Almonds ✻

TAKE a Pound of *Jordan* Almonds, do not blanch them, or but one Half of them; beat the White of an Egg very well, and pour it on your Almonds, and wet them all over; then take half a Pound of double-refin'd Sugar, and boil it to Sugar again; and put your Almonds in, and ſtir them till as much Sugar hangs on them as will; then ſet them on Plates, and put them into the Oven to dry after Bread is drawn, and let them ſtay in all Night. They will keep the Year round if you keep them dry, and are a pretty Sweetmeat.

(*E. Smith's* Compleat Houſewife, *Williamſburg,* 1742. Prov'd *Market Square Tavern* Kitchen, 1937.)

A

*A Method to make All Sorts of Light, Seed,
And Other Cakes**

IT may not be improper to obferve, that before
you proceed to make any Sort of Cakes, that
Care fhould firft be taken to have all your Ingredients ready before you begin, then beat your Eggs
well, and not leave them till you have finifhed the
Cakes, for by fuch Neglect, they would go back,
and your Cakes would not be light; if your Cakes
are to have Butter in, take Care you beat it to a
fine Cream before you put in your Sugar, for if you
beat it twice the Time after it will not anfwer fo
well.

(Court & Country Confectioner. London, 1770.
From <i>Tucker</i> Houfe, <i>Williamfburg.</i>)

Williamfburg *Almond Cakes**

CREAM together one Cupful of Sugar and one
half Pound of Butter, add three well-beaten
Eggs, one Teafpoonful of Mace or of Cinnamon
and one Wine-glafs of Brandy. Sift in enough Flour
to make a Dough which will roll out very thin. Cut
your Cakes, place them on unbuttered Tins,
fprinkle with chopped Almonds and bake in moderate Oven.

(Old Recipe from Richmond, Virginia.
Adapted <i>Market Square Tavern</i> Kitchen, 1937.)

To make little hollow Bifkets

BEAT fix Eggs very well with a Spoonful of
Rofe-water, then put in a Pound and two
Ounces of Loaf-fugar beaten and fifted; ftir it to-
gether

gether till 'tis well mixed in the Eggs; then put in as much Flour as will make it thick enough to lay out in Drops upon Sheets of white Paper; ſtir it well together till you are ready to drop it on your Paper; then beat a little very fine Sugar and put into a Lawn Sieve, and ſift ſome on them juſt as they are going into the Oven; to bake them, the Oven muſt not be too hot, and as ſoon as they are baked, whilſt they are hot, pull off the Papers from them, and put them in a Sieve, and ſet them in an Oven to dry; keep them in Boxes with Papers between.

(*E. Smith's* Compleat Houſewife, *Williamſburg,* 1742.)

Empire Biſcuits *

SIFT well ſix heaping Tableſpoons of Flour, four Tableſpoons of Sugar, one Teaſpoon of Cinnamon. Cut into this one fourth of a Pound of Butter. Knead together lightly, roll out thin. Prick all over with a Fork and cut with ſmall round Cutters. Bake in moderate Oven on greaſed Papers about twenty Minutes. Cool. Put Currant Jelly between two Biſcuits, ſpread the Top with a flavored white Icing then decorate with candied Angelica or Cherries.

(Old *Richmond* Recipe. Prov'd
Market Square Tavern Kitchen, 1937.)

Williamſburg *Naples Biſcuits* *

BEAT the Whites of three Eggs very light adding gradually one third of a Cup of powdered Sugar, beating conſtantly. Fold in three well-beaten Egg Yolks. Sift in and mix lightly, one third Cup

Cup of Flour ſifted with a Pinch of Salt. Add one half Teaſpoon of Vanilla. Shape carefully into Fingers on unbuttered Paper; ſprinkle with finely powdered Sugar and bake ten Minutes in a moderate Oven.

(Mrs. *Randolph's* Recipe, 1831.
Adapted *Market Square Tavern* Kitchen, 1937.)

Palais Royal *Biſcuits*

TAKE eight Eggs, break them and put the Yolks in one Pan, and the Whites in another; then weigh half a Pound of Sugar, which you put in the Pan where the Yolks are, beat well your Yolks and the Sugar together with a Spoon, till it makes a white Paſte; weigh ſix Ounces of Flour which you put on a white Sheet of Paper; when your Yolks of Eggs are well-beaten with the Sugar, and your Flour weighed, and put on a Sheet of Paper, take a ſmall Whiſk, beat well your Whites of Eggs till they come up like a Syllabub, and they are so hard that your Whiſk can ſtand upright in them; then take your Yolks which are like a Paſte, and put them with the Whites, and mix them in, turning them gently with your Whiſk. When both the Yolks and Whites are well mixed, take a Sieve, put your Flour in it, and ſift it gently over your Mixture, and continue ſtirring till you ſee all is well mixed, and there is no Lump of Flour in your Paſte; when your Compoſition is finiſhed, have little Paper Moulds made long and ſquare, fill them with that Paſte, and ſift on the Top of each of them a little of fine pounded Loaf Sugar, which is called the Icing of them, then put them in the Oven.

(Court & Country Confectioner. *London*, 1770.
From *Tucker* Houſe, *Williamſburg*.)

Tavern

Tavern Biſcuits ✻

TO two Cups of Flour, add one Cup of Sugar, one Cup of Butter, ſome Mace and Nutmeg powdered, and a Glaſs of Brandy or Wine; wet it with Milk, and when well kneaded, roll it thin, cut it in Shapes, and bake it quickly.

(Mrs. *Mary Randolph's* Recipe, 1831.
Adapted *Market Square Tavern* Kitchen, 1937.)

Coffee-Cream Bomboons

TAKE about a Pint of Coffee made with Water, put in it a Pound of loaf Sugar, ſet it on the Fire, and boil it to the ninth Degree, then you add a full Pint of double Cream, and let it boil again, keeping continually ſtirring till it comes to Caramel Height; to know when it is come to that Point, you muſt have a Baſon of Water by you, dip your Finger in it, and put it quickly in your Sugar, then in the Water again to remove the Sugar, which will have ſtuck to it; take a Bit of it in your Teeth, if it is hard in its Crackling take it off, it is to the Height required; pour it upon a buttered Tin Plate, and roll it thin with a buttered Rolling-pin. When it is warm you may cut it in little Squares, or Lozenges, or any other ſhapen Paſtiles, and draw a few Strokes over them with a Knife.

(Court & Country Confectioner, *London*, 1770.
From *Tucker* Houſe, *Williamſburg.*)

Currant Squares*

HEAT until warm, but not hot, one Cupful of Cream on a very low Fire, ſtir in one half Cupful of melted Butter, add one Cup of Sugar, then three well beaten Eggs. Add one ſmall Yeaſt Cake diſſolved in a little Milk-warm Water. Sift in four Cups of Flour, one Tableſpoon of powdered Mace, one Teaſpoon of Salt. Beat well for at leaſt fifteen Minutes. Pour into ſhallow buttered Baking-pans and let riſe until double in Bulk. Bake in a quick Oven, ſprinkle with powdered Sugar and Cinnamon juſt before removing from Oven. Cool a little and cut into Squares.

(Old *Henrico* County Recipe.
Prov'd *Market Square Tavern* Kitchen, 1937.)

Cookies of 1812*

CREAM one Cup of Butter with two Cups of fine Sugar. Beat the Yolks of four Eggs very light, then combine with the well-beaten Whites and add to creamed Mixture. Sift in two Cups of Flour, one Teaſpoon of Cream of Tartar, one half Teaſpoon of Nutmeg. Add two Tableſpoons of ſweet Milk, one half Teaſpoon of Soda in a little warm Water, one Teaſpoon of Vanilla. Mix well, adding more Flour if neceſſary to make Dough ſtiff enough to roll out thin. Bake in moderate Oven, a delicate brown. This Dough may be made into ſmall Rolls, chilled Overnight and ſliced into ſmall Cakes for baking.

(Traditional *Virginia* Recipe.
Adapted *Market Square Tavern* Kitchen, 1937.)

Dough

Dough Nuts—*A* Yankee *Cake*❊

DRY half a Pound of good brown Sugar, pound it, and mix it with two Pounds of Flour, and ſift it; add two Spoonfuls of Yeaſt, and as much new Milk as will make it like Bread; when well riſen, knead in half a Pound of Butter, make it in Cakes the Size of a half Dollar, and fry them a light brown in boiling Lard.

(Mrs. *Mary Randolph's* Virginia Houſewife, 1831.)

Another Way❊

SIFT together five Cups of Flour, one Teaſpoon of Salt, one and three fourth Teaſpoons of Soda, the ſame of Cream of Tartar, one half Teaſpoon of Nutmeg and one fourth Teaſpoon of Cinnamon. Cut in one Tableſpoon of Butter; beat one Egg well with one Cup of Sugar, add one Cup of ſour Milk. Knead ſlightly, roll out one fourth Inch thick, cut with a Doughnut-cutter. Fry in deep Fat, drain on brown Paper.

(*Market Square Tavern* Kitchen, 1937.)

To make Dutch *Gingerbread*❊

TAKE four Pounds of Flour, and mix with it two Ounces and half of beaten Ginger, then rub in a quarter of a Pound of Butter, and add to it two Ounces of Carraway-ſeeds, two Ounces of Orange-peel dry'd and rubb'd to Powder, a few Coriander-ſeeds, bruiſed, two Eggs, then mix all up in a ſtiff Paſte with two Pounds and a quarter of Treacle; beat it very well with a Rolling-pin, and make it up into thirty Cakes; put in a candied Citron;

Citron; prick them with a Fork; butter Papers
three double, one white, and two brown; waſh
them over with the White of an Egg; put 'em into
an Oven not too hot for three quarters of an Hour.

(*E. Smith's* Compleat Houſewife, *London*, 1739.)

Soft Ginger Cakes *

CREAM together one Cup Sugar, one half Cup
of Lard. Add one Cup black Molaſſes. Diſſolve
one Teaſpoon Soda in one Cup ſour Milk. Add
enough Flour to make Batter ſtiff. Sift with Flour,
one Teaſpoon ground Ginger, one Teaſpoon Cinnamon. Drop from Spoon. Bake in moderate Oven
on greaſed Tins.

(Old *Richmond* Recipe. Prov'd
Market Square Tavern Kitchen, 1937.)

Gingerbread Cakes

TAKE three Pounds of Flour, a Pound of Sugar,
the ſame Quantity of Butter rolled in very
fine, two Ounces of Ginger beat fine, and a large
Nutmeg grated. Then take a Pound of Treacle, a
quarter of a Pint of Cream, and make them warm
together. Make up the Bread ſtiff, roll it out, and
make it up into thin Cakes. Cut them out with a
Teacup or ſmall Glaſs or roll them round like Nuts,
and bake them in a ſlack Oven on tin Plates.

(*John Farley's* London Art of Cookery, 1787.
From *Brookbury, Cheſterfield* County.)

Mrs. J. Randolph Page's *Ginger Cakes*

TWO Quarts of Flour, one Teacupful of Sugar,
one Pint of Molaſſes, half a Pound of Lard,
four Tableſpoonfuls of ground Ginger, one Tableſpoonful

ſpoonful of ground Cloves, and one Teaſpoonful of Salt. Let any one try this Recipe who wants to be convinced that the beſt Things are not always the moſt expenſive. The Dough muſt be juſt as ſtiff as it can be to handle well, and rolled out to Wafer-like Thickneſs. Stick as you do Biſcuits, and bake quickly without burning. Cut out alſo with a plain round Biſcuit Cutter.

(Mrs. *Mary Stuart Smith's* Virginia Cookery Book, 1885.)

Williamſburg *Ginger Cakes*⁎

CREAM one half Cup of Lard with two Cups of brown Sugar, ſtir in two Cups of light Mo-laſſes. Sift into this four Cups of Flour, two Table-ſpoons of Ginger, one half Teaſpoon of Salt, one Teaſpoon of Soda. Add enough Flour to make a ſtiff Dough which can be rolled very thin. Cut with ſmall round or fancy Cutters and bake in buttered Tins in a quick Oven. They will burn eaſily.

(Adapted and prov'd *Market Square Tavern* Kitchen, 1937.)

Jumbles⁎

ONE Pound of Flour, one of Sugar, half Pound of Butter, three Eggs, a little Cinnamon. Mix firſt the Flour and Sugar and let them dry a little. Beat the Eggs, then mix the Butter and Eggs to-gether—then mix them all and knead them well, roll the Dough ſmall and long. Form them like a Hoop. Dip them in pounded Sugar, bake them on Paper.

(Manuſcript Cook Book, prior 1839.
Morton Family of *Charlotte* County *Virginia*.)

Williamſburg

Williamſburg *Jumbals* ⁕

MIX one third of a Cup of Butter and the ſame of fine Sugar, together. Add one well beaten Egg. Sift in three fourths of a Cup of Flour with one fourth Teaſpoonful of Salt, and one Teaſpoonful of powdered Mace. Drop by Spoonfuls far apart on a buttered Tin, ſpread thin, and bake in moderate Oven about ten Minutes.

(Mrs. *E. Smith's* Recipe, 1742.
Adapted *Market Square Tavern* Kitchen, 1937.)

Macaroon Cakes

ONE Pound of blanched Almonds, one of double refined Sugar—the Whites of four Eggs— beaten to Froth, a Spoonful Brandy or Roſe-water —mix the Ingredients well together, ſift Sugar over them and bake them.

(Manuſcript Cook Book, prior 1839.
Morton Family of *Charlotte* County, *Virginia*.)

To Candy Orange Chips

PARE your Oranges and ſoak the Peelings in Water two Days, and ſhift the Water twice; but if you love them bitter ſoak them not: Tie your Peels up in a Cloth, and when your Water boils, put them in, and let them boil till they are tender; then take what double refin'd Sugar will do, and break it ſmall and wet it with a little Water, and let it boil till' tis near Candy-high, then cut your Peels of what Length you pleaſe, and put 'em into the Syrup; ſet 'em on the Fire and let 'em heat well thro', then let them ſtand a while, heat them
twice

twice a Day, but not boil: Let them be ſo done till they begin to candy, then take them out and put them on Plates to dry, and when they are dry, keep them near the Fire.

(Mrs. *E. Smith's* Compleat Houſewife, *Williamſburg*, 1742.)

King's Arms *Pecan Confections*＊

BEAT one Egg White to a ſtiff Froth, add gradu- ally one Cupful of brown Sugar, one Pinch of Salt, one level Tableſpoonful of Flour. Stir in one Cupful of chopped Pecans, drop on greaſed Tins by ſmall Spoonfuls far apart. Bake in very ſlow Oven for fifteen Minutes. Remove from Tin when partly cooled. Makes two Dozen.

(Old Recipe. Adapted *Travis* Houſe, *Williamſburg*.)

Petticoat Tails＊

SIFT together ſeveral Times five Cups of Flour and one Cup of fine powdered Sugar. Cut and knead into this two Cups of Butter. Shape the Dough in Rolls and chill overnight. Slice thin and bake in moderate Oven.

(Old Recipe, *Sparta, Virginia*. Prov'd *Market Square Tavern* Kitchen, 1937.)

Williamſburg *Ratafia Cakes*＊

TAKE one half Pound of Almond Paſte, and three eighths of a Pound of Sugar together on a marble Slab and work them together ſlowly with a broad flat Knife until they are ſmooth. Add ſlowly

ſlowly the Whites of three Eggs well beaten. Drop
from a Spoon on buttered Paper and bake in a ſlow
Oven about fifteen Minutes.

(Court & Country Confectioner *London*, 1770.
Adapted *Market Square Tavern* Kitchen, 1937.)

Scotch *Shortbread*⁂

BEAT one Pound Butter to a Cream. Mix together and gradually ſift in two Pounds Flour,
one fourth Pound Cornſtarch. Then add one fourth
Pound granulated Sugar, one Ounce Almonds,
blanched and cut in ſmall Pieces. Work the Paſte
quite ſmooth. Cut ſmall Pieces off and roll into
three Inch Squares about one Inch thick. Pinch up
the Edges and prick well with a Fork. Ornament
with a Strip of Orange-peel. Bake in moderate
Oven twenty five or thirty Minutes.

(Old *Richmond* Recipe. Prov'd
Market Square Tavern Kitchen, 1937.)

Shrewſbury *Cakes*

BEAT half a Pound of Butter to a fine Cream,
and put in the ſame Weight of Flour, one Egg,
ſix Ounces of beaten and ſifted Loaf-ſugar, and
half an Ounce of Carraway-ſeeds. Mix them into a
Paſte, roll them thin, and cut them round with a
ſmall Glaſs or little Tins; prick them, lay them on
Sheets of Tin, and bake them in a ſlow Oven.

(*John Farley's* London Art of Cookery, 1787.
From *Brookbury, Cheſterfield* Co., *Virginia*.)

Shrewſbury

Shrewſbury *Cakes*

TAKE to one Pound of Sugar three Pounds of the fineſt Flour, a Nutmeg grated, ſome beaten Cinnamon, the Sugar and Spice muſt be ſifted into the Flour, and wet it with three Eggs, and as much melted Butter as will make it of a good Thickneſs to roll it to a Paſte. Cut it into what Shape you pleaſe, perfume them and prick them before they go into the Oven.

(Manuſcript Cook Book, c-1825, of Miſs *Margaret Prentis* of *Williamſburg*. Owned by *Robert H. Webb*, Eſq., *Charlotteſville*.)

Shrewſbury *Cakes* *

MIX a Pound of Sugar with two Pounds of Flour and a large Spoonful of pounded Coriander-ſeeds; ſift them, add three quarters of a Pound of melted Butter, ſix Eggs, and a Gill of Brandy; knead it well, roll it thin, cut it in Shapes, and bake without diſcolouring it.

(Mrs. *Mary Randolph's* Virginia Houſewife, 1831.)

All Sorts of Seed Cakes *

MIX one Cup of Sugar in three fourths of a Cup of well-creamed Butter, add three ſlightly beaten Eggs, one fourth of a Cup of Brandy, and two Cups of Flour. Roll out thin, ſprinkle with Seeds, roll again, cut in Shapes and bake ſlowly a light golden Color. Pounded Cardamon-ſeeds, Coriander-ſeeds, Bene-ſeeds or Carraway-ſeeds were the old Favorites.

(The four Recipes preceding adapted *Market Square Tavern* Kitchen, 1937.)

Of

Of CAKES

FROM Chriſtenings to Funerals, Cakes were moſt intimately aſſociated with family and ſocial Life. There was a ſpecial Cake for each happy or ſad Occaſion—Pancakes for St. *Valentine's* Day, Bride's Cakes for Weddings, large Fruit Cakes for *Chriſtmas* Holidays, elaborately decorated Twelfthnight Cakes, and laſt of all the Funeral Cake (uſually provided by the Eſtate of the Deceaſed).

Even the *Engliſh* Language itſelf defers to the Cake, and the Word has become a Symbol for the prized Things in Life: One cannot have one's Cake and eat it. To have *Cakes and Ale* is to enjoy Mirth and good Living—a winning Perſon *takes the Cake*, and when one has failed his *Cake's all Dough.*

In the Memoirs of *William Wirt* there is this elegant Deſcription of the Bride's Cake at the beautiful Miſs *P*———'s Wedding in *Williamſburg* in April, 1806:

> . . . It was paſt eleven when the Sanctum Sanctorum of the Supper-room was thrown open —although I don't know but that the Deſignation of the Sanctum would be better applied to another Apartment in the Houſe—and it was near twelve when it came to my Turn to ſee the Show. And a very ſuperb one it was, I aſſure you. The Tree in the centre Cake was more ſimply elegant than anything of the Kind I remember to have ſeen.

seen. It was near four Feet high: the Cake itself, the Pedestal, had a rich—very rich—Fringe of white Paper surrounding it: the Leaves, Baskets, Garlands, &c., &c., were all very naturally done in white Paper, not touched with the Pencil, and the Baskets were rarely ornamented with silver Spangles. At the Ends of the Tables were two lofty Pyramids of Jellies, Syllabubs, Ice-creams, &c.—the which Pyramids were connected with the Tree in the centre Cake by pure white Paper Chains, very prettily cut, hanging in light and delicate Festoons, and ornamented with Paper Bow-knots. Between the centre Cake and each Pyramid was another large Cake made for Use: then there was a Profusion of Meats, Cheese-cakes, Fruits, &c., &c.

But there were two unnatural Things at Table; —a small silver Globe on each Side of the Tree, which might have passed—if Charlotte, to enhance their Value, had not told us that they were a Fruit—whose Name I don't recollect—between the Size of a Shaddock and an Orange, covered with silver Leaf;—which was rather too outlandish for my Palate. All the Grandees of the Place were there.

All Sorts of Cakes

Beefsteak Cake *

CREAM two Cups of Sugar and one half Cup of Butter. Add three well-beaten Eggs. Sift in three and one fourth Cups of Flour, two Teaspoons baking Powder, one scant Teaspoon of Salt, alternately with one Cup of sweet Milk. Add one Teaspoon of Vanilla. Grease and flour three Layer-cake Tins

Tins and fill two of them. To the remaining Third of the Batter add three Tableſpoons Molaſes, one Tableſpoon of Allſpice and one Teaſpoon each of Cloves and Cinnamon and one Cup of chopped Raiſins. Bake in a moderate Oven about thirty Minutes. Ice with brown Sugar Icing.

(Recipe from *Cole* Family, *Williamſburg.*
Adapted *Market Square Tavern* Kitchen, 1937.)

Brown Sugar Icing*

BRING to Boil one Cup brown Sugar, one Cup white Sugar, one Cup rich Milk, one Tableſpoon Corn Syrup, one Tableſpoon Butter, and Pinch of Salt. Continue cooking until Syrup forms ſoft Ball in Water. Cool and beat until creamy. Add one Teaſpoon Vanilla, one fourth Teaſpoon baking Powder—beat until ready to ſpread on Cake.

(*Market Square Tavern* Kitchen, 1937.)

Black Walnut Cake*

CREAM one Pound of Butter with one Pound of Sugar, then add one Egg Yolk. Blend thoroughly, then add another, and ſo on until all nine Yolks are thoroughly mixed and creamed. Sift one Pound of Flour in gradually, and finally add ſtiffly beaten Egg Whites. Dredge one Pound of black Walnut-meats in ſmall amount Flour and add to Batter. Bake in very ſlow Oven for two and one half to three Hours, in a deep Mould.

(Recipe from *Diſputanta, Virginia,* c-1729.)

To

To make a Bride Cake Mrs. Raffald's *Way*

TAKE four Pounds of fine Flour well dried, four Pounds of freſh Butter, two Pounds of loaf Sugar, pound and ſift fine a quarter of an Ounce of Mace, the ſame of Nutmegs, to every Pound of Flour put eight Eggs, waſh four Pounds of Currants, pick them well and dry them before the Fire, blanch a Pound of ſweet Almonds (and cut them lengthway very thin) a Pound of Citron, one Pound of candied Orange, the ſame of candied Lemon, half a Pint of Brandy; firſt work the Butter with your Hand to a Cream, then beat in your Sugar a quarter of an Hour, beat the Whites of your Eggs to a very ſtrong Froth, mix them with your Sugar and Butter, beat your Yolks half an Hour at leaſt, and mix them with your Cake, then put in your Flour, Mace, and Nutmeg, keep beating it well till your Oven is ready, put in your Brandy, and beat your Currants and Almonds lightly in, tie three Sheets of Paper round the Bottom of your Hoop to keep it from running out, rub it well with Butter, put in your Cake, and lay your Sweet-meats in three Lays, with Cake betwixt every Lay, after it is riſen and coloured, cover it with Paper before your Oven is ſtopped up; it will take three Hours baking.

(Court & Country Confectioner. *London*, 1770.
From *Tucker* Houſe, *Williamſburg*.)

To make Almond Iceing for the Bride Cake

BEAT the Whites of three Eggs to a ſtrong Froth, beat a Pound of *Jordan* Almonds very fine with Roſe-water, mix your Almonds with the Eggs lightly

lightly together, a Pound of common Loaf-ſugar
beat fine, and put in by Degrees, when your Cake
is enough, take it out and lay your Icing on, and
put it in to brown.

(Court & Country Confectioner. *London*, 1770.
From *Tucker* Houſe, *Williamſburg.*)

Buttermilk Cake*

BLEND well together three Cups of Sugar and
one Cup of Butter. Beat in four Eggs, adding
one at a Time and beating the Mixture well each
Time. Sift in three Cups of Flour with one Teaspoon
of baking Powder alternately with one Cup of
Buttermilk. The Buttermilk ſhould have one Teaſpoon of Soda diſſolved in it. Add one Teaspoon
Vanilla and bake in three well-greaſed Tins in a
moderate Oven about forty Minutes. An Orange
Icing is good with this Cake.

(Mrs. *Cole's* Recipe, c-1837. Prov'd
Market Square Tavern Kitchen, 1937.)

Orange Icing*

TO three Cups of Confectioner's Sugar add one
third of a Cup of Butter and mix well together.
Thin with Orange-juice which has ſome finely
grated freſh Orange-peel in it until it is right to
ſpread. A Decoration of candied Orange-peel about
the Edge is nice. (*Market Square Tavern* Kitchen, 1937.)

Glazed Cocoanut Cake*

SIFT together ſeveral Times, one and three
fourths Cups of Flour, one Cup of Sugar, one
fourth Teaspoon of Salt, two and one half Teaſpoons

ſpoons of Baking-powder. Melt one third of a Cup
of Butter and mix it with two thirds of a Cup of
warm (not hot) Milk. Add to Flour Mixture then
beat in two Eggs. Beat well, add one Teaſpoonful
of Vanilla. Pour into a large Layer-cake Tin. Bake
for ten Minutes in a moderately quick Oven and
reduce the Heat for the next fifteen Minutes. Turn
your Cake out onto a Rack, with the Top up.
Glaze: Six Tableſpoonfuls of melted Butter mixed
with ſix Tableſpoonfuls of brown Sugar, three
Tableſpoons of Cream, and one half Cupful of
grated Cocoanut. Spread on hot Cake, put under
Broiler to brown. Do not burn. Serve warm.

(*Richmond* Recipe, c-1840.
Prov'd *Blair* Kitchen, 1938.)

A Faſhion Cake

MIX a Handful of Flour with a Pint of good
Cream, half a Pound of Beef-ſuet, melted
and ſifted, a quarter of a Pound of Sugar-powder,
half a Pound of Raiſins ſtoned and chopped, dried
Flowers or Orange, a Glaſs of Brandy, a little Coriander and Salt; bake it as all other Cakes, about
an Hour, and glaze or garniſh it.

(Court & Country Confectioner. *London*, 1770.
From *Tucker* Houſe, *Williamſburg*.)

Mrs. Governor Floyd's Good but Cheap Cake

THREE Cups of Sugar, three Eggs, three Cups
of ſifted Flour, one Cup of ſour Cream, one
Teaſpoonful of Soda. Add the Cream and Soda
laſt.

laſt. The Batter will be uncommonly ſtiff. Half fill Cups with it, and bake in a quick Oven. Flavor with what you like.

(Mrs. *Mary Smith's* Virginia Cookery Book, 1885.)

Another Way*

BEAT together one Tableſpoon of Butter and one Cup of Sugar. Add three Eggs and beat well, add one Cup of ſour Cream and beat ſlightly. Sift in one and three fourths Cups of Flour, one half Teaſpoon of Salt, one Teaſpoon of Soda and one half Teaſpoon of Mace. Mix together but do not over mix. Pour into a well-greaſed Loaf-pan and bake in a moderately ſlow Oven about three quarters of an Hour. Half a Cup of *Engliſh* Walnuts may be added at the laſt if deſired.

(Mrs. *Floyd's* Recipe. Adapted *Market Square Tavern* Kitchen, 1937.)

Dried Prune Cake*

FIRST ſtew your Prunes, then work them through a coarſe Colander to take out the Seeds. Take two thirds of a Cup of the Prune Pulp and cool. Cream one half Cup of Shortening with one and one half Cups of Sugar. Beat in two Eggs and the Prunes. Sift in one and one half Cups of Flour with one half Teaſpoon each of Cinnamon, Nutmeg, Allſpice alternately with two thirds of a Cup of ſour Milk. One third of a Cup of broken *Engliſh* Walnut Meats may be added. Bake in one well-greaſed large Pan in a moderate Oven about twenty-five

twenty-five Minutes. This may be ſerved warm
with a Syllabub of flavored, whipped Cream, or
with hard Sauce ſent up in a Boat. For Icing, uſe
Wine Icing (page 180).

(Mrs. *Cole's* Recipe, c-1837.
Adapted *Blair* Kitchen, 1938.)

Mrs. Garrett's *Ten-minute Cake* ✳

TAKE two Teaſpoonfuls of Cream of Tartar
and mix it, by ſifting, with one Pint of dry
Flour, one even Teaſpoonful of Soda, diſſolved in
a Teacupful of Milk; rub a Piece of Butter the
Size of an Egg into the dry Flour; then beat up one
Egg and a Teacupful of Sugar; mix all well together
and bake without Delay. Have your Oven ready
heated before you begin mixing, and you can make
and bake the Cake in ten Minutes.

(From Mrs. *Smith's* Virginia Cookery Book, 1885.
Prov'd *Market Square Tavern* Kitchen, 1937.)

Hurry-up Gingerbread ✳

BEAT together well one half Cup of Sugar, one
half Cup of Butter and one Egg. Add one Cup
of Molaſſes, then ſift together two Cups of Flour,
one Tableſpoon of Ginger, one Teaſpoon of Cinnamon, one half Teaſpoon of Salt. Add theſe alternately with one Cup of ſour Milk to which you
have added one Teaſpoon of Soda. Bake in a ſhallow greaſed Pan in moderate Oven about thirty
Minutes.

(Old Recipe, *Sparta, Virginia.*)

Another

Another Way*

Inftead of the four Milk you may diffolve your Soda in boiling Water and add it at the laft.

(*Williamsburg* Family Recipes
in *Barlow* and *Cole* Family Cook Books.)

Robert E. Lee *Cake**

B EAT nine Egg Yolks very light then flowly beat in one Pound of Sugar. Fold in the well-beaten Egg Whites. Sift in one half Pound of Flour with one half Teafpoon of Salt and mix lightly together, ftir in one Tablefpoonful of Lemon-juice. Bake in a flow Oven in three ungreafed Layer-pans.

FILLING: Squeeze the Juice of two Lemons and three Oranges over two Cups of Sugar and flavour with a little of the grated Rinds. Add a Cup of grated Cocoanut and put between Layers and on Top. Sprinkle with dry Cocoanut.

(*Lane* Family Recipe, c-1870, *Williamsburg*.
Prov'd *Market Square Tavern* Kitchen, 1937.)

Lemon Jelly *Cake**

M IX well one Cup of Sugar and one half Cup of Butter. Add five well beaten Egg Yolks and beat until light. Sift into this two Cups of Flour with one Teafpoon of Soda and one and a half Teafpoons of Cream of Tartar, alternately with one Cup of fweet Milk. Flavor as you choofe. Add well-beaten Whites of the Eggs and bake in two or three Layers in a moderate Oven.

JELLY: Take the Juice and Rind of two Lemons and one Cup of Sugar. Cook until Sugar is diffolved and

and add three well-beaten Eggs. Cook this over
boiling Water until thick. Spread between Layers
and ſprinkle Top of Cake and Sides with powdered
Sugar.   (Old Recipe, *Bridgetown, Virginia.*)

A Liſbon *Cake*

IN order to make this Cake, get four or five
Pounds of fine Flour, and make a good Puff-
Paſte; that being done, roll it as thin as a half crown
Piece. Then put over it a Diſh of the Bigneſs of the
Cake you deſign to make, cut your Paſte round it,
and put this Piece of Paſte to cut round upon a
Sheet of Paper. Cut out in the ſame Manner ſeven
or eight Abbeſſes more, cutting one of them into
ſeveral Figures, to be placed on the Top of your
Cake. This being done, let them be baked ſeparately, then glaze the Abbeſs cut out into Figures
and make your Cake as follows: Put over one of
theſe Abbeſſes a Laying of Apricot Marmalade;
then over this another Abbeſs with a Laying of Jelly
of Currants; again, another Abbeſs over the Laſt
with Jelly of Gooſeberries. Continue after the ſame
Manner to place the Reſt of your Abbeſſes, putting
between them your ſeveral Layings of preſerved
Raſpberries, Apple Jelly, etc., placing on the Top
your figured and glazed Abbeſs, ſo that the Reſt
may not be ſeen: To which Purpoſe, your Cake
muſt be glazed with a white Glaze, a green Glaze,
and a Cochineal-colour Glaze, that it may appear
no more than one Abbeſs. Make the Glaze thus, viz.
beat together in an earthen Veſſel with a wooden
Spoon about a Pound of powder Sugar, the White
of

of two Eggs, and the Juice of half a Lemon. If this
Mixture proves to be too thin, put some more
Sugar in it; then divide this Composition into three
Parts: in the First, put Nothing, but leave it white
as it is; in the Second, put a Cochineal, to make it
red; and the Third green, with some Juice of Spinage. Glaze your Cake from Top to Bottom, first,
with a Streak of your white Composition, then
with a Streak of the Red, and afterwards with a
Streak of the Green; following the same Order till
your Cake is entirely glazed. Then to dry your
Icing, put your Cake for a little While, in a warm
Oven, or before the Fire, turning it round now and
then. Your Cake being as it should be, you lay it
in its Dish, and serve it up. It may be made as small
or as large as you please.

(Court & Country Confectioner. *London,* 1770.
From *Tucker* House, *Williamsburg.*)

Molasses Cake *

TAKE one Cup of Butter or Lard and mix well
with one Cup of Sugar, then beat in three
Eggs. Add two Cups of Molasses, one Cup of sour
Milk alternately with three and one half Cups of
Flour sifted with two Teaspoons of Soda, one half
Teaspoon of Salt and one Tablespoon of Ginger.
Bake in a slow Oven in a greased Tin about forty
Minutes.

(Old Recipe, *Richmond, Virginia*
Prov'd *Market Square Tavern* Kitchen, 1937.)

Orange

Orange Cake*

TAKE one Cup of Sugar, half a Cup of Butter, two Cups of Flour, half a Cup of ſweet Milk, a Teaſpoonful of baking Powder ſifted with the Flour. Rub the Butter and Sugar to a Cream, add two Eggs, the Whites and Yolks beaten ſeparately, then the Milk, then the Flour. Bake in Jelly-pans in moderate Oven about thirty Minutes. Squeeze the Juice from an Orange, add to it the grated Rind, make it ſtiff with powdered Sugar, and ſtir in the White of one Egg well-beaten. Spread this on the Cakes and lay one on another, like Jelly Cake.

(Mrs. *Cole's* Recipe, c-1837. Prov'd
Market Square Tavern Kitchen, 1937.)

Williamſburg *Orange Wine Cake**

CHOP very fine or grind, one medium-ſized, tender Orange-rind and one Cup of Raiſins. Add one half Cup of coarſely-chopped *Engliſh* Walnuts.

Cream one half Cup of Butter with one Cup of Sugar, add two beaten Eggs, one Teaſpoon of Vanilla and chopped Mixture. Sift two Cups of Flour with one Teaſpoon of Soda, one half Teaſpoon of Salt and add alternately with one Cup of ſour Milk. Pour into well-greaſed ſquare Cake-pan and bake in moderate Oven about thirty or forty Minutes. While hot this Cake may be glazed by ſpreading over it one Cup of Sugar mixed with one third of a Cup of Orange-juice and returning it to the Oven.

Oven. Others prefer this Cake ſerved warm with a
Syllabub of frothed Cream and ſtill others ſerve
it with

*Wine Icing**

MIX well one third of a Cup of Butter with two
Cups of Confectioner's Sugar. Add Sherry
to this, ſlowly beating well, add ſome finely-grated
Orange-peel, and when thick enough, ſpread on the
Cake. Beating the White of an Egg into this Icing
much improves its Texture.

(Old *Williamſburg* Recipe.   Prov'd
Market Square Tavern Kitchen, 1937.)

*Little Plumb Cakes**

CREAM one Cup of Shortening with one and
one half Cups of brown Sugar, add two well-
beaten Eggs. Sift together three Cups of Flour,
one Teaſpoon of Soda, one Teaſpoon of Cinnamon,
one half Teaſpoon each of Allſpice and Ginger.
Mix well, add one Cup of Raiſins, one half Cup of
Nut Meats broken, and (if deſired) two Table-
ſpoonfuls of chopped, candied Orange-peel or
Lemon-peel. Drop by Spoonfuls on greaſed baking
Tin and bake about twenty Minutes in a moderate
Oven. This makes between four and five Dozen
Cakes.

(Mrs. *Randolph's* Recipe, 1831.
Adapted *Blair* Kitchen, 1938.)

Pork

Pork Cake*

CUT fine one Pound of salt Pork and pour over it two Cups of boiling Water. Add two Cups of Molaſſes, one Cup of brown Sugar. Sift together ſeven Cups of Flour, two Tableſpoons each of Cinnamon and Allſpice, two Teaſpoons each of Cloves, Nutmeg and Soda, and beat well into the Batter. Add one Pound of well-cleaned Currants and one and one half Pounds of Raiſins (which have ſoaked overnight in one Cup of Brandy if you chooſe). Bake in three large Loaf-pans in a very ſlow Oven about one Hour.

(Old Recipe, *Highland Springs, Virginia.*)

Pound Cake*

BEAT one Cup of Butter to a Cream, ſlowly beat in one and one third Cups of Sugar. Add one Teaſpoonful of Mace and beat in five whole Eggs adding them one at a Time. Sift in two Cups of Flour, turn at once into a greaſed and floured Pan or Mould and bake ſlowly for one Hour.

(Recipe from *Wicomico* Church, c-1754.)

Mount Vernon *Pound Cake*

WASH all the Salt from a Pound of Butter, then put it dry between the Folds of a clean Cloth and ſet away in a cold Place. Sift one Pound of Paſtry Flour and ſeparate the Yolks and Whites of twelve Eggs. Cream the Butter and Flour together very thoroughly and beat the Yolks of the Eggs to a thick, almoſt white, Froth with one Pound

Pound of granulated Sugar. Add one Teaſpoonful of Vanilla and a Grating of Mace. Gradually add the creamed Butter and Flour to the Sugar and Egg Mixture and whip well, then fold in the ſtiffly beaten Whites of the Eggs, pour into a well-greaſed and floured Tube-pan, ſcatter a little grated Lemon or Orange-rind over the Top and bake in a moderate Oven about one and a quarter Hours.

(Old Recipe, *Chaſe City, Virginia.*)

Williamſburg *Pound Cake**

CREAM one Pound of Butter and one Pound of Sugar together, add the well beaten Yolks of twelve Eggs, and the ſtiffly beaten Whites and one Pound of Flour (ſifted twice) alternately to the Sugar and Butter Mixture. Beat until *very light.* Pour into a well-greaſed and floured Mold and bake in a moderate Oven. The Secret of this Cake lies in careful Baking.

(Prov'd *Market Square Tavern* Kitchen, 1937.)

Savoy *or Spunge Cake**

TAKE twelve freſh Eggs, put them in the Scale, and balance them with Sugar: take out half, and balance the other half with Flour: ſeparate the Whites from the Yelks, whip them up very light, then mix them, and ſift in, firſt Sugar, then Flour, till both are exhauſted; add ſome grated Lemon-peel; bake them in Paper Caſes, or little Tin Moulds. This alſo makes an excellent Pudding, with Butter, Sugar and Wine, for Sauce.

(Mrs. *Mary Randolph's* Virginia
Houſewife, 1831. Prov'd 1937.)

Williamſburg

Williamſburg *Sponge Cake**

BEAT three Egg Yolks until very light, ſlowly beat in one third of a Cup of Sugar. Add one Teaſpoonful of Lemon-juice. Stir in lightly three well-beaten Egg Whites. Sift in one third of a Cup of Flour and one fourth Teaſpoon of Salt. Bake in ſmall buttered Muffin Tins, or in a ſmall Cake-pan in a very moderate Oven about twenty-five Minutes.

(Mrs. *Randolph's Recipe.*
Adapted *Blair* Kitchen, 1938.)

*Silver Cake**

CREAM together three Cups of ſifted Sugar and one Pound of waſhed Butter. Add alternately one Pound of Flour ſifted three Times and the Whites of fourteen Eggs beaten to a ſtiff Froth. Flavor with one Teaſpoon of Almond Extract and bake in a ſlow Oven.

(*Coleman* Family Recipe, c-1840.
From *Cheſter, Virginia.*)

*Spice Cake**

TAKE one Cup of brown Sugar and beat it well with one fourth Pound of Butter. Add well beaten Yolks of two Eggs. Sift together one and one fourth Cups of Flour, one half Teaſpoon each of Cloves, Cinnamon, Nutmeg and baking Powder, add this to your Mixture alternately with one half Cup of ſour Milk in which you have mixed one half Teaſpoon of Soda. Pour your Batter in a ſmall
well-greaſed

well-greaſed ſquare Pan, and ſpread it with a
Meringue made by beating the two Egg Whites
with one Cup of ſifted brown Sugar. Sprinkle with
one third Cup of chopped *Engliſh* Walnuts. Bake
in moderate Oven about thirty-five Minutes. This
may be ſerved warm.

(Old *Richmond* Recipe, adapted 1937.)

Sponge Cake *

WEIGH ten Eggs, take the Weight of the Eggs
in Sugar, one half the Weight of the Eggs in
Flour, Juice and Rind of one freſh Lemon and two
Teaſpoons of Vanilla. Beat Yolks well, add Sugar
gradually, Lemon-juice and Rind, then Flour, one
half Teaſpoon of Salt and Flavoring. Fold in
beaten Whites and bake in a flow Oven for about
twenty-five Minutes.

(Old *Richmond* Recipe. Prov'd
Market Square Tavern Kitchen, 1937.)

Tipſy Cake *

TAKE two Layers of Sponge Cake and ſoak
them well in Sherry and chill well. Take a
Quart of cold boiled Cuſtard and pour Part of it
over one Layer. Add the ſecond Layer and ſtuff
the Top with ſplit blanched Almonds and pour the
remaining Cuſtard over it. On the Top of the Cake
put frothed Cream and a few chopped toaſted
Almonds.

(Traditional *Williamſburg* and *Virginia* Recipe.
Prov'd *Market Square Tavern* Kitchen, 1937.)

Tipſy

Tipſy Squire*

INSTEAD of making a large Cake you may cut your Sponge in ſquare Portions and ſend it up in ſeparate Sauce Diſhes for each Serving.

(Traditional *Williamſburg* and *Virginia* Recipe.
Prov'd *Travis* Houſe, 1938.)

George Waſhington *Cake—1780*

RUB two Cups of Butter and two Cups of Sugar to a light Cream. Beat four Egg Yolks very light with one Cup of Sugar and ſtir together. Sift together four Cups of Flour, one Teaſpoon of Mace two Tableſpoons of baking Powder, and add alternately with one Cup of Milk. Stir in one Cup of Raiſins, one half Cup of Currants and one fourth Cup of finely-cut Citron. Fold in the well-beaten Whites. Bake in ſquare ſhallow Pan in moderate Oven about one Hour; when cold ice with white Icing.

(Old *Williamſburg* Family Cook Book.)

Of DESSERTS

DESSERTS were made to pleaſe the Eye as well as the Palate, and ſometimes, one might ſuſpect, the Eye had the Preference. Elaborate Flummeries, molded Blanc-manges, exuberantly decorated Puddings were important Diſhes upon every well-ſet and compleat Table.

If the Pudding ſmacked ſtrongly of the "Spinage"

age" that had been uſed to make it a lively Green,
or if the Flavour of the Beets was as predominant
as the Colour, it was politely overlooked by the
pleaſed Gueſt, who ſaw ſuch culinary Miracles as
Solomon's Temple in Flummery riſe from the Center of the Table.

It was a painſtaking Age. From the yellowed
Pages of the finely-written little Cook Book of
Frances Bland Tucker Coalter, a *Williamſburg*
Bride, one can viſualize the young Houſekeeper
ſupervising the Preparation of a *Hen's Neſt* for
ſome ſpecial Occaſion. Firſt a Blanc-mange was
prepared, laboriouſly, with Iſinglaſs to congeal it;
then ſeveral Dozen Eggs were blown and filled
with it. A Neſt was made by partly filling a Bowl
with Jelly, on the Top of which a Straw made of
ſhredded Orange and Lemon-peel was placed—
then the Eggs were laid in the Straw and Jelly was
poured over to hold them in Place. This realiſtic
Sculpture in Jelly was then turned out in a *China*
Diſh and garniſhed with green Sweetmeats.

In this Matter of dreſſing Victuals to pleaſe the
Eye, *Beverley* ſaid of the *Virginians* in 1705:

> . . . They have their Graziers, Seedſmen, Gar-
> diners, Brewers, Bakers, Butchers, and Cooks
> within themſelves: they have a great Plenty and
> Variety of Proviſions for their Table; and as for
> Spicery, and other things that the Country don't
> produce, they have conſtant Supplies of 'em from
> *England*. The Gentry pretend to have their
> Victuals dreſt, and ſerv'd up as Nicely, as at the
> beſt Tables in *London*.

That Nothing was lacking in Spicery or other
Table Delicacies to prevent the *Virginia* Cook from
attempting

attempting the most elegant and genteel Exploits in Cookery is evidenced by a small Order for Sundries by Lord *Dunmore*, from the Governor's Palace in *Williamsburg*, to *John Norton & Sons*, Merchants of *London*, on the twelfth of June in 1773: Invoice of Sundries for the Earl of *Dunmore*.

    15 Dozen bottles of Strong Beer
    15 Do. of Ale.
     3 Hogsheads of Porter
    12 large *Cheshire* Cheese
     2 Dozen *Gloucester* do.
   100 lb. Currants
    50 lb. Jar Raisins
     4 lb. Mace
     2 lb. Nutmegs
     1 lb. Cloves
     1 lb. Cinnamon
    24 lb. Black Pepper
     6 lb. *Jamaica* do.
     2 Boxes Hand Soap
     2 Casks of Barley
    24 Bottles Mustard
    20 lb. Isinglass
   100 lb. Rice
   100 lb. Split Peas
    50 lb. Maccaroni
    20 Dozen Packs of Cards
     1 Barrel of good Vinegar
     1 Dozen Wine and Beer Cocks
    30 lb. Almonds
    12 Bottles of Olives
     6 Do. of Capers
     4 Dozen pint Bottles of best Oil
    12 Bottles small pickled Onions
    12 Do. of small pickled Cucumbers
    12 Dozen Wine Glasses
     6 Do. Tumblers
     6 Do. Quart Bottle Decanters with Handles
     3 Do. 2 Quart Decanters

To

Defferts

To make an Almond Pudding

TAKE a Pound of the beft *Jordan* Almonds blanched in cold Water, and beat very fine with a little Rofe-water; then take a Quart of Cream, boiled with whole Spice, and taken out again, and when 'tis cold, mix it with the Almonds, and put to it three Spoonfuls of grated Bread, one Spoonful of Flour, nine Eggs, but three Whites, half a Pound of Sugar, a Nutmeg grated; mix and beat thefe well together, put fome Puff-pafte at the Bottom of a Difh; put your Stuff in, and here and there ftick a Piece of Marrow in it. It muft bake an Hour, and when 'tis drawn, fcrape Sugar on it, and ferve it up.

(Mrs. *E. Smith's* Compleat Houfewife,
Williamfburg, 1742.)

Apple Dumplings*

HAVING pared your Apples, take out the Core with an Apple-fcraper, and fill the Hole with Quince or Orange Marmalade, or Sugar, as may fuit you beft. Then take a Piece of cold Pafte, and make a Hole in it, as if you were going to make a Pie. Lay in your Apple, and put another Piece of Pafte in the fame Form, and clofe it up round the Side of your Apple, which is much better than

gathering

gathering it in a Lump at one End. Tie it in a Cloth and boil it three quarters of an Hour. Serve them up, with melted Butter poured over them.

(*John Farley's* London Art of Cookery, 1787. From *Brookbury, Cheſterfield* County, *Virginia*.)

To make Apple Fritters

TAKE the Yolks of eight Eggs, the Whites of four, beat them well together, and ſtrain 'em into a Pan; then take a Quart of Cream, warm it as hot as you can endure your Finger in it; then put to it a quarter of a Pint of Sack, three quarters of a Pint of Ale, and make a Poſſet of it; when your Poſſet is cool, put to it your Eggs, beating them well together; then put in Nutmeg, Ginger, Salt and Flour to your Liking: Your Batter ſhould be pretty thick; then put in Pippins ſliced or ſcraped; fry them in good Store of hot Lard with a quick Fire.

(Mrs. *E. Smith's* Compleat Houſewife. *Williamſburg*, 1742.)

Williamſburg *Apple Fritters* *

PEEL and core ſix Apples and cut them in thin Slices. Soak them for two Hours in Brandy (or Lemon Juice). Dip them in Batter and fry them in a Kettle of boiling Fat, or you may ſauté them in Butter.

BATTER: Beat two Egg Yolks and add one fourth Cup of rich Milk, one fourth Cup of cold Water, one Tableſpoonful of Brandy (or Lemon Juice) and one Tableſpoonful of melted Butter.
Sift

Sift in one Cup of Flour, two Tableſpoonfuls of Sugar, and one fourth Teaſpoonful of Salt. Mix quickly, then ſtir in lightly two well-beaten Egg Whites.

(Mrs. *Mary Randolph's* Recipe, 1831.
Adapted *Blair* Kitchen, 1938.)

*A Pupton of Apples**

PARE a Dozen and half of fine, ſound, well-taſted Apples, and quartering them take out the Cores.

Put them into a Sauce-pan and pour over them three Spoonfuls of Water; duſt on five Ounces of the fineſt Sugar powdered, and ſet them over a gentle Fire in a Stove; ſtir them about from Time to Time, and when they are tender put in half a Teaſpoonful of powdered Cinnamon.

Let them keep on ſome Time longer, and they will grow thick and like Marmalade; then pour the Whole into a *China* Bowl, and let it cool.

Grate ſome Bread very fine, and beat up ſix Yolks of Eggs; mix with this a quarter of a Pound of freſh Butter, and ſome of the Crumb of Bread: When this and the Apples are both cold mix them together, and put the Whole into a Silver Diſh, or Baking-pan; ſet it in a ſlow Oven, and half an Hour will very well do it; turn it upſide down into the Diſh, and ſerve it up hot: Send up with it ſome Slices of freſh Butter in a Saucer, with freſh Parſley.

(Mrs. *Martha Bradley's* Britiſh Houſewife.)

Apple

Apple Pudding

HALF a Pound of Apples boiled, and ſqueezed through a hair Sieve half a Pound of Butter—beaten to a Cream and mixed with the Apples before they are cold, ſix Eggs well beaten, half a Pound of fine Sugar—the Rind of two Lemons—or Oranges—boiled well ſhifting the Water ſeveral Times—then beat all togather—bake them on a Cruſt. Half an Hour will bake it.

(Manuſcript Cook Book, prior 1839.
Morton Family of *Charlotte* County, *Virginia.*)

To make an Apple Tanſy *

TAKE three Pippins, ſlice them round in thin Slices, and fry them with Butter; then beat four Eggs, with ſix Spoonfuls of Cream, a little Roſe-water, Nutmeg, and Sugar, and ſtir them together, and pour it over the Apples: Let it fry a little, and turn it with a Pye-plate. Garniſh with Lemon and Sugar ſtrew'd over it.

(Mrs. *E. Smith's* Compleat Houſewife,
Williamſburg, 1742.)

Blanc Mange

TO an Ounce of Iſinglaſs pour a Pint of boiling Water to ſtand Overnight. Next Morning add three Pints of ſweet Milk, a Pound and a quarter of loaf Sugar, and a Tableſpoonful or two of Roſe-water. Put it in Braſs Kettle, boil fifteen or twenty Minutes very faſt; wet your Moulds and pour it in.

(Old *Williamſburg* Recipe, c-1837.
Mrs. *Elizabeth Labbé Cole's* Colleǎion)

Williamſburg *Blanc Mange*✻

SCALD two and one quarter Cups of Milk. Mix well three fourths of a Cup of cold Milk, one fourth of a Cup of Cornſtarch, two Tableſpoontfuls of Sugar and a Pinch of Salt. Add to the hot Milk and cook very ſlowly until thick and the Cornſtarch is well cooked. Then add one Egg which has been beaten well with two Tableſpoonfuls of Sugar, and finiſh cooking for a Minute or two. Flavor with Vanilla. Pour into a Mould and chill well. Unmould and ſerve with a Sauce of cruſhed freſh Fruit or a well-flavored Cuſtard Sauce.

(Mrs. *Cole's* Recipe, c-1837.
Adapted *Blair* Kitchen, 1938.)

A baked Bread Pudding✻

TAKE a Penny-loaf, cut it in thin Slices, then boil a Quart of Cream or new Milk, and put in your Bread, and break it very fine; put five Eggs to it, a Nutmeg grated, a quarter of a Pound of Sugar, and half a Pound of Butter; ſtir all theſe well together; butter a Diſh, and bake it an Hour.

(Mrs. *E. Smith's* Compleat Houſewife,
Williamſburg, 1742.)

Williamſburg *Carrot Pudding*✻

TAKE one Cup of grated raw Carrots, one half Pound of fine dry Bread Crumbs, one Teaſpoonful of Nutmeg, two of Cinnamon and one fourth of Salt. Over this pour one fourth Cup of Sherry.
Beat

Beat four Eggs very light with one half Cup of
Sugar, add four large Tableſpoonfuls of melted
Butter. Bake in moderate Oven in buttered Bak-
ing-diſh about forty-five Minutes. Serve hot with
Pudding Sauce.

(Mrs. *E. Smith's* Recipe, 1742.
Adapted *Market Square Tavern* Kitchen, 1937.)

Clouted Cream

TAKE a Gill of new Milk, and ſet it on the Fire
and take ſix Spoonfuls of Roſe-water, four or
five Pieces of large Mace, put the Mace on a
Thread; when it boils, put to them the Yolks of
two Eggs very well beaten; ſtir theſe very well together; then take a Quart of very good Cream, put
it to the Reſt, and ſtir it together, but let it not
boil after the Cream is in. Pour it out of the Pan
you boil it in, and let it ſtand all Night; the next
Day take the Top off it, and ſerve it up.

(Mrs. *Hannah Glaſſe's* Art of Cookery,
London, 1774.)

Cocoanut Pudding

TAKE three quarters of a Pound of Sugar, the
ſame of Butter—creamed together, the Whites
of twelve Eggs beat them to a Froth—add them to
the Butter and Sugar—add three quarters of a
Pound of grated Cocoanut—half a Glaſs of Brandy
bake on a thin Cruſt.

(Manuſcript Cook Book, prior 1839.
Morton Family of *Charlotte* County, *Virginia*.)

To

To make baked Cuſtards*

ONE Pint of Cream boiled with Mace and Cinnamon; when cold take four Eggs, two Whites left out, a little Roſe and Orange-flower Water and Sack, Nutmeg and Sugar to your Palate; mix them well together, and bake them in *China* Cups.

(Mrs. *Hannah Glaſſe's* Art of Cookery, *London*, 1774.)

Ice Cuſtard

TO one Quart of new Milk put three Eggs with Sugar a little cold Water to the Eggs and Sugar after it is beaten before put to the boiling Milk— to prevent it from turning take the Kettle off the Fire when the Eggs are ſtirred in—freeze it as you do Ice Cream.

(Manuſcript Cook Book, prior 1839. *Morton* Family of *Charlotte* County, *Virginia*.)

Cuſtard Ice Cream*

SCALD a Cup and a half of Milk, ſtir in three fourths of a Cup of Sugar and a Pinch of Salt. Pour ſlowly over two or three beaten Egg Yolks. Cook very ſlowly until thick. Cool, add one Tableſpoonful of Vanilla and one Pint of rich Cream which has been whipped to a Froth and freeze.

(Mrs. *Coalter's* Recipe, c-1801. Adapted *Blair* Kitchen, 1938.)

Cream Puffs*

PUT one half Cup of Butter and one Cup of boiling Water in a Sauce-pan when it comes to a Boil ſift in one Cup of Flour, ſtirring well. Remove

move from Fire and beat in four Eggs one at a
Time. Drop on buttered Tins by ſmall Spoonfuls
and bake in a quick Oven about half an Hour.
Theſe may be filled with thick boiled Cuſtard, or
flavored whipped Cream.

(Mrs. *Cole's* Recipe, c-1837, *Williamſburg.*
Adapted *Market Square Tavern* Kitchen, 1937.)

Delicate Pudding *

BEAT one half Cup of Sugar with two Egg Yolks.
Pour over this one and one half Cups of ſcalded
Milk. Add one and one half Tableſpoons of Gela-
tine diſſolved in one half Cup of cold Water. When
cool, add the ſtiffly beaten Whites of the Eggs, one
half Cup of Cream which has been whipped, and
one Teaſpoonful of Vanilla. Pour into Moulds and
chill.

(Mrs. *Cole's* Recipe, c-1837, *Williamſburg.*
Adapted *Market Square Tavern* Kitchen, 1937.)

Dutch Puff Pudding *

MIX together well one half Cup of Flour, one
half Cup of Sugar, one half Teaſpoon of Salt
and one Quart of Milk. Add four well beaten Eggs.
Pour into a buttered Pudding Diſh and bake in a
moderate Oven.

Sauce *

POUR two Cups of boiling Water over one Cup
of brown Sugar, half an Orange Rind dried and
grated, and one Teaſpoon of Flour. Boil well for
five Minutes and ſerve hot over the Pudding.

(Recipe, c-1700, from *Wicomico Church, Virginia.*
Prov'd *Market Square Tavern* Kitchen, 1937.)

Eve's

Eve's Pudding*

CHOP and mix one half Pound of Beef-fuet, one half Pound of Apples, with one half Pound of fine Bread Crumbs, one Cup of Flour, one grated Nutmeg, one Teafpoon of Salt. Beat five Egg Yolks well, flowly beating in one Cup of Sugar. Add one Cup of ftoned Raifins and one Ounce each of finely cut Citron and Lemon-peel which have foaked Overnight in a Glafs of Brandy. Mix all, adding laft the Whites of the Eggs beaten to a ftiff Froth. Butter a Mould well and fteam for three Hours, then bake about fifteen Minutes in a moderate Oven.

(Traditional *Virginia* Recipe. Prov'd *Market Square Tavern* Kitchen, 1937.)

The floating Ifland, a pretty Difh for the Middle of a Table at a fecond Courfe, or for Supper

YOU may take a Soop-difh, according to the Size and Quantity you would make, but a pretty deep Glafs is beft, and fet it on a *China* Difh; firft take a Quart of the thickeft Cream you can get, make it pretty fweet with fine Sugar, pour in a Gill of Sack, grate the yellow Rind of a Lemon in, and mill the Cream till it is all of a thick Froth, then as carefully as you can, pour the Thin from the Froth, into a Difh; take a *French* Roll, or as many as you want, cut it as thin as you can, lay a Layer of that as light as poffible on the Cream, then a Layer of Currant Jelly, then a very thin Layer of Roll, and then Hartfhorn Jelly, then *French* Roll, and over that whip your Froth which you faved off the Cream very well milled up, and

lay

lay at Top as high as you can heap it; and as for the Rim of the Diſh, ſet it round with Fruit or Sweetmeats, according to your Fancy. This looks very pretty in the Middle of a Table with Candles round it, and you may make it of as many different Colours as you fancy, and according to what Jellies and Giams or Sweetmeats you have; or at the Bottom of your Diſh you may put the thickeſt Cream you can get; but that is as you fancy.

(Mrs. *Hannah Glaſſe's* Art of Cookery, *London,* 1774.)

Williamſburg *Floating Iſland* *

TAKE two Cupfuls of cuſtard Sauce (page 211) and place it in your Baking-diſh. Beat three egg Whites very ſtiff and ſlowly beat in three Tableſpoonfuls of Sugar and one fourth Teaſpoonful of Salt, flavor with a few Drops of Almond Extract. Drop by Spoonfuls on the Cuſtard, leaving Spaces between each Iſland. Bake in a hot Oven for about two Minutes until the Iſlands be ſlightly browned.

(Mrs. *Cole's* Recipe, c-1837.
Adapted *Blair* Kitchen, 1938.)

To make a Grateful Pudding

TAKE a Pound of fine Flour, and a Pound of white Bread grated, take eight Eggs but half the Whites, beat them up, and mix with them a Pint of new Milk, then ſtir in the Bread and Flour, a Pound of Raiſins ſtoned, a Pound of Currants, half a Pound of Sugar, a little beaten Ginger; mix all well together, and either bake or boil it. It will take

take three quarters of an Hour's Baking. Put Cream in, inſtead of Milk, if you have it. It will be an Addition to the Pudding.

(Mrs. *Hannah Glaſſe's* Art of Cookery, *London*, 1774.)

Caramel Ice Cream*

MELT one and three fourths Pounds dark brown Sugar in an iron Skillet. Add one Pint of Water, diſſolve and ſtrain. Make Cuſtard of two Quarts of Milk and ten Eggs. Cool both Mixtures, mix, add one Quart of Cream and freeze.

(Old Recipe, *Diſputanta, Virginia.*)

Williamſburg *Lemon Cream**

GRATE two Teaſpoonfuls of Lemon-rind onto two Cups of Sugar. Boil for five Minutes with three fourths of a Cup of Lemon-juice and one fourth Teaſpoon of Salt. Freeze until muſhy. Then add two ſtiffly beaten Egg Whites and freeze until firm.

(Mrs. *Coalter's* Recipe, c-1801
Adapted *Travis* Houſe, 1938.)

Solomon's *Temple in Flummery*

DIVIDE a Quart of ſtiff Flummery into three Parts, and make one Part a pretty thick Colour with a little Cochineal bruiſed fine, and ſteeped in *French* Brandy. Scrape an Ounce of Chocolate very fine, diſſolve it in a little ſtrong Coffee, and mix it with another Part of your Flummery, to make it a light Stone Colour. The laſt Part muſt be White. Then wet your TempleMould, and

ſet

ſet it in a Pot to ſtand even. Fill the Top of the
Temple with red Flummery for the Steps, and the
four Points with white. Then fill it up with Choco-
late Flummery, and let it ſtand till the next Day.
Then looſen it round with a Pin, and ſhake it looſe
very gently; but do not dip your Mould in warm
Water, as that will take off the Gloſs, and ſpoil the
Colour. When you turn it out, ſtick a ſmall Sprig of
Flowers, down from the Top of every Point, which
will not only ſtrengthen it, but alſo give it a pretty
Appearance. Lay round it Rock-candy Sweetmeats.

(*John Farley's* London Art of Cookery, 1787.
From *Brookbury, Cheſterfield* County, *Virginia.*)

Indian *Meal Pudding—Mrs.* Hopkins

TAKE eight Ounces Muſh, good Weight, ſix
Ounces Butter, ſix Ounces Sugar, the Yolks of ſix
Eggs and White of one. Mix the Butter in the Muſh
while ſtill warm, beat the Eggs light, mix the Sugar
with them, and add them to the Muſh when cool.
Put Mace, Nutmeg, and Wine to your Taſte.

(Manuſcript Cook Book, c-1801,
of Mrs. *Frances Bland Tucker Coalter.*
Owned by Dr. *St. George Tucker Grinnan, Richmond.*)

Frozen Plumb Pudding*

MAKE a Cuſtard of one Quart of Milk, two
Cups of Sugar and four Eggs. Cool. Add two
Cups of chopped Raiſins, one Cup of chopped
Nuts, one half Cup of brandied Cherries, one Cup
of

of chopped preſerved Pineapple, and two Tableſpoons of Orange Marmalade. Beat one Quart of
Cream, mix with Cuſtard and Fruits and freeze.

(Old *Richmond* Recipe.
Prov'd *Market Square Tavern* Kitchen, 1937.)

Another Way*

MAKE a Cuſtard of three Cups of Milk, Yolks
of ten Eggs, two Cups of Sugar, little Salt.
When cool add one and one half Pints Cream or
more, three fourths Cup candied Fruit, one third
Cup Raiſins, one half Cup blanched Almonds, one
half Cup pounded Macaroons, one half Cup Sherry.
Freeze. This makes about three Quarts.

(Old *Richmond* Recipe. Prov'd 1937.)

King's Arms *Green-gage Plum Ice Cream**

SKIN, ſeed and maſh one Pint of preſerved Green-
gage Plums, add the Juice of two Lemons, two
Cups of Sugar, one and one half Quarts of Milk
and one Quart of Cream with a Pinch of Salt.
Freeze.

Hunting Pudding

MIX eight Eggs beat up fine with a Pint of good
Cream, and a Pound of Flour. Beat them
well together, and put to them a Pound of Beef-
ſuet finely chopped, a Pound of Currants well
cleaned, half a Pound of Jar Raiſins ſtoned and
chopped ſmall, two Ounces of candied Orange cut
ſmall, the ſame of candied Citron, a quarter of a
Pound

Pound of powdered Sugar, and a large Nutmeg
grated. Mix all together with half a Gill of Brandy,
put it into a Cloth, tie it up close, and boil it four
Hours.

(*John Farley's* London Art of Cookery, 1787.
From *Brookbury, Chesterfield* County, *Virginia.*)

Lemon Ice Cream

THE Juice of six Lemons to two Quarts Water,
(or two Cups bottled Juice). Steep the Peels
for sometime in the Water (or some Lemon Conserve if you have not fresh Peels) and strain it.
Mix into it two Pounds white Sugar and the Whites
of twenty-four Eggs beat till they will adhere to
the Bowl. The Freezer must be kept in Motion till
y^r Cream is of the Consistence of Snow.

(Manuscript Cook Book, c-1801,
of Mrs. *Frances Bland Tucker Coalter.*
Owned by *St. George Tucker Grinnan, Richmond.*)

Lemon Pudding

HALF a Pound of beaten Sugar—the same
Quantity of Flour dried and sifted, half Pound
of Butter, the Yolks of ten Eggs well beaten, add
the Rine of one Lemon grated—Mix the Juice of
the Lemon with half a Glass of Brandy beat them
together bake them on a Crust or as Fancy may
direct.

(Manuscript Cook Book, prior 1839.
Morton Family of *Charlotte* County, *Virginia.*)

Potatoe Pudding—Irish

TAKE one half Pound Potatoes, finely mashed, one half Pound Sugar, one half Pound Butter, fix Eggs with the Whites—beat them. Cream the Butter mix all together and beat very light. You may add Orange or Lemon-peel or Mace and a large Wine-glafs of Wine.

(Manufcript Cook Book, c-1801,
of Mrs. *Frances Bland Tucker Coalter*.
Owned by Dr. *St. George Tucker Grinnan, Richmond*.)

Clear Sauce for Puddings*

MIX Wine, Sugar and melted Butter to yʳ Tafte. Stir them together, taking Care to fkim off the Salt as it rifes.

(Manufcript Cook Book, c-1801,
of Mrs. *Frances Bland Tucker Coalter*.
Owned by Dr. *St. George Tucker Grinnan, Richmond*.)

Pudding Sauce*

HEAT one half Cup Milk and one half Cup Cream on a low Fire. Beat two Egg Yolks till thick. Add two Tablefpoons Sugar. Pour Milk and Cream gradually on Egg Mixture, beating conftantly, and cook flowly till thick. Add two Tablefpoons Brandy or Wine, one half Teafpoon Vanilla and a Bit of Salt. Pour over the two Egg Whites beaten till ftiff.

(Old Recipe, *Richmond, Virginia*.
Prov'd, *Blair* Kitchen, 1938.)

Snow

Snow a nice Dressing for a boiled Custard

TAKE the Whites of four Eggs, some beaten Sugar and a little Rose-water, whip them to a Froth, have ready some boiling Milk and Water, throw in the Froth, dip it up as quick as you can, and dress the Custard on the Top and tip it about with a little red Currant Jelly.

(Manuscript Cook Book, prior 1839.
Morton Family of *Charlotte* County, *Virginia*.)

To make an Orange Pudding

TAKE the out-side Rind of three *Sevil* Oranges, boil them in several Waters till they are tender; then pound them in a Mortar with three quarters of a Pound of Sugar; then blanch and beat half a Pound of Almonds very fine, with Rose-water to keep them from oiling; then beat sixteen Eggs, but six Whites, and a Pound of fresh Butter; beat all these together very well till 'tis light and hollow; then put it in a Dish, with a Sheet of Puffpaste at the Bottom, and bake it with Tarts; scrape Sugar on it, and serve it up hot.

(Mrs. *E. Smith's* Compleat Housewife,
Williamsburg, 1742.)

A Quire of Paper

TAKE three Spoonfuls of fine Flour, a Pint of Cream, six Eggs, three Spoonfuls of Sack, one of Orange-flower Water, a little Sugar, half a Nutmeg grated, and half a Pound of melted Butter almost cold. Mix all well together, and butter the
Pan

Pan for the firſt Pancake. Let them run as thin as poſſible, and when they be juſt coloured, they will be enough. In this Manner all the fine Pancakes ſhould be fried.

(*John Farley's* London Art of Cookery, 1787.
From *Brookbury*, *Cheſterfield* County, *Virginia*.)

Quire of Paper-pancakes

TAKE the Yolks of four Eggs well beat, mix in one half Pint of Milk, three Spoonfuls Flour, three Ounces Sugar, four Ounces freſh Butter, melted & cooled, (this muſt not be put in until the others are well mixed) and three Spoonfuls white Wine. Greaſe your Pan once with freſh Butter which will be ſufficient for all.

(Recipe in the Handwriting of *Lelia Tucker* in a
Letter written by *St. George Tucker* from
Williamſburg, 6th February [1804],
to his Daughter *Frances Coalter*.)

Another Way *

BEAT the Yolks of four Eggs well, add one Cup of rich Milk, ſift in three Tableſpoons of Flour, one fourth Cup of Sugar, one half Cup of melted Butter, three Spoonfuls white Wine. Butter a Griddle once, and do not cook too faſt. Serve at once.

(Mrs. *Coalter's* Recipe [1804],
Adapted *Market Square Tavern* Kitchen, 1937.)

Pink coloured Pancakes

BOIL a large Beet tender—beat it fine in a marble Mortar add the Yolks of four Eggs three Spoonfulls of Cream—two Pounds of Flour;
ſweeten

ſweeten to Taſte, half a Nutmeg, Glaſs of Brandy
—beat all togather half an Hour, fry them with
Butter, garniſh with Sweetmeats.

(Manuſcript Cook Book, prior 1839.
Morton Family of *Charlotte* County, *Virginia*.)

To make a Quaking Pudding

TAKE a Pint of Cream, and boil it with Nutmeg
and Cinnamon and Mace; take out the Spice
when 'tis boiled; then take the Yolks of eight Eggs,
and four of the Whites; beat them very well with
ſome Sack, and mix your Eggs with your Cream,
with a little Salt and Sugar, and a ſtale Half-penny
white Loaf, and one Spoonful of Flour, and a
quarter of a Pound of Almonds blanch'd and beat
fine, with ſome Roſe-water; beat all theſe well together, and wet a thick Cloth, and flour it, and put
it in when the Pot boils. It muſt boil an Hour at
leaſt. Melt Butter, Sack, and Sugar, for the Sauce;
ſtick blanch'd Almonds and candied Orange-peel
on the Top.

(*E. Smith's* Compleat Houſewife, *Williamſburg*, 1742.)

Quaking Pudding

TAKE one Pint of Cream out of which take two
or three Spoonfuls and mix quite ſmooth with
a Spoonfull of fine Flour. Set the Reſt to boil—
when it has boiled take it off and ſtir in the cold
Cream and Flour very well. When it is cool beat
five Yolks and two Whites of Eggs—ſtir in Nutmeg or Mace and a little Salt—Sweeten to your
Taſte—butter a wooden Bowl or other Veſſel and

put

put it in—tie a Cloth over and boil it half an Hour.
It muſt be put into boiling Water and turned about
a few Minutes to prevent the Egg going to one Side
—when done turn it into a Diſh and pour over it a
Sauce of melted Butter, Wine and Sugar. You may
dreſs it with Citron or other Sweetmeats.

(Manuſcript Cook Book, c-1801, of *Frances Bland
Tucker Coalter.* Owned by Dr. *St. George
Tucker Grinnan, Richmond.*)

Queen of Puddings *

POUR one Quart of Milk over two Cups of fine
dry Bread-crumbs. Beat four Egg Yolks add one
half Cup of Sugar, then combine them with one
half Cup of Butter creamed with one Cup of Sugar.
Add a Spoonful of Flavoring and pour into a ſhallow buttered Baking-diſh and bake until ſet in a
moderate Oven. Spread the Top with a thick Layer
of freſh or preſerved Strawberries or Raſpberries.
If freſh Berries are uſed, ſtrew well with Sugar, if
Preſerves, uſe no Sweetening. Spread over the Top
a light Meringue made by whipping the four Egg
Whites to a Froth with two Tableſpoonfuls of
powdered Sugar. Return to moderate Oven and
cook until the Meringue is ſet and ſlightly browned.

(Old *James City* County, *Virginia*, Recipe.
Adapted *Market Square Tavern* Kitchen, 1937.)

Rice Blanc Mange *

BOIL a Teacupfull of Rice in a very ſmall Quantity of Water, till it is near burſting—then add
half a Pint of Milk, boil it to a Muſh, ſtirring all
the

the Time; ſeaſon it with Sugar, Wine and Nutmeg; dip the Mould in Water, and fill it; when cold, turn it in a Diſh, and ſurround it with boiled Cuſtard ſeaſoned, or Syllabub—garniſh it with Marmalade.

(Mrs. *Mary Randolph's* Virginia Houſewife, 1831.)

Williamſburg *Rice Blanc Mange* ❊

BOIL one Cup of Rice in four Cups of Water with one fourth Teaſpoon of Salt until well done. Add one Pint of Milk and boil it to a Muſh, ſtirring all the Time. Seaſon with one fourth Cup of Sugar, one fourth Cup of Wine or Brandy, one Teaſpoon of Nutmeg. Dip a Mould in Water, fill it and chill. Turn out on a Diſh, cover with Cuſtard Sauce or Syllabub (Page 211).

(Mrs. *Randolph's* Recipe, 1831.
Adapted *Market Square Tavern* Kitchen, 1937.)

A Carolina *Rice Pudding*

TAKE half a Pound of Rice, waſh it clean, put it into a Saucepan, with a Quart of Milk, keep it ſtirring till it is very thick; take great Care it don't burn; then turn it into a Pan, and grate ſome Nutmeg into it, and two Teaſpoonfuls of beaten Cinnamon, a little Lemon-peel ſhred fine, ſix Apples, pared and chopped ſmall: mix all together with the Yolks of three Eggs, and ſweetened to your Palate; then tie it up cloſe in a Cloth; put it into boiling Water, and be ſure to keep it boiling all the Time; an Hour and a quarter will boil it. Melt
Butter

Butter and pour over it, and throw some fine Sugar all over it; and a little Wine in the Sauce will be a great Addition to it.

(Mrs. *Glasse's* Recipe, 1774.
Manuscript Copy in Cook Book of Miss
Margaret Prentis, Williamsburg, c-1828.)

*Sippet Pudding**

CUT a Loaf of Bread as thin as possible, put a Layer of it in the Bottom of a deep Dish, strew on some Slices of Marrow or Butter, with a Handful of Currants or stoned Raisins; do this till the Dish is full; let the Currants or Raisins be at the Top; beat four Eggs, mix with them a Quart of Milk that has been boiled a little and become cold, a quarter of a Pound of Sugar, and a grated Nutmeg—pour it in, and bake it in a moderate Oven—eat it with Wine Sauce.

(Mrs. *Mary Randolph's* Virginia Housewife, 1831.
Prov'd *Market Square Tavern* Kitchen, 1937.)

To make Steeple Cream

TAKE five Ounces of Hart's-horn, and two Ounces of Ivory, and put them into a Stone-bottle, and fill it up with fair Water to the Neck, and put in a small Quantity of Gum-arabick, and Gum-dragant; then tie up the Bottle very close, and let it into a Pot of Water with Hay at the Bottom, let it boil six Hours; then take it out and let it stand an Hour before you open it, lest it fly in your Face; then strain it in, and it will be a strong Jelly; then take a Pound of blanch'd Almonds, and beat them very fine, and mix it with a Pint of thick Cream, and let it stand a little; then strain it

out

out and mix it with a Pound of Jelly; ſet it over
the Fire till 'tis ſcalding hot, ſweeten it to your
Taſte with double-refin'd Sugar; then take it off,
and put in a little Amber, and pour it out into
ſmall high Gallipots like a Sugar-loaf at Top; when
'tis cold turn it out, and lay whipt Cream about
them in Heaps.

(Mrs. *E. Smith's* Compleat Houſewife,
Williamſburg, 1742.)

A Sweetmeat Pudding

MAKE a Quart of Flour into Puff-paſte; when
done, divide into three Parts of unequal
Size; roll the largeſt out ſquare and moderately
thin, ſpread over it a thin Layer of Marmalade,
leaving a Margin; then roll the ſmalleſt, and put it
on the other two, ſpreading Marmalade; fold it
up, one Fold over the other, the Width of your
Hand—preſs the Ends together, tie it in a Cloth
ſecurely, and place it in a Kettle of boiling Water,
where it can lie at Length without doubling; boil it
quickly, and when done, pour melted Butter with
Sugar and Wine in the Diſh.

(Mrs. *Mary Randolph's* Virginia Houſewife, 1831.)

Sweet Potato Pudding*

BOIL one Pound of ſweet Potatos very tender,
rub them while hot through a Colander; add
ſix Eggs well beaten, three quarters of a Pound of
powdered Sugar, three quarters of Butter, and
ſome grated Nutmeg and Lemon-peel, with a Glaſs
of Brandy; put a Paſte in the Diſh, and when the
Pudding

Pudding is done, sprinkle the Top with Sugar, and cover it with Bits of Citron. *Irish* Potato Pudding is made in the same Manner, but is not so good.

(Mrs. *Mary Randolph's* Virginia Housewife, 1831.
Prov'd *Market Square Tavern* Kitchen, 1937.)

Grated Potato Pudding *

BEAT four Eggs very light, add gradually two Cups of Sugar, two Cups of grated sweet Potato, two Cups of scalded Milk, one fourth Pound of melted Butter, two Teaspoonfuls of Ginger and one Tablespoon of Corn Starch dissolved in cold Water. Cook slowly, stirring constantly, on Top of Stove for about half an Hour until Mixture thickens. Bake in buttered Baking-dish in moderate Oven fifteen or twenty Minutes. Serve warm with whipped Cream.

(Old *Williamsburg* Recipe.)

Tansey Pudding

BEAT seven Eggs very light, mix with them a Pint of Cream and nearly as much Spinach Juice, with a little Juice of Tansey; add a quarter of a Pound of powdered Crackers or pounded Rice made fine, a Glass of Wine, some grated Nutmeg and Sugar; stir it over the Fire to thicken, pour it into a Paste and bake it, or fry it like an Omelette.

(Mrs. *Mary Randolph's* Virginia Housewife, 1831.)

Tipsy Cake *

CUT a Loaf of Sponge Cake in two-inch Squares. Split Squares in half. Saturate each Piece with Sherry. Cover each Piece with a rich Custard and top with whipped Cream and whole Almonds.

Custard

Custard Sauce ❊

BEAT three Egg Yolks lightly with one fourth of a Cup of Sugar. Pour slowly over these one Pint of scalded Milk. Return to Fire and cook very slowly, stirring continually until thick. Flavor as you choose with Vanilla or Rum, and Nutmeg.

(*Market Square Tavern* Kitchen, 1937.)

To make a Trifle ❊

COVER the Bottom of your Dish with *Naples* Biscuits broke in Pieces, Mackaroons, and Ratafia Cakes, just wet them all with Sack, pour on a good boiled Custard when cold, then a whipt Syllabub over that.

(Court & Country Confectioner, *London*, 1770.
From *Tucker* House, *Williamsburg*. Prov'd
Market Square Tavern Kitchen, 1937.)

Boiled Custard ❊

SCALD one Quart of Milk in a Double-boiler, beat six Eggs slightly and add to the Milk; add one-half Cup of Sugar and one-eighth Teaspoon of Salt, combined. Cook until Custard thickens. It will form a Coat on a clean silver Spoon when done.

(*Market Square Tavern* Kitchen, 1937.)

A

A MORAL AND PHYSICAL THERMOMETER: or, A SCALE of the Progrefs of TEMPERANCE and INTEMPERANCE.—LIQUORS, with their EFFECTS in their ufual Order.

WATER   TEMPERANCE.

Scale	Liquors	Effects
70	WATER	
		Health, Wealth,
60	Milk and Water	Serenity of mind,
		Reputation, long Life, and
50	Small Beer	Happinefs
40	Cider and Perry	Cheerfulnefs
		Strength and
30	Wine	Nourifhment, when taken only
		at meals, and in moderate
20	Porter	quantities.
10	Strong Beer	
0		

INTEMPERANCE.

Scale	Liquors	VICES.	DISEASES.	PUNISHMENTS.
10	Punch	Idlenefs	Sicknefs	
			Puking, and	
		Peevifhnefs	Tremors of the Hands in the Morning	Debt
20	Toddy and Crank	Quarrelling	Bloatednefs	Black Eyes
		Fighting	Inflamed Eyes	Rags
30	Grog		Red Nofe and Face	
		Lying	Sore and fwelled Legs	Hunger
		Swearing	Jaundice	Hofpital
40	Flip Shrub	Obfcenity	Pains in the Limbs, and burning in the Palms of the Hands, and Soles of the Feet	Poor-houfe
	Bitters infus'd in Spirits	Swindling		Jail
50	Ufquebaugh Hyfteric water	Perjury	Dropfy	Whipping
			Epilepfy	
	Gin, Annifeed, Brandy, Rum, and Whifky in the *Morning*	Burglary	Melancholy Madnefs	The Hulks
60		Murder	Palfy	Botany Bay
			Apoplexy	
70	Do. during the *Day and Night.*	Suicide	DEATH.	GALLOWS

Of HEALTH DRINKING

IT was a Matter of some Concern to the early
Virginia Lawmakers that no one should be suf-
fered "to drink more than was necessary." To this
End they passed many Acts for the Suppression of
notorious Drunkenness, and for the Restraint of
Ordinaries and Tippling Houses, that these Latter
might not cherish Idleness and encourage loose and
careless Persons to neglect their Callings and mis-
spend their Times in Drunkenness. Ordinary Keepers were permitted to extend only limited Credit
to their Patrons, (a Prohibition which they were
careful not to apply in the Capital while the
Courts and General Assembly were sitting).

There was an early Rule in the House of Bur-
gesses fining any of its Members who should, by the
major Part of the House, be adjudged "to be dif-
"guised with overmuch Drinke."

Students at the College of *William and Mary*
were enjoined from Drinking to Excess or in a Way
contrary to good Manners. A Letter from *John
Allison* to *St. George Tucker*, Professor of Law at the
College, written on *March* 2, 1816, shows clearly
the Problems that confronted the Parents of the
Students who overstepped these Bounds. The Dif-
cussion

cuffion of *William's* unbecoming Conduct con-
cludes:

> P.S. I hope *William* did not get drunk by himfelf,
> becaufe that would evince a total Difregard of
> Decency and Decorum.

The Gentlemen who made the Laws for the
Colony provided alfo for the Drinking they con-
fidered neceffary and polite. Ordinary Keepers
were not permitted to charge extraordinary Rates
for their Wines and Spirits—the County Courts
regulating the Price for Liquors, Diet, Lodging,
Stableage, &c. Diftinctions were made between
domeftic and imported Liquors, and in fome Coun-
ties, fuch as *Ifle of Wight*, the Court made fome
Judgment of Quality, rating "good *Barbaaoes*
"Rum" at 10 Shillings, and "*New England* and other
"bad Rum" at 5 Shillings per Gallon.

Neceffary Drinking included the "fmall Drink"
ufed at the Table, which confifted of a Variety of
Wines, Beer and Ale. Their ftrong Wine was
chiefly *Madeira*, a noble Wine which the
Reverend *Hugh Jones* faid was fitteft to cheer the
fainting Spirits in the Heat of Summer, and to
warm the chilled Blood in the bitter Colds of Winter. There was alfo Punch, made of Rum from the
Caribbee Iflands, or of Brandy diftilled from *Virginia* Apples and Peaches; befides *French* Brandy
and all Kinds of *French* and *European* Wine, efpe-
cially Claret and Port.

Chriftenings, Birthnight Feftivities, *Eafter*, *Chriftmas*, and all other Occafions for focial Gatherings,
were Occafions alfo for Health-drinking or Toaft-
ing. One Writer has obferved that Rum and Funeral
Wines

Wines were as neceſſary a Part of the Funeral as the Corpſe.

When Governor *Alexander Spotſwood* led a Company of Gentlemen, Rangers, and *Indians* beyond the *Blue Ridge* Mountains, the Expedition was well-prepared to obſerve the neceſſary Niceties. One of the higheſt Peaks of the Ridge was named Mount *George* for his Majeſty, and the Journal of *John Fontaine* records:

> September 6, 1716.
> We had a good dinner. After dinner we got the men all together and loaded all their arms and we drunk the King's health in Champagne, and fired a volley; the Prince's health in Burgundy, and fired a volley; and all the reſt of the Royal Family in Claret, and a volley. We drunk the Governor's health and fired another volley. We had ſeveral sorts of liquors, namely Virginia Red Wine and White Wine, Iriſh Uſquebaugh, Brandy, Shrub, two sorts of Rum, Champagne, Canary, Cherry punch, Cider, Water &c.

From ſuch a Beginning was inſtituted the *Order of the Golden Horſeſhoe* to which any Gentleman who had drunk his Majeſty's Health on Mount *George* was admitted.

The Cellars which ſupplied the neceſſary Refreſhment for ſuch Occaſions were ample—and among the largeſt and beſt-ſtocked in the Colony were thoſe in the Governor's Palace in *Williamsburg*.

After Lord *Botetourt's* Death in 1770, the Appraiſers made an Inventory of the Palace Cellars, which had been depleted, of courſe, by the Demands of the ſtate Funeral and had not been repleniſhed.

pleniſhed. At that Time the Cellars contained Hogſheads, Caſks, and Bottles holding more than 2,566 Gallons of a choice Aſſortment of Beer, Ale, Cider, Arrack, Brandy, Porter, Burgundy, Champagne, Claret, Hock, *Madeira* (almoſt one thouſand Gallons of this Favorite), Port, Rum, old Spirits and white Wine.

It was natural that one of the moſt noted and well-accuſtomed Taverns in *Virginia*, the *Raleigh*, ſhould have been known for the Excellence of its Bar. Travellers ſpoke of "the exceeding good *Ma-"deira"* for which the *Raleigh* was famous, and two hundred Acres of *Goochland* County Land bear Teſtimony to the Excellence of Keeper *Henry Wetherburn's* Punch. In the Year 1738, *William Randolph* of *Tuckahoe* deeded the Land to *Thomas Jefferſon's* Father, *Peter*, for "*Henry Wetherburn's* "biggeſt Bowl of Arrack Punch."

The beſt Summary of the *Virginian's* Attitude toward Conviviality is to be found carved and gilded above the Mantel in the *Raleigh's* hiſtoric *Apollo* Room, "*Hilaritas Sapientiae et Bonae Vitae "Proles"*—"Jollity—the Offspring of Wiſdom and "good Living."

Caudles, Punches, &c.

Apple Toddy*

TO one Gallon of Apple Brandy or Whiſkey, add one and a half Gallons of hot Water, well ſweetened, one Dozen large Apples, well roaſted,

two

two grated Nutmegs, one Gill of Allspice, one Gill of Cloves, a Pinch of Mace. Season with half a Pint of good Rum. Let it stand three or four Days before using. (Old Recipe, *Pittsylvania* County, *Virginia.*)

An Arrack Punch*

MELT one half Pound Sugar in enough hot Water to dissolve it well, pour it over the grated Rind, of two Lemons. Add the Juice of four Lemons; one Pineapple peeled, sliced and pounded, six Cloves, twenty Coriander-seeds, one small Stick of Cinnamon, one Pint of Brandy, one Pint *Jamaica* Rum, one Cup of Arrack, one Cup of strong green Tea, one Quart boiling Water. Strain well into a clean Bottle, cork well and steep it overnight. Add one Quart of hot Milk and the Juice of two more Lemons. When cool, ice and serve.

Arrack Punch*

MIX two Quarts of Arrack, one Gallon of Spirits, one Gallon of plain Syrup (made with one Pound of Sugar and one Gallon of Water), one third of a Cup of Tincture of Lemon-peel. This Punch may be iced and served immediately or will keep well if bottled.

Another Way*

POUR the strained Juice of two large Oranges over three-fourths of a Pound of Loaf-sugar. Add a little of the outside Peel cut in very thin Slices. Pour over it one Quart of boiling Water, one
Pint

Pint of Arrack and a Pint of hot red *French* Wine.
Stir together. This may be ferved when cold and
will improve with Age.

(As Mr. *Wetherburn* might have made it.)

For Bitters (*very fine*)

TO a Gallon of Brandy put four Ounces *Sevil*
Orange-peel, four Ounces Gentian cut fine,
two Ounces Cardimun-feed and one Ounce Coche-
neill, the Orange-peel, the Gentian and Cardemun
to be bruifed—the Cochen[eal] powdered.

(Manufcript Cook Book, c-1825, of Mifs *Margaret
Prentis* of *Williamfburg*. Owned by *Robert H.
Webb*, Efq., *Charlottefville*.)

Blackberry Cordial *

TO two Quarts Blackberry Juice add one Pound
Loaf-fugar, four grated Nutmegs, one-quarter
Ounce ground Cloves, one-quarter Ounce ground
Allfpice, one-quarter Ounce ground Cinnamon.
Simmer all together, for thirty Minutes, in a Stew-
pan clofely covered. Strain through a Cloth when
cold and add a Pint of the beft *French* Brandy.

(Old *Virginia* Recipe.)

A fine Caudle

TAKE a Pint of Milk, turn it with Sack; then
ftrain it, and when 'tis cold, put it in a Skillet,
with Mace, Nutmeg, and fome white Bread fliced;
let all thefe boil, and then beat the Yolks of four
or five Eggs, the Whites of two, and thicken your
Caudle,

Caudle, ſtirring it all one Way for fear it curdle;
let it warm together, then take it off, and ſweeten
it to your Taſte. (Mrs. *E. Smith's* Compleat Houſewife,
Williamſburg, 1742.)

Caudle ✳

PUT a Handfull of Allſpice in a Quart of Water,
& put it on the Fire to boil, beat well three or
four Eggs with as much Sugar as will make it ſweet
enough; pour the boiling Water to the Sugar, and
Eggs, very ſlowly, to prevent them curdling, rake
the Fire from under the Stew-pan, then pour the
Caudle back in it, ſtir it untill it is done, add a little
Wine or Rum when cool.

(Manuſcript Cook Book, prior 1839.
Morton Family of *Charlotte* County, *Virginia*.)

Cherry Shrub

GATHER ripe *Morello* Cherries, pick them from
the Stalk, and put them in an earthen Pot,
which muſt be ſet into an iron Pot of Water; make
the Water boil, but take Care that none of it gets
into the Cherries; when the Juice is extracted, pour
it into a Bag made of tolerably thick Cloth, which
will permit the Juice to paſs, but not the Pulp of
your Cherries; ſweeten it to your Taſte, and when
it becomes perfectly clear, bottle it—put a Gill of
Brandy into each Bottle, before you pour in the
Juice—cover the Corks with Roſin. It will keep all
Summer, in a dry cool Place, and is delicious mixed
with Water.

(Mrs. *Mary Randolph's* Virginia Houſewife, 1831.)

Morello

Morello *Cherry Bounce*

GATHER and pick your Cherries when perfectly ripe, put them into a Tub and mash them with a Rolling-pin, Stones and all, and to every five Pints of Cherries put a Quart of Rum, let it stand a Week; strain it through a Flannel Bag, to every Gallon of Bounce put three fourths of a Pound of brown Sugar. Cheap Rum at 75 Cents or 50 Cents a Gallon answers equally as well as the best Spirit for Bounce.

(Manuscript Cook Book, *Charlottesville*, 1836. Owned by Mrs. *Virginia Grasty Griffin*.)

Cordial Water

TWO Gallons of Brandy add of Water one fourth of the Quantity of Brandy. Two Dozen Lemons sliced and sweetened and six of the Peelings, eight Tablespoons white Sugar, and two Tablespoons of good brown Sugar candied—from Mrs. *Dunbar*.

(Manuscript Cook Book, c-1825, of Miss *Margaret Prentis* of *Williamsburg*. Owned by *Robert H. Webb*, Esq., *Charlottesville*.)

To make Whipt Cream

TAKE a Quart of thick Cream, and the Whites of eight Eggs beaten with half a Pint of Sack; mix it together, and sweeten it to your Taste with double-refin'd Sugar: You may perfume it if you please with some Musk or Ambergrease tied in a Rag, and steeped a little in the Cream; whip it up
with

with a Whisk, and a bit of Lemon-peel tied in the
Middle of the Whisk; take the Froth with a Spoon,
and lay it in your Glasses or Bason.

(Mrs. *E. Smith's* Compleat Housewife,
Williamsburg, 1742.)

Currant Shrub*

GATHER your Currants when full ripe, on a
dry Day. Mash them; then put them into a
flannel (or cotton) Bag and when the Juice has all
run out, to every Pint put twelve Ounces of Loaf-
sugar and half a Pint of Rum. Bottle and seal it
and set it away for Use. This Receipt answers
equally well for Cherries. The Shrub is indifferent
unless the Rum is good.

(Manuscript Cook Book, *Charlottesville,* 1836.
Owned by Mrs. *Virginia Grafty Griffin.*)

To make a Custard Posset

TAKE fourteen Eggs, beat them very well, and
put to them twelve Spoonfuls of Sack, nine of
Ale, and half a Pound of Sugar.

Set them upon some Coals and warm them, then
strain them, and set them on again, and heat them
till they begin to thicken; and if you please, you
may add a little Nutmeg.

Take one Quart of Cream and boil it, pour it
into the Eggs, cover it up, and let it stand half an
Hour; then serve it up.

(Mrs. *Martha Bradley's* British Housewife.)

Damson

Damſon Cordial

GET the Juice from the Fruit, ſee Jelly—ſtrain it and put a Pound of Sugar to a Pint of Juice, and boil it—throw in a Few of the Kernels, & ſome Orange-peel, one Quart of Peach Brandy to two of Syrup.

(Manuſcript Cook Book, prior 1839.
Morton Family of *Charlotte* County, *Virginia*.)

A good Dram*

TO a Gallon of Brandy put a Quart of Water, one Pound of Sugar, three Spoonfuls of beaten Orange-peel and a Gill of Milk.

(Manuſcript Cook Book, *Charlotteſville*, 1836
Owned by Mrs. *Virginia Graſty Griffin*.)

Eggnog*

BEAT well the Yolks of three Dozen Eggs, then ſlowly beat in two and one half Pounds of fine Sugar. Add ſlowly, Drop by Drop, one Pint of choice *French* Brandy, and let it ſtand while you beat the Whites of the Eggs very light with one half Pound of Sugar. Add to the Yolks two Quarts of Milk, two Quarts of Cream and one Gallon of Brandy. Add the Egg Whites and grate in a freſh Nutmeg.

(Old Recipe, *Lynchburg, Virginia*.)

Weſtmoreland *Club Eggnog* *

SEPARATE the Yolks and Whites of two Dozen Eggs. Beat the Yolks well, then beat in one Pound of finely pulverized Sugar. Pour over this very ſlowly one half Gallon of Brandy and one half Pint

Pint of Rum, ſtirring ſlowly and ſteadily. Pour in one Quart of rich Cream, add the well-beaten Whites, and ſtir until they diſappear. Serve very cold with grated Nutmeg.

[Eggnog is better if it is made ſome Days before it is to be uſed and is kept in a very cold Place. It muſt be well ſhaken and mixed before ſerving.]

Fiſh Houſe Punch *

MAKE a Syrup of three Quarts of Water, one Pound of brown Sugar, pour hot over the Rinds and Juice of a Dozen or a Dozen and a half Lemons. Cool. Add two Quarts *Jamaica* Rum, one Quart of Brandy, daſh well with Peach Brandy to make it mellow and extra fine. Serve in a Bowl of cruſhed Ice. (By uſing three Pounds of brown Sugar this Punch may be prepared for Bottling and will improve with Age.) To ſerve immediately, ſome add one Quart of Pineapple-juice inſtead of one of the three Quarts of Water.

[Note: This Recipe is an old one in the *Taylor* Family of *Norfolk*. This Copy was given by Mrs. *Taylor*, Wife of Colonel *Walter Herron Taylor*, Adjutant General of the Army of Northern *Virginia*, C. S. A. (on General *Lee's* Staff), to Mrs. *Philip Alexander Bruce*. At the Bottom of the Recipe is written "*Walter* ſays 'look out for ſwell "Head next Morning'."]

(*Taylor* Family Recipe, prior 1862, *Norfolk, Virginia*.)

To make fine *Milk-punch*∗

TAKE two Quarts of Water, one Quart of Milk, half a Pint of Lemon Juice, and one Quart of Brandy, Sugar to your Taſte; put the Milk and Water together a little warm, then the Sugar, then the Lemon Juice, ſtir it well together; then the Brandy; ſtir it again, and run it through a Flannel Bag till 'tis very fine; then bottle it; it will keep a Fortnight or more.

(Mrs. *E. Smith's* Compleat Houſewife,
Williamſburg, 1742.)

Punch∗

THE Juice of three good Lemons—two ſmall Coffee-cups Rum ſweetened as for Toddy (one Pound brown Sugar to each Gallon of Spirit), one do. of F. [*French*] Brandy and white Sugar—to your Taſte, will make three Quarts Punch—or one ſmall Coffee-cup of bottled Juice in place of freſh Lemons. Five good Limes equal to three Lemons.

(Manuſcript Cook Book, c-1801,
of Mrs. *Frances Bland Tucker Coalter.*
Owned by *St. George Tucker Grinnan, Richmond.*)

King's Arms *Froſted Fruit Shrub*∗

MIX the Juice of four Lemons and ſix Oranges with one Cup of Pineapple Juice, one Cup of Juice from pickled Fruit and one half Cup of Spice Syrup. Chill. Serve in ſmall Glaſſes topped with Orange Sherbet.

Spice Syrup: To one Cup of granulated Sugar, add one Cup of Water, one Tableſpoon of clear
Corn

Corn Syrup, one Tablespoon of whole Cloves, two Pieces of Cinnamon Bark. Stir over hot Water until Sugar is dissolved, then simmer fifteen Minutes. Strain and cool.

To make a true Mint Julep*

THERE is only one approved and authentic Method of making a *Virginia* Mint Julep—and to this Truth every good *Virginian* will agree. After many Years of Study and patient Investigation the Author is able to report that on this precise Method, few *Virginians* are able to agree. A Symposium held with some of the better Julep-makers finds them in Agreement with the following:

A Julep Glass or Goblet is not the proper Container in which to serve Salads composed of Oranges, Pineapples, Lemons, Cherries and other outlandish Fruits, such as are commonly found in some Establishments which pretend to serve Juleps.

Two Things will inevitably ruin any Julep, the first of which is too much Sugar, and the second, too little Whisky. Having observed carefully the foregoing, take a long, thin, glass Tumbler or a Silver Goblet and place it on a Tray. In the Bottom place the Leaves from a Sprig of Mint and add one half Tablespoonful of powdered Sugar. Crush the Mint well with the Sugar, and dissolve in a Tablespoonful of Water. Pack the Glass full with very finely-crushed Ice, trying not to wet the Outside of the Glass. Pour into this a Glass of Whisky (Whisky distilled from Corn is traditional but that made from Rye or other Grain is permissible). Some Authorities, having packed the Glass well with Ice, pour in the
Whisky

Whiſky until the Glaſs is full. Stir gently until the
Glaſs is well-froſted on the Outſide. Decorate on
Top with three Sprigs of Mint and ſerve.

(A *Williamſburg* Sympoſium 1699-1938.)

A Negus *

RUB a ſmall Lump of Sugar over a Lemon until
it is well-flavored. Put it in a heavy Glaſs and
add two Teaſpoons of Lemon Juice. Pour into this
a large Wine Glaſsful of Port or Sherry. Fill the
Glaſs with freſh boiling Water and ſerve up with
grated Nutmeg on Top.

(Recipe derived from one firſt popularized
by Colonel *Francis Negus*, who died in 1732.
This popular Drink was known in *England* and
her Colonies by this Name.)

Panada *

PUT the Crumbs of Bread in a Bowl, add a Glaſs
of Wine or a Spoonfull of Rum—or Vinegar, as
may ſuit beſt—ſome grated Nutmeg, Butter, and
Sugar, Spice as Fancy may direct—pour the Water
on boiling hot.

(Manuſcript Cook Book, prior 1839.
Morton Family of *Charlotte* County, *Virginia*.)

To make Orange Wine

TO every Gallon of Water put two Pounds &
half of Sugar, beat the Whites of two Eggs well
& put them to the Water & Sugar, let it boil one
Hour & ſcum it well; to a Gallon of this Water put
the Juice and Inſide of eight Oranges, pare them
very thin; when the Water is almoſt cold put it all
together

together with a little Yeast, let it stand two or three Days, stirring it twice a Day, then strain it & put it into the Vessell; if you please you may add a Pint of Brandy to each Gallon. If it is ten or twelve Gallons let it stand five or six Months & in proportion according to the Quantity you make.

(Wines & Cookery. *English* Manuscript Book, c-1740. Owned by *Colonial Williamsburg*.)

Orgeat

A Necessary Refreshment at all Parties

BOIL two Quarts of Milk with a Stick of Cinnamon, and let it stand to be quite cold, first taking out the Cinnamon, blanch four Ounces of the best sweet Almonds, pound them in a Marble Mortar with a little Rose-water; mix them well with the Milk, sweeten it to your Taste, and let it boil a few Minutes only, lest the Almonds should be oily; strain it through a very fine Sieve till quite smooth, and free from the Almonds, serve it up either cold or lukewarm, in Glasses with Handles.

(Mrs. *Randolph's* Virginia Housewife, 1831.)

Peach Cordial

GATHER ripe cling-stone Peaches, wipe off the Down, cut them to the Stone in several Places and put them in a Cask; when filled with Peaches, pour on as much Peach Brandy as the Cask will hold; let it stand six or eight Weeks, then draw it off, put in Water until reduced to the Strength of Wine; to each Gallon of this, add one Pound of good

good brown Sugar—diſſolve it, and pour the Cordial into a Caſk juſt large enough to hold it—when perfectly clear, it is fit for Uſe.

(Mrs. *Randolph's* Virginia Houſewife, 1831.)

To make a Poſſet with Ale, King William's Poſſet

TAKE a Quart of Cream and mix with it a Pint of Ale, then beat the Yolks of ten Eggs, and the Whites of four; when they are well beaten, put them to your Cream and Ale; ſweeten it to your Taſte, and ſlice ſome Nutmeg in it; ſet it over the Fire, and keep it ſtirring all the While, and when 'tis thick, and before it boils, take it off, and pour it into the Baſon you ſerve it in to the Table.

(Mrs. *E. Smith's* Compleat Houſewife, *Williamſburg,* 1742.)

Mulled Wine*

GRATE one half a Nutmeg into a Pint of Wine and ſweeten to your Taſte with Loaf-ſugar. Set it over the Fire and when it boils take it off the Fire to cool. Beat the Yolks of four Eggs very well, ſtrain them and add to them a little cold Wine, then mix them with yᵣ hot Wine gradually. Pour it backward and forward ſeveral Times till it looks fine and light, then ſet it on the Fire and heat it very gradually till it is quite hot and pretty thick, and pour it up and down ſeveral Times. Put it in Chocolate Cups and ſerve it with long, narrow Toaſt.

(Manuſcript Cook Book, c-1801, of Mrs. *Frances Bland Tucker Coalter.* Owned by Dr *St. George Tucker Grinnan, Richmond.*)

Quince

Quince Wine

TAKE twenty large Quinces, gathered when they be dry and full ripe. Wipe them clean with a coarſe Cloth, and grate them with a large Grate or Raſp as near the Cores as you can; but do not touch the Cores. Boil a Gallon of Spring-water, throw in your Quinces, and let them boil ſoftly about a quarter of an Hour. Then ſtrain them well into an earthen Pan on two Pounds of double-refined Sugar. Pare the Peel off two large Lemons, throw them in, and ſqueeze the Juice through a Sieve. Stir it about till it be very cool, and then toaſt a thin bit of Bread very brown, rub a little Yeſt on it, and let the Whole ſtand cloſe-covered twenty-four Hours. Then take out the Toaſt and Lemon, put the Wine in a Caſk, keep it three Months, and then bottle it. If you make a twenty-gallon Caſk, let it ſtand ſix Months before you bottle it; and remember, when you ſtrain your Quinces, to wring them hard in a coarſe Cloth.

(*John Farley's London* Art of Cookery, 1787.
From *Brookbury, Cheſterfield County, Virginia.*)

Raſpberry Vinegar

MEASURE your Raſpberries into a Bowl, and pour over them an equal Quantity of Vinegar. The next Day take out the Fruit and add as much more to the ſame Vinegar. The Day following, re-move the Raſpberries as before and again replace them with Freſh and on the fourth Day put to each Pint of Liquid Pound a of Loaf-ſugar—place it in a
Skillet

Skillet on a gentle Fire, ſimmer and ſkim it for a
ſhort Time when it will be ready to bottle for Uſe
—Seal it down well.

(Manuſcript Cook Book, *Charlotteſville*, 1836.
Owned by Mrs. *Virginia Graſly Griffin.*)

Regent Punch*

TO one Pint of ſtrong black Tea (in which put
the Rind of four Lemons cut very thin). Two
Pounds of Sugar, Juice of ſix Lemons, Juice of ſix
Oranges, one Pint of *French* Brandy, one Pint of
Rum, two Quarts of Champagne. Serve in a Bowl
with plenty of Ice.

(Early nineteenth Century Recipe, *Charlotte* County, *Virginia.*)

Roman *Punch*

TO make a Gallon take one and a half Pints of
Lemon Juice, Rinds of two Lemons grated on
Sugar, one Pint of Rum, half a Pint of Brandy,
two Quarts of Water, three Pounds of Loaf-ſugar,
a Pint-bottle of Champagne. Mix all together, and
chill.

(Old *Richmond* Recipe.)

To make Rum or Brandy Shrub*

TO a Gallon of Rum put a Quart of Orange Juice,
one Pound & half of double-refined Sugar &
the Ryne of two Oranges cut very thin. Let ſtand
in a Caſk ſix or ſeven Days, or till 'tis fine, then
bottle it off for Uſe.

(Wines & Cookery. *Engliſh* Manuſcript Book, c-1740.
Owned by Colonial *Williamſburg.*)

To

PLATE IV.

The King's Arms in the Duke of Gloucester Street at Williamsburg.

E. JONES.

To make Shrub*

TAKE two Quarts of Brandy, and put it in a large Bottle, and put into it the Juice of five Lemons and Peels of two, half a Nutmeg, ſtop it up, and let it ſtand three Days, and add to it three Pints of White-wine, a Pound and half of Sugar; mix it, and ſtrain it twice thro' a Flannel, and bottle it up; 'tis a pretty Wine and a Cordial.

(Mrs. *E. Smith's* Compleat Houſewife, *Williamſburg*, 1742.)

Shrub

TAKE one Pint Juice, two Pounds brown Sugar, three Pints Spirit, of this Mixture put one Wine-glaſs in yᵣ Toddy Meaſure which then fill up with yᵣ ſweetened Toddy Spirit, and add two more Meaſures of the ſame Spirit and about one third of a Wine-glaſs of powdered Sugar. Theſe will make three Quarts of excellent Toddy. Note. When you mix your Fruit do it in a Stone Pot taking out the Seed of the Fruit which will give a Bitterneſs. Stir the Mixture well—tie it up very cloſe and let it ſtand two Days. It will then have a curdled Appearance and the Clear will be very pure. Strain thro' a Flannel, and bottle for Uſe.

(Manuſcript Cook Book, c-1801, of Mrs. *Frances Bland Tucker Coalter.* Owned by Dr. *St. George Tucker Grinnan, Richmond.*)

Tea Punch*

TO three Cups of ſtrong green Tea put the Rind of ſix Lemons, pared very thin, one and one-half Pounds of Sugar, Juice of ſix Lemons. Stir together

gether a few Minutes, then ſtrain, and laſtly add
one Quart of good Rum. Fill the Glaſſes with
cruſhed Ice when uſed. It will keep bottled.

(Old *Williamſburg* Recipe.)

To make very fine Syllabubs

TAKE a Quart and half a Pint of Cream, a Pint
of *Rheniſh*, half a Pint of Sack, three Lemons,
near a Pound of double-refin'd Sugar; beat and
ſift the Sugar and put it to your Cream, grate off
the yellow Rind of your three Lemons and put that
in; ſqueeze the Juice of the three Lemons into your
Wine, and put that to your Cream; then beat all
together with a Whiſk juſt half an Hour; then take
it up all together with a Spoon, and fill your
Glaſſes. It will keep good nine or ten Days, and is
beſt three or four Days old. Theſe are called *The
everlaſting Syllabubs*.

(Mrs. *E. Smith's* Compleat Houſewife, *Williamſburg*, 1742.)

To make whipt Syllabubs

TAKE a Quart of Cream, not too thick, and a
Pint of Sack, and the Juice of two Lemons;
ſweeten it to your Palate, and put it into a broad
earthen Pan, and with a Whiſk whip it, and as the
Froth riſes, take it off with a Spoon, and lay it in
your Syllabub Glaſſes; but firſt you muſt ſweeten
ſome Claret, or Sack, or White-wine and ſtrain it,
and put ſeven or eight Spoonfuls of the Wine into
your Glaſſes, and then gently lay in your Froth.
Set them by. Do not make them long before you
uſe them.   (Mrs. *E. Smith's* Compleat Houſewife,
                         Williamſburg, 1742.)

To

To make Toddy — Mrs. Tucker*

TAKE one Gallon of Rum and one Pound of Sugar, brown, well mixed in a Pot, kept cloſely stopped till clear—ſay two Days—and then carefully racked off in a Jug.

(Manuſcript Cook Book, c-1801,
of Mrs. *Frances Bland Tucker Coalter*.
Owned by Dr. *St. George Tucker Grinnan, Richmond*.)

Of Chriſtmas in VIRGINIA

Now *Chriſtmas* comes, 'tis fit that we
   Should feaſt and ſing, and merry be
Keep open Houſe, let Fiddlers play
   A Fig for Cold, ſing Care away
And may they who thereat repine
   On brown Bread and on ſmall Beer dine

(*Virginia* Almanack, 1766.)

IN this Manner the old Almanack-maker heralded the Advent of that Holiday of all Holidays in *Virginia*—*Chriſtmas*—a Holiday not obſerved with juſt one Day of Feſtivity, but with a Round of Church-going, Feaſting, Drinking, Dancing, Hunting and Celebration, which began a full Week before *Chriſtmas* and extended until the Sixth of January, or *Twelfth Night*.

Scholars at the College of *William and Mary* contrived to lengthen their *Chriſtmas* Holidays by barring-out their Preſident and Maſters until
pledged

pledged an early Releaſe from Claſſes. After ſubmitting meekly to the Barring-out, the Faculty entered the College Buildings to partake of Food and other Entertainment; and often provided Funds for Ammunition for *Chriſtmas* Guns.

Houſeholds always noted for their generous Hoſpitality, at this Seaſon extended an even fuller Meaſure of Diverſion to Travellers and Others. Monſieur *Durand,* a *Frenchman* journeying through *Virginia* in the *Chriſtmas* holiday Seaſon in 1686, wrote:

> The *Chriſtmas* holidays were drawing near; Monſieur *Parker* . . . wiſhed to ſpend *Chriſtmas* Day in *Maryland.* As it was but five or ſix Leagues away, we had no Intention of letting him go alone. Conſequently we decided to paſs the Night at Colonel *Fichoux'* [*Fitzhugh's*], whoſe Houſes ſtand along the Banks of the great *Pethomak* [*Potomac*] River . . .
>
> Monſieur *Wormeley* is ſo well beloved and eſteemed in this Country that all the honeſt people in the neighborhood came to ſee him and would not leave him, ſo we rode twenty ſtrong to Colonel *Fichoux'* [*Fitzhugh's*], but he has ſuch a large eſtabliſhment that he did not mind. We were all of us provided with Beds, one for two men. He treated us royally, there was good Wine and all kinds of beverages, ſo there was a great deal of carouſing. He had ſent for three Fiddlers, a Jeſter, a tight-rope Dancer, an Acrobat who tumbled around, and they gave us all the Entertainment one could wiſh for. It was very cold, yet no one ever thinks of going near the Fire, for they never put leſs than a Cartload of wood in the Fireplace and the whole Room is kept warm.

From

From Plantation to Plantation the Scene was one of Excitement and Feſtivity. *Philip Vickers Fithian*, a young Tutor from *Princeton*, who was in charge of the little School at *Nomini* Hall, the *Carter* Plantation, ſaid that for a Week or more nothing had been heard in Converſation but the Balls, Fox-hunts, fine Entertainments and good Fellowſhip which were to be exhibited at the approaching *Chriſtmas*. His Fellow-tutor, Mr. *Goodlet*, had been barred-out of his School for the Holidays.

In his Diary on December 18, 1773, young *Fithian* wrote:

> . . . When the Candles were lighted, we all repaired, for the laſt Time, into the Dancing Room; firſt each Couple danced a Minuet; then all joined as before in the Country Dances, theſe continued till half after ſeven when at the Propoſal of ſeveral, we played Button, to get Pawns for Redemption; here I could join with them, and indeed it was carried on with Sprightlineſs, and Decency; in the Courſe of redeeming my Pawns I had ſeveral Kiſſes of the Ladies! Half after eight we were rung into Supper. The Room looked luminous and ſplendid; four very large Candles burning on the Table where we ſupped; three others in different Parts of the Room; a gay, ſociable Aſſembly, and four well inſtructed Waiters! So ſoon as we roſe from Supper, the Company formed into a Semicircle round the Fire, and Mr. *Lee*, by the Voice of the Company was choſen Pope, and the Reſt of the Company were appointed Friars, in the Play called "Break the "Pope's Neck." Here we had great Diverſion in the reſpective Judgments upon Offenders, but we were all diſmiſſed by ten, and retired to our ſeveral Rooms.

Fithian

Fithian related exciting Events that were held that *Chriſtmas*. Mrs. *Carter* gave a Ball for her Friends and on *Chriſtmas* Eve when Guns were fired throughout the Neighbourhood "the Negroes "ſeemed inſpired with new Life." Early *Chriſtmas* Morning, Guns were fired all round the Houſe.

The Negroes, excuſed from all but houſehold Duties, were given new Clothes and Shoes, they appeared at the great Houſe to wiſh each Perſon "Joyful *Chriſtmas*" and to collect ſmall Sums of Money for their *Chriſtmas* Boxes. The Coachman, the Barber, the Laundreſs, the waiting Boys, the Poſtillions came—a conſtant Proceſſion.

The Fire-crackers which ſtill pop loudly in *Virginia* at this Seaſon are remindful of the old Cuſtom of *Chriſtmas* Guns. In December, 1804, *Robert Mitchell*, Eſq., the Mayor of *Richmond*, wrote, aſſuring the Governor of *Virginia* that he would do his beſt to follow the Governor's Advice to prevent the Evil of unlawful Gaming, then added:

> . . . but it does appear to me to be impoſſible to prevent firing what is called *Chriſtmas* Guns, being an old eſtabliſhed Cuſtom, although there is an Ordinance of the City Police fixing a Fine of 5s. for every Offence of firing Guns within this City.

The Church was decked with Cedar, Holly, Miſtletoe, and Evergreens and became the Orbit about which Life in Town and Country revolved—but in the Houſehold the real Center of Activity was the Kitchen. Here the buſy Houſe-wife and all the Houſehold Servants entered into a ritualiſtic Preparation of Plum Puddings, Fruit Cakes, Egg Nogs, and Mincemeat Pies, bringing

out

out for the Purpose ancient Recipes that were as
valued a Part of the Family Inheritance as Great-
grandfather's Sword, or Great-grandmama's best
silver Spoon.

William Byrd, writing to his Friend, Sir *John
Randolph*, in 1736, of the *Randolphs'* Impatience to
return to *Williamsburg* after a Holiday Visit at
Westover, seems to attribute their hasty Departure
over the wintry Roads to Lady *Randolph's* im-
patient Desire to preside over the Holiday Cookery
of her own Household:

> In hopes you may be safe at *Williamsburg* by
> this Time and my Lady up to the Elbow in Sassages
> & Black Puddings, I can't forbear Greeting you
> well, and signifying our Joy at your Arrival in
> your own Chimney Corner. We have had the
> good Nature to be in Pain for you ever since you
> left us, 'tho in good Truth your Obstinacy in ex-
> posing your Wife and Children to be starved with
> Cold and buried in the Mire, hardly deserved it.
> No doubt you were obliged to have Pioneers to
> clean the Way before you as far as Mr. *Custis'*
> Plantation, and you needed four Yokes of Oxen,
> as they do in the deep Roads of *Sussex* to drag you
> thro' the Dirt. I dare say notwithstanding your
> fine Horses you were not able to go along faster
> than Mr. *Attorney* walks.

The *Williamsburg* to which the *Randolphs* re-
turned has always made much of the Holiday of
Holidays. It was a Tradition that carried un-
changed through even the genteely-decaying Years
of the early nineteenth Century. The *Christmas*
Spirit which pervaded the old City is best told in
the Story of the first *Christmas* Tree in *Williamsburg*.

In

In 1842, before the Custom of decorating a *Christmas* Tree had found its Way from the old World to this Region of the new, a young political Exile from *Germany* was a Guest in the *Tucker* House. He had been released from a long Prison Confinement and had fled to this Country with sixty cheap Volumes of the Classics his only worldly Goods. He taught for a While in *Philadelphia* and then came to the College of *William and Mary* as Professor of Ancient Languages.

The sympathetic Friendship of the Family and its Friends made young *Charles Frederick Ernest Minnigerode* welcome in the *Tucker* Household, but as the Holiday Season approached, he talked longingly of *Christmas* in his native *Germany*, of Carols, and of Fir Trees decorated with Tinsel and Stars and Candles.

The young *Tucker* Children asked that such a *Christmas* Tree be brought to their House, and eagerly improvised Ornaments from Twists of colored Paper, Fruit and a gilded Paper Star. When *Christmas* came, other Children of the Neighborhood gathered and thrilled to the Innovation—there were Hymns and Carols and *Christmas* Spirit enough to link young *Minnigerode* forever to his adopted Country.

* * *

To return again to the old *Virginia* Almanack Makers, we can find in their Pages of Penny Wisdom the warmest of *Christmas* Wishes, the most expressive

preſſive of Greetings for the Seaſon, with which we here conclude:

> We wiſh you Health, and good Fires; Victuals, Drink and good Stomachs, innocent Diverſion, and good Company; honeſt Trading, and good Succeſs; loving Courtſhip, and good Wives, and laſtly a merry CHRISTMAS and a happy NEW YEAR.

For Chriſtmas

Roaſt Turkey *

AFTER waſhing the Fowl and putting it in Salt Water to ſtand for ſome Hours, pour ſome hot Water into the Body of the Turkey to heat it well. Wipe it dry inſide and out, then fill the Body and Breaſt of the Turkey with Dreſſing which has already been made. For Dreſſing, prepare Bread in Quantity proportioned to the Size of the Fowl. A twelve-pound Turkey will require a Quart Loaf to ſtuff it properly; a ſmall Hen only half as much. Break up the Bread between your Hands, mixing well with it a Tableſpoonful of Butter and Seaſoning of black Pepper, Salt and a Tableſpoonful of Butter and Seaſoning of black Pepper, Salt and a Teaſpoonful of bruiſed Celery-ſeed; make the Dreſſing hold together with a little hot Water, or Yolk of an Egg and Water. After filling with the Dreſſing, ſew it up, rub it all over with fine Salt, tie the Legs and Wings cloſe down and put it to roaſt with a moderate Fire. In about half an Hour baſte

it

it all over with Butter and duft on the Flour. Do this three or four Times while roafting; it will make it look nice and brown. Pour the Gravy each Time into a Bowl to keep it from burning. For a Turkey of about ten Pounds, roaft about three Hours.

(Recipe ufed by *Dorothea Dandridge Henry*, Wife of *Patrick Henry*, at *Red Hill*, *Charlotte* County, *Virginia*.)

Old Virginia *Roaft Pig*✻

A FAT Pig about three Weeks old is beft for a Roaft. Wafh it out thoroughly infide and out. Chop the Liver fine with Bread-crumbs, Onions, Parfley, Pepper, Salt, and Potatoes boiled and mafhed. Make into a Pafte with Butter and Egg. Put the Stuffing into the Pig and few it up. Put in a Baking-pan with a little Water and roaft over a bright Fire, bafting well with Butter; rub frequently, alfo, with a Piece of Lard tied in a clean Rag. When thoroughly done, lay the Pig Back up in a Difh, and put a red Apple or pickled Mango in the Mouth. Make a Sauce with fome of the Stuffing, a Glafs of Wine, and fome of the Dripping. Serve with the roaft Pig, and alfo in a Gravy Boat.

(Old Recipe from *Highland Springs*.)

Pork Pot Pie

A Favorite Chriftmas *Difh with* Virginia *Negroes*

CHINES and Spare-ribs are generally ufed for this Difh, but any Part of lean Pork will anfwer. Crack the Bones and cut into Pieces two Inches long. Line the Pot with Paftry. Put in the

Meat,

Meat, ſprinkle with Salt and Pepper, then a Layer
of parboiled *Iriſh* Potatoes, ſliced, and ſo continue
until the Pot is nearly full. Then pour in a Quart of
cold Water and put on the upper Cruſt, cutting a
ſmall round Hole out of the Middle of the Cruſt,
through which you can pour hot Water ſhould the
Gravy boil away too faſt. Put on the Cover of the
Pot and boil about two Hours. When done, remove
the upper Cruſt carefully, turn out the Meat and
Gravy into a Bowl, and take out the lower Cruſt.
Put this upon a hot Diſh, put the Meat and Potatoes upon it, pour the Gravy over it, and cover
with the top Cruſt. This can be browned by holding
over it a red-hot Oven Lid or Stove Plate.

(Old Recipe, *Richmond, Virginia.*)

Cheſs Cakes*

CREAM one Pound of Butter and one Pound
of Sugar well together. Beat the Yolks of
twelve Eggs light in Color and add to the Butter
and Sugar. Put in one-eighth Teaſpoon of Salt
and ſtir in three-fourths of a Cup of good white
Wine. Bake in ſmall Paſtry Shells rolled thin in
Muffin Tins. Fill the Shells about three-fourths
full. Bake in a moderately hot Oven. Serve cold.
Will keep for ſeveral Days in a cool Place.

(Old *Morgan* Family Recipe.
Prov'd *Market Square Tavern* Kitchen, 1937.)

Egg Nog*

BEAT Yolks of twelve Eggs well. Add two and
a fourth Cups of Sugar and continue to beat
well. Add one Quart of good Brandy, one Pint of
Jamaica

Jamaica Rum alternately and ſlowly. To this add three Quarts of heavy Cream and fold in half of the beaten Egg Whites. Beat remaining ſix Egg Whites very ſtiff and add one Cup powdered Sugar. Then ſtir lightly into this one Quart of Cream and fold this Mixture into the other Ingredients. Let ſtand from ſix to twelve Hours in a cold Place before ſerving.

(Old *Virginia* Recipe.
Adapted *Blair* Kitchen, 1938.)

Fruit Cake*

CREAM one and a half Pounds of unſalted Butter, and ſift in one and a half Pounds of Flour. Beat the Yolks of eighteen Eggs very light, then beat into them ſlowly a Pound and a half of Sugar, then mix with them the ſtiffly beaten Whites. Combine. Add one-fourth Pound each of finely cut candied Orange-peel and Lemon-peel, candied Cherries; three fourths of a Pound of finely cut Citron and three Pounds of well-cleaned Currants which have ſoaked Overnight in one Cup of Brandy. Add the Fruits to the Batter and bake ſlowly in Pans lined with well-greaſed brown Paper for ſeveral Hours.

(Recipe prior to 1776, *Graves* and *Hatcher* Families.)

Fruit Cake*

CREAM one Pound of Butter with one Pound of Sugar, add the beaten Yolks of twelve Eggs, and one Cup of Molaſſes. Clean two Pounds of Currants and two of Raiſins and cut fine one Pound of Citron, one-half Pound of blanched Almonds, one-fourth Pound of Orange-peel, one-
fourth

fourth Pound of Lemon-peel, one-half Pound of candied Cherries, one-half Pound of Figs, and ſift over them one Pound of Flour in which there are two Teaſpoons of Allſpice, two grated Nutmegs, two Teaſpoons of Cinnamon, one of Cloves, one ſcant Teaſpoon of Soda and three of baking Powder. Work the Fruits, Almonds, Flour and Spice well together before adding to Butter Mixture. Thin with one Cup of Sherry and laſtly add the beaten Egg Whites. If the Batter is too firm, add more Sherry. Fill the well-greaſed tube Pans (which have been lined with greaſed brown Paper) two-thirds full. Bake very ſlowly four or five Hours.

(Old Recipe, c-1829, *Sparta, Virginia.*)

Another Way*

FOLLOWING the above Directions make your Cake of the following Materials: one Dozen Eggs, two Pounds of Sugar, one Pound of Butter, four Pounds of Raiſins, two Pounds of Currants, one-half Pound of Citron, one-half Pound of Dates, one Teaſpoon each of Cinnamon, Cloves, Allſpice, Ginger, Nutmeg and one Pint of Sherry.

(Recipe, c-1737, *Courtland, Virginia.*)

Williamſburg *Fruit Cake**

TAKE two Pounds of ſeeded Raiſins, two Pounds of ſeedleſs Raiſins, two Pounds of Currants (white Raiſins are not ſo gritty and may be uſed), three fourths of a Pound of Dates, one Pound of Citron, one fourth Pound each of Lemon-peel and Orange-peel, one fourth Pound of blanched Almonds cut in long Strips, one fourth Pound of
Engliſh

English Walnuts cut fine, one half Pound
of candied Cherries, one Glafs of Currant Jelly.
Clean and prepare thefe the Day before you bake
your Cake. Cut Cherries and Dates in Quarters,
fhred Citron and other Peel. Blanch Almonds and
foak in hot Water before cutting in long Slips.
Mix together with the Jelly, pour over this a Pint
of Peach or Apple Brandy and ftore in a covered
Crock or Bowl Overnight.

To make the Cake: Cream one Pound of Butter
with one half Pound of Sugar. Beat the Yolks of
one Dozen Eggs well, and beat into them one half
Pound of Sugar. Combine. Add the well-beaten
Whites and mix with the Fruits. Sift together one
Pound of Flour, two Teafpoons of Allfpice, two
Teafpoons of Cinnamon, one Teafpoon each of
Nutmeg, Cloves, Mace and Salt and ftir in with
one Cup of Sherry. Enough Flour will be needed
to make a ftiff Batter. Pack firmly into tube Cake-
Pans lined with greafed brown Paper and fteam
about three Hours. Bake in a moderate Oven and
teft with a Straw, twenty-five Minutes fhould be
enough. Store in covered Tins or Crocks and
moiften occafionally with a little Sherry and the
Cakes will keep indefinitely.

(The Author's own Recipe.
Adapted from a *Virginia* Recipe, c-1723.)

A rich Fruit Cake*

HAVE the following Articles prepared, before
you begin the Cake: four Pounds of Flour
dried and fifted, four Pounds of Butter, wafhed to
free it from Salt, two Pounds of Loaf-fugar,
pounded,

pounded, a quarter of a Pound of Mace, the same of Nutmegs powdered; wash four Pounds of Currants clean, pick and dry them; blanch one Pound of sweet Almonds, and cut them in very thin Slices; stone two Pounds of Raisins, cut them in two, and strew a little Flour over to prevent their sticking together, and two Pounds of Citron sliced thin; break thirty Eggs, separating the Yelks and Whites; work the Butter to a Cream with your Hand—put in alternately, Flour, Sugar, and the Froth from both Whites and Yelks, which must be beaten separately, and only the Froth put in. When all are mixed and the Cake looks very light, add the Spice, with half a Pint of Brandy, the Currants and Almonds: butter the Mould well, pour in Part of the Cake, strew over it some Raisins and Citron —do this until all is in: set it in a well-heated Oven: when it has risen, and the Top is coloured, cover it with Paper; it will require three Hours' baking— it must be iced.

(Mrs. *Randolph's* Virginia Housewife, 1831.)

White Fruit Cake*

CREAM one half Pound of Butter with one Pound of Sugar, add four well-beaten Egg Yolks. Cut one Pound of blanched Almonds in fine Strips and the following Fruits in small Pieces: one fourth Pound of candied Cherries, one half Pound of candied Pineapple, one half Pound of Citron, one Pound of white Raisins. Dredge Fruit well with Part of one Pound of Flour, add remaining Flour and one small Cup of Sherry alternately.
Stir

Stir in one half Pound of grated Cocoanut and the floured Fruit. Fold in the well-beaten Egg Whites. Bake in a flow Oven about four Hours.

(Recipe, c-1830, from *Richmond, Virginia.*)

*Another Way**

SIFT one Pound of Flour with one Teaspoonful of Soda, two Teaspoonfuls Cream of Tartar. Cream one-half Pound of Butter, add one Pound white Sugar, and beat it awhile; then add the well-beaten Whites of twelve Eggs and the Flour. After beating the Batter fufficiently, add about one third of the Fruit, referving the Reft to add in Layers, as you put the Batter in the Cake-moulds. For the Fruit ufe two Pounds Citron, cut in thin, long Strips; two Pounds Almonds, blanched and cut in Strips and one large Cocoanut, grated. Bake flowly and carefully, as you do other Fruit Cake.

(Traditional *Virginia* Recipe.)

*To make Mince Pies the beft Way**

TAKE three Pounds of Suet, fhred very fine, and chopped as fmall as poffible, two Pounds of Raifins, ftoned and chopped as fine as poffible, two Pounds of Currants, nicely picked, wafhed, rubbed and dried at the Fire, half a hundred of fine Pippins, pared, cored and chopped fmall, half a Pound of fine Sugar, pounded fine, a quarter of an Ounce of Mace, a quarter of an Ounce of Cloves, two large Nutmegs; all beat fine, put all together into a great Pan, and mix it well together with half a Pint of Brandy, and half a Pint of Sack; put it

it down clofe in a Stone-pot, and it will keep good
four Months. When you make your Pies, take a
little Difh, fomething bigger than a Soup-plate, lay
a very thin Cruft all over it, lay a thin Layer of
Meat, and then a thin Layer of Citron cut very
thin, then a Layer of Mince-meat, and a thin Layer
of Orange-peel cut thin, over that a little Meat,
fqueeze half the Juice of a fine *Seville* Orange or
Lemon, and pour in three Spoonfuls of red Wine;
lay on your Cruft, and bake it nicely. Thefe Pies
eat finely cold. If you make them in little Patties,
mix your Meat and Sweetmeats accordingly. If you
chufe Meat in your Pies, parboil a Neat's Tongue,
peel it, and chop the Meat as fine as poffible, and
mix with the Reft; or two Pounds of the Infide of
a   Sirloin of Beef boiled.

(Mrs. Hannah Glaffe's Art of Cookery, London, 1774.)

To make Mincemeat for Pies*

BOIL either Calves' or Hogs' Feet till perfectly
tender, rub them through a Colander; when
cold, pafs them through again, and it will come out
like pearl Barley; take one Quart of this, one of
chopped Apples, the fame of Currants, wafhed and
picked, Raifins ftoned and cut, of good brown
Sugar, Suet nicely chopped, and Cider, with a Pint
of Brandy; add a Teafpoonful of pounded Mace,
one of Cloves and of Nutmegs; mix all thefe together intimately. When the Pies are to be made,
take out as much of this Mixture as may be neceffary; to each Quart of it, add a Teafpoonful of
pounded black Pepper, and one of Salt; this
greatly improves the Flavour, and can be better
mixed

mixed with a small Portion than with the whole
Mass. Cover the Moulds with Paste, put in a Suffi-
ciency of Mincemeat, cover the Top with Citron,
sliced thin, and lay on it a Lid garnished around
with Paste cut in fanciful Shapes. They may be
eaten either hot or cold, but are best when hot.

(Mrs. *Randolph's* Virginia Housewife, 1831.)

Mince Pies*

TAKE two Pounds of Beef, two and a half of
Beef-suet, twelve large Apples, two Pounds of
Raisins stoned and chopped, two Pounds of Currants, half an Ounce of Cinnamon, one Nutmeg,
half a Pound of brown Sugar; half an Ounce of
Cloves, a small Quantity of Mace, one Pound of
Citron not cut up very fine, one Quart of Brandy,
one of Wine—the half of these Ingredients, that is
the half of each of them, will do for a small Family—if the Weather is cool they will keep some
Time. (Manuscript Cook Book prior to 1839, *Morton* Family
of *Charlotte* County, *Virginia*.)

Mince Pies*

TAKE three Pounds of Suet shred very fine &
chopped as small as possible, two Pounds of
Raisins stoned & well chopped, two Pounds of Currants nicely picked, washed & rubbed & dried at
the Fire, half a Hundred of fine Pippins pared,
cored & chopped small, half a Pound of fine Sugar,
a quarter of an Ounce of Mace, a quarter of an
Ounce of Cloves, two large Nutmegs all beat fine.
Put all together into a great Pan & mix it well with
half

half a Pint of Brandy, half a Pint of Sack, put it down cloſe in a Stone Pot & it will keep good four Months. When you bake your Pies take a little Diſh ſomething bigger than a Soup-plate & lay a thin Cruſt all over it, lay a thin Layer of Meat & then a thin Layer of Citron cut very thin, then a Layer of Mincemeat, & then a thin Layer of Orange-peel cut thin, over that a little Meat, & pour in three Spoonfuls of red Wine, lay on your Cruſt, & bake it nicely. Theſe Pies eat finely cold. If you chuſe Meat in your Pies chop in two or three Pounds of a Sirloin of Beef boiled.

(Manuſcript Cook Book. *Charlotteſville*, 1836. Owned by Mrs. *Virginia Graſty Griffin*.)

Mince Meat for Pies*

SIMMER two Pounds of Beef ſlowly until ten-der; cool and chop fine. Mix with it two Pounds of ſtoned Raiſins; two Pounds of ſeedleſs Raiſins; two Pounds of cleaned Currants; one Pound of finely cut Citron; one and a half Pounds of finely cut candied Lemon-peel; four Pounds of Apples which have been peeled, cored and cut fine; two Pounds of finely chopped Beef-ſuet; two Pounds of light brown Sugar; one Tableſpoon each of Cloves and Mace; two Tableſpoons of Cinnamon; two grated Nutmegs and one Teaſpoon of Salt. Mix all together well, add one Pint of Brandy. Store in a covered ſtone Jar in a cool Place.

(*Cuſtis & Lee* Family Recipe, c-1760. From *Cheſter*, *Virginia*.)

Plumb

Plumb Cake—Mrs. Cary—*or Pudding**

TAKE one and a fourth Pounds Flour, one
Pound Sugar, one Pound Butter, twelve Eggs.
Cream the Butter and Flour together till quite
light. Beat the Yolks and Whites of Eggs ſeparately,
beat the Sugar into the Yolks and when light add
the Whites, then mix them with the Butter and
Flour. Put in one and a fourth Pounds ſtoned Raiſins, cut up, or the ſame of Currants with three
Spoonfuls beaten Mace and two Wine-glaſſes
French Brandy. It muſt be baked in a quick Oven
and the Top muſt be hot enough to turn it unleſs
covered with Paper. It is very nice as a Pudding
but too large for a moderate Company.

(Manuſcript Cook Book, c-1801,
of Mrs. *Frances Bland Tucker Coalter.*
Owned by Dr. *St. George Tucker Grinnan, Richmond.*)

Plumb Porridge

THIS is a famous old *Engliſh* Diſh, and though
at preſent difuſed in *London*, yet as there are
many Families in the Country who ſtill keep up the
Cuſtom of Hoſpitality, and admit this among the
Entertainments of the Seaſon, we ſhall not leave
the Cook at a Loſs how to make it.

Chuſe a fine and fleſhy Leg of Beef with the
Shin, crack the Bone in ſeveral Places, and put it
into a clean Copper with eight Gallons of Water:
Let there be a moderate Fire; add nothing to the
Meat and Water, but let them boil together till the
Meat is ready to fall from the Bones, and the Broth
is

is very strong; then strain it out, pressing the Meat hard to get out the last of the Gravy.

Wipe the Copper, and pour in the Broth.

Cut off the Tops and the Bottoms of Half a Dozen Penny-loaves, slice them, and put them into a Pot with as much of the Broth out of the Copper as will cover them; let them stand half an Hour to soak, and then set them over the Fire to boil.

When the Bread is thoroughly soft pour the Whole into the Copper to the Rest.

Let this boil up a quarter of an Hour.

While this is doing wash and pick five Pounds of Currants, put them in, and make it boil up again.

While the Currants are boiling in the Broth, stone six Pounds of Raisins, and a Pound and half of Prunes, put these in, and let them boil till they are plumped up and perfectly tender.

Then put in ten Blades of Mace, a Dozen and a half of Cloves, and half an Ounce of Nutmegs, all bruised together in a Mortar.

When the Spices have boiled up two or three Times take away the Fire, and let the Whole cool: When it is so cool that it can be tasted put in three Pounds of double-refined Sugar powdered, some Basket Salt, and a Quart of Sack.

Stir it all about, and then taste it. The Salt is the nice Article; take Care that it be neither briny nor insipid; when it is rightly seasoned put in a Quart of red Port Wine, and squeeze in three Lemons.

Stir all up very well together, and taste it once again to see if it be rightly seasoned: The Palate must judge of this; if there want more Wine, more Sugar, or more Lemon Juice, add these till it is right;

right; if it be too fharp a little Sugar takes that off, and if too fweet the Juice of Lemon is a Remedy for that: When it is thus well fuited to the Palate, ladle it out into earthen Pans, and fet it by: A proper Quantity is to be heated occafionally, and fent up to Table.

The *French* laugh outrageoufly at this old *Englifh* Difh, and to be fure it is an odd Medley: It puts one in Mind of thofe famous Medicines of Antiquity, the *Mithridate* and *Venice* Treacle, into which the Inventors ftrove to put every Thing that was good, without confulting how the feveral Things would agree with one another; there are, however, yet many good old *Englifh* Palates which are well affected to the cordial Broth.

(Mrs. *Bradley's* Britifh Houfewife, *London.*)

Plumb Pudding*

PUT in a ftone Crock or large Bowl one Pound of Currants, one Pound of *Sultana* Raifins, one half Pound of Orange-peel, one half Pound of Lemon-peel, one half Pound of Citron and one quarter of a Pound of Walnuts all chopped fine. Pour over this one Cupful of good Brandy and cover well. Soak Overnight. Mix one Pound of ground Suet, one half Pound of fifted Bread-crumbs, one Teafpoon Salt, one Pound of brown Sugar, one half Pound of Flour with one Teafpoon Cinnamon, and one fourth Teafpoon each of Nut-meg, Mace, Ginger and Cloves. Beat eight Eggs well. Stir all your Pudding very well together. Pour into buttered Molds, tie down with a clean fcalded Cloth

Cloth and boil gently for ten Hours but do not let the Water boil over it.

This Pudding will keep indefinitely, especially if moistened with Brandy. It should be reheated for three Hours in boiling Water and served with Hard Sauce.
(The Author's own Recipe.
Adapted from a *Virginia* Recipe, c-1725.)

Christmas *Pudding*※

THIS Pudding is made like the Preceding but with the following Ingredients: One Pound of Beef-suet; one Pound of seeded Raisins; one Pound of *Sultana* Raisins; one Pound of Currants; one Pound of brown Sugar; one half Pound blanched and chopped *Jordan* Almonds; one half Pound each of candied Lemon-peel and Orange-peel; one half Pound of Citron; three fourths of a Pound of fine Bread-crumbs; one fourth of a Pound of Flour; two Teaspoons each of Cinnamon, Cloves and Nutmeg, twelve Eggs and one Pint of Brandy.

(Old Recipe, *Richmond, Virginia*. Prov'd.)

Plumb Pudding※

ONE Pound of Flour—half a Pound of Butter, half a Pound of Sugar, two Whites and eight Yolks of Eggs, half Pound of Raisins stoned and cut up. The Flour and Butter rubbed well together, the Eggs and Sugar beaten tite together, one Pint of Milk, the Flour, Butter and Sugar mixed all and beat them well together dip a Cloth in boiling Water flour it thickly; pour it in, tie it

up

up—put in a Pot that boils quickly; it muſt not
ceaſe boiling a Moment—keep turning the Bag—
leſt the Fruit ſettle—Two and a half Hours will
boil it. Uſe Butter, Sugar and Wine Sauce.

(Manuſcript Cook Book, prior 1839, Morton Family
of Charlotte County, Virginia.)

Plumb Pudding

TAKE a Pound of beſt Flour, ſift it and make it
up before Sunriſe—with ſix Eggs beaten light
—a large Spoonfull of good Yeaſt and as much Milk
as will make it the Conſiſtance of Bread—let it riſe
well, knead into it half a Pound of Butter, a grated
Nutmeg, one Pound of Raiſins, ſtoned and chopped
up, mix all togather, wet the Cloth, flower it, tie
looſly, ſo the Pudding may have Room to riſe. The
Raiſins ſhould be rubbed in Flower.

(Manuſcript Cook Book, prior 1839, Morton Family
of Charlotte County, Virginia.)

Cold Sauſe*

MIX an equal Quantity of freſh Butter and
pounded Sugar—Cream together—Nutmeg
or Lemmon Drop if you like, colour it with the Sirrup
of Strawberries or Damſons Preſerves. Set it in the
Icehouſe untill cold enough to cut with a Knife.

(Manuſcript Cook Book, prior 1839, Morton Family
of Charlotte County, Virginia.)

Fine Plumb Pudding*

TAKE a Pound of Flour, one half Pound But-
ter, one half Pound Sugar, eight Yolks and two
Whites of Eggs, one Pint of Milk, one half Pound
Currants

Currants or Raiſins, ſtoned (tho three-fourths will make it better), one half a Nutmeg. The Flour and Butter muſt be rubbed together. The Milk, Flour and Butter then mixed together and beat light. The Eggs and Sugar beat together and then the other Ingredients all mingled and beat till quite light. Flour the Bag and put them in. The Pot muſt boil briſkly and muſt not be ſuffered to ceaſe for a Moment. Keep turning the Bag leaſt the Fruit ſettle to one Side. Two and half Hours will boil it. Butter and Wine with a Part of the Sugar weighed for the Pudding for Sauce, a Tea-kettle of Water ſhould be kept boiling to repleniſh the Pot if neceſſary.

(Manuſcript Cook Book, c-1801,
of Mrs. *Frances Bland Tucker Coalter.*
Owned by Dr. *St. George Tucker Grinnan, Richmond.*)

Plumb Pudding—Mrs. C. Jones*

TAKE one Pound grated Bread, one Pound Suet, two Pounds Plums, eight Eggs, Flour and Milk enough to make it of a proper Conſiſtence. Add a ſmall Quantity of Mace and Citron, a Glaſs of F. [*French*] Brandy and one of Wine. It will require four or five Hours to boil.

(Manuſcript Cook Book, c-1801,
of Mrs. *Frances Bland Tucker Coalter.*
Owned by Dr. *St. George Tucker Grinnan, Richmond.*)

Williamſburg *Plum Pudding**

MIX together one Pound of ground Beef-ſuet; one Pound of Currants; two Pounds ſeeded and cut Raiſins; one Pound of Figs cut fine; one Pound of finely-cut blanched Almonds; and one Pound

Pound of fine dry Bread-crumbs. Dredge over the Fruits ſome Flour mixed with one Teaſpoon of All-ſpice, one half Teaſpoon of Salt, two Teaſpoons of Ginger and two grated Nutmegs. Beat the Yolks of twelve Eggs very light and ſlowly beat in one Pound of brown Sugar, mix with well-beaten Whites of Eggs. Combine both, then thin with two Cups of ſweet Milk, one and one half Cup of Wine. Pack into ſmall tin Molds which are well greaſed and floured. Fill to one Inch of Top and put on a tight Cover. Stand in boiling Water for ſix Hours. Will keep any Length of Time. Reheat in boiling Water to ſerve.

(Old *Virginia* Recipe. Prov'd *Blair* Kitchen, 1938.)

To make a Yorkſhire Chriſtmas *Pie*

FIRST make a good ſtanding Cruſt, let the Wall and Bottom be very thick; bone a Turkey, a Gooſe, a Fowl, a Partridge, and a Pigeon. Seaſon them all very well, take half an Ounce of Mace, half an Ounce of Nutmegs, a quarter of an Ounce of Cloves, and half an Ounce of black Pepper, all beat fine together, two large Spoonfuls of Salt, and then mix them together. Open the Fowls all down the Back, and bone them; firſt the Pigeon, then the Partridge, cover them; then the Fowl, then the Gooſe, and then the Turkey, which muſt be large; ſeaſon them all well firſt, and lay them in the Cruſt, ſo as it will look only like a whole Turkey; then have a Hare ready caſed, and wiped with a clean Cloth. Cut it to Pieces; that is joint it; ſeaſon it, and lay it as cloſe as you can on one Side; on the
other

other Side Woodcocks, Moor Game, and what Sort of wild Fowl you can get. Season them well, and lay them close; put at least four Pounds of Butter into the Pie, then lay on your Lid, which must be a very thick one, and let it be well baked. It must have a very hot Oven, and will take at least four Hours.

This Crust will take a Bushel of Flour. In this Chapter you will see how to make it. These Pies are often sent to *London* in a Box as Presents; therefore the Walls must be well built.

(Mrs. *Hannah Glasse's* Art of Cookery, *London*, 1774.)

An

An Account of the BOOKS consulted in this WORK:

The Art of COOKERY made plain and easy, by a Lady. [Mrs. *Hannah Glasse*]. London, 1774. (Owned by *Harvard* University, *Cambridge, Massachusetts*.)

The *British* HOUSEWIFE: or, The Cook, Housekeeper's and Gardiner's Companion . . . by Mrs. *Martha Bradley*. London, printed for *S. Crowder* and *H. Woodgate* . . . [n. d.]. (Owned by Institute for Research in Social Science, *Chapel Hill, North Carolina*.)

A Collection of above three hundred Receipts in COOKERY, PHYSICK and SURGERY for the Use of all good Wives, tender Mothers, and careful Nurses, by several Hands. *London*, printed for *Henry Lintot*, 1749. (Owned by *Harvard* University, *Cambridge, Massachusetts*.)

The compleat City and Country COOK: or accomplish'd Housewife, by *Charles Carter*. London, printed for *A. Bettesworth* and *C. Hitch*, 1732. (Owned by *Harvard* University, *Cambridge, Massachusetts*.)

The compleat HOUSEWIFE: or, accomplish'd Gentlewoman's Companion: being a Collection of upwards of six Hundred of the most approved Receipts, by *E. Smith*. Ninth Edition. *London*, printed for *J. and J. Pemberton*, 1739. (Owned by *Harvard* University, *Cambridge, Massachusetts*.)

The Compleat HOUSEWIFE: or, accomplish'd Gentlewoman's Companion: being a Collection of several Hundred of the most approved Receipts . . . by *E. Smith*. Collected from the fifth Edition. *Williamsburg*, printed and sold by *William Parks*, 1742. (First *American* Book on Cookery. Copy —one of four extant—owned by *Colonial Williamsburg*, Incorporated.)

The court and country CONFECTIONER: or, The House-Keeper's Guide; to a more speedy, plain, and familiar Method of of understanding the whole Art of Confectionary, Pastry, Distilling, and the Making of fine flavoured *English* Wines from all Kinds of Fruits, Herbs and Flowers . . . by an ingenious Foreigner, now head Confectioner to the *Spanish* Ambassador in *England. London*, printed for *G. Riley* and *A. Cooke* . . . 1770. (Owned by Mr. and Mrs. *George P. Coleman, Tucker* House, *Williamsburg*.)

Directions for COOKERY in its various Branches, by Miss *Leslie.* [*Philadelphia, E. L. Carey & A. Hart*, 1838]. (Owned by Mrs. *H. D. Cole, Williamsburg*.)

HOUSEKEEPING in old *Virginia*. Containing Contributions from two hundred and fifty of *Virginia's* noted Housewives, distinguished for their Skill in the culinary Art and other Branches of domestic Economy. Edited by *Marion Cabell Tyree* . . . *Louisville, Kentucky, John P. Morton & Company*, 1890. (Owned by Miss *Emma Lou Barlow, Williamsburg*. With manuscript notes added.)

THE LADY'S COMPANION. Containing upwards of three thousand different Receipts in every Kind of Cookery: and those the best and most fashionable; being four Times the Quantity of any Book of this Sort . . . The sixth Edition, with large Additions. *London*, printed for *J. Hodges* . . . and *R. Baldwin*, 1753. (This Copy, owned by Miss *Anna Maria Dandridge* in 1756, now owned by Mrs. *Neville Mitchell Smith* of *York, Pennsylvania*.)

The *London* Art of COOKERY, and Housekeeper's complete Assistant, on a new Plan . . . by *John Farley*. Fourth Edition. *London*, printed for *J. Scatcherd* and *J. Whitaker*, 1787. (Owned by Mrs. *E. L. Bemiss, Brookbury, Chesterfield* County, *Virginia*.)

Virginia COOKERY-BOOK. Compiled by *Mary Stuart Smith. New York, Harper*, 1885. (Owned by University of *Virginia*.)

Virginia COOKERY BOOK: traditional Recipes. *Richmond Virginia* League of Women Voters, *Richmond*, 1922. (Owned by Mrs. *W. P. Clements, Richmond, Virginia*.)

The *Virginia* HOUSEWIFE: or, methodical Cook, by Mrs. *Mary Randolph* . . . Stereotype Edition, with Amendments and Additions. *Baltimore, Plaskitt & Cugle*, [1831]. (Owned by University of *Virginia*.)   **The**

The *Virginia* HOUSEWIFE: or, the methodical Cook. *Philadelphia,* published by *E. H. Butler & Company,* 1855. (Owned by *Colonial Williamsburg,* Incorporated.)

The whole DUTY OF A WOMAN: or, an infallible Guide to the fair Sex. Containing Rules, Directions, and Observations, for their Conduct and Behaviour through all Ages and Circumstances of Life, as Virgins, Wives, or Widows. With Directions, how to obtain all useful and fashionable Accomplishments suitable to the Sex. In which are comprised all Parts of good HOUSEWIFERY, particularly Rules and Receipts in every Kind of Cookery. *London,* printed for *T. Read,* 1737. (Owned by *Harvard* University, *Cambridge, Massachusetts.*)

Manuscript Cook Book of *English* WINES AND COOKERY. c. 1740. (Owned by *Colonial Williamsburg,* Incorporated.)

Manuscript COOK BOOK. c. 1801, of Mrs. *Frances Tucker Coalter,* of *Williamsburg.* (Owned by Dr. *St. George Tucker Grinnan, Richmond, Virginia.*)

Manuscript COOK BOOK. c. 1836, *Charlottesville, Virginia.* (Owned by Mrs. *Virginia Grasty Griffin, Richmond, Virginia.*)

Manuscript RECIPES. c. 1837, of Mrs. *Elizabeth Labbé Cole.* (Owned by Mrs. *H. D. Cole, Williamsburg, Virginia.*)

Manuscript COOK BOOK, prior to 1839, of the *Morton* Family of *Charlotte* County, *Virginia.* (Deposited at the College of *William and Mary, Williamsburg.*)

Manuscript COOK BOOK. c. 1825 of Miss *Margaret* [*Margaretta*] *Prentis* of *Williamsburg.* (Owned by *Robert H. Webb,* Esq., University of *Virginia.*)

Recipes contributed by Mrs. *Doris Morgan Macomber* (who conducted the experimental Kitchen in the *Market Square Tavern,* under the Direction of *John Green,* Esq., and Miss *Alice Carter*), Mrs. *Archibald Bolling Shepperson,* Miss *Jeane Lee,* Mrs. *Frank Armistead,* Mrs. *H. B. Stryker,* Mrs. *L. W. Lane,* Jr., Mrs. *Philip Nelson,* Miss *Tony Bracher,* Miss *Genevieve Yost,* Mrs. *H. Norton Mason,* Mrs. *Sarah E. Sumner,* Mrs. *Sybil Tripp,* Miss *Mildred Moss,* Mrs. *Gracie Mason* and *Robert A. Lancaster,* Esq.

THE

THE
INDEX.

Chestnut

Cutlets,

Peel

A Note to the READER.

Colonial Williamsburg's interest in early American cookery began with the desire to serve foods based on early Virginia recipes at the Travis House and the Williamsburg Inn. Home economics clubs at Virginia high schools were approached for old family recipes, local housewives offered present-day favorites that had been handed down for generations, and recipes were culled from cookbooks known to have been owned by eighteenth-century Williamsburg residents.

When Helen Bullock compiled this volume, Colonial Williamsburg owned only two early cookbooks. Mrs. Bullock persuaded rare book librarians at the Library of Congress, Harvard University, and the University of Virginia to loan early printed and manuscript cookbooks for research purposes, promising to keep the borrowed volumes in a fireproof building at all times.

Some of the recipes were tested in an experimental kitchen and somewhat modernized so that today's cooks can reproduce tipsy cake, chicken pot-pie, and tansies. Recipes for dishes such as "An Egg as Big as Twenty" and "Solomon's Temple in Flummery" were reprinted in their
original

original form for their historical and antiquarian interest. Mrs. Bullock also included introductory remarks about early Virginia food and drink and commented on Virginia hospitality.

When Colonial Williamsburg published this compilation of traditional recipes and historical notes in 1938, Mrs. Bullock anticipated it would interest readers and hoped as well that a facsimile-type edition would sell widely. No one imagined that demand for this now classic volume would grow steadily for over half a century.

The typographical style, reminiscent of *The Compleat Housewife, or Accomplish'd Gentle-woman's Companion,* published by William Parks in Williamsburg in 1742, adds to the cookbook's charm. The text is set in Caslon, an eighteenth-century type similar to one used by Parks, the paper resembles paper manufactured at Parks's mill near Williamsburg, and the illustrations by Richmond artist Elmo Jones are drawn with line cuts in imitation of a technique used by eighteenth-century engravers.

Patricia A. Gibbs
Historian, Colonial Williamsburg Foundation